RE
PRE
SENT
!

Frederik Dhaenens

Studies of Diversity
and Popular Media
Culture

ACADEMIA
PRESS

Contents

INTRODUCTION 7

CHAPTER 1 | Concepts, debates, and approaches 19
1. Identity and diversity in Western society 20
   1.1 About identity 20
   1.2 Social constructionist perspective 21
   1.3 Sociocultural diversity, inequality, and identity politics 22
   1.4 Intersectionality 25
   1.5 And what about woke and cancel culture? 28

2. Researching diversity and popular media culture 32
   2.1 Divergent paradigmatic perspectives 32
   2.2 Communication sciences: Realism and socialisation 34
   2.3 Media and cultural studies: Ideology and sense-making practices 36

3. Representation 39
   3.1 Politics of representation 39
   3.2 Stereotyping 42
   3.3 Trans-coding strategies 44

CHAPTER 2 | Gender 51
1. Sex, gender, and feminisms 55
   1.1 Disentangling sex from gender 55
   1.2 Masculinities and femininities 56
   1.3 Feminism(s) 58

2. Researching gender and popular media culture **62**
   2.1 Communication sciences: Stereotypes and cultivation **63**
   2.2 Media and cultural studies: Ideology **66**

3. Gender, the music industry, and rock music **68**
   3.1 The music industry and hegemonic masculinity **68**
   3.2 Female artists navigating a music culture shaped by hegemonic masculinity **69**
   3.3 The music press, the rock canon, and audiences **71**
   3.4 Small changes **76**

4. Pornography and the sex wars **80**
5. Trans representation in media **84**

CHAPTER 3 | Sexual orientation **89**

1. Sexuality, sexual identity, and sexual diversity **93**
   1.1 Conceptualisations **93**
   1.2 Changing discourses about nonheterosexuality in Western society **94**

2. Researching sexual diversity and popular media culture **99**
   2.1 Cultivation-theory-informed communication research **101**
   2.2 Queer-theory-informed media and cultural studies **103**

3. Representing sexual diversity in film and television fiction **108**
   3.1 Absent images and coded representation **109**
   3.2 Stereotyping **112**
   3.3 Between heteronormativity and queerness **115**

4. Queer practices of fan audiences **120**

CHAPTER 4 | Race, ethnicity, and diaspora **123**

1. On race, ethnicity, and diaspora **127**
   1.1 About race and racialisation **127**
   1.2 About ethnicity and diaspora **129**

2. Researching racial and ethnic diversity and popular media culture **135**
3. Racial and ethnic diversity in the production of popular media culture **139**
   3.1 Capitalism, media and cultural industries, and racial and ethnic diversity **139**
   3.2 Diversity initiatives and policies **142**
   3.3 Pitfalls, pressures, and pervasive whiteness **145**

4. A historical outline of black popular music **150**

CHAPTER 5 | Dis/ability **159**

1. About dis/ability **163**
   1.1 Terminology **163**
   1.2 Changing discourses about impairment and disability **165**
   1.3 Disablism and ableism **169**

2. Researching dis/ability and popular media culture **170**
3. Representing dis/ability **173**
   3.1 Underrepresentation and disablist stereotypes **173**
   3.2 Ableist representations of disability **182**
   3.3 Accurate and critical representations **184**

4. Accessibility and access to production **188**

CHAPTER 6 | Social class **191**

1. Reflections on social class **194**
   1.1 Modern class theory: Marx, Althusser, and Bourdieu **195**
   1.2 Contemporary reflections **202**

2. Researching social class and popular media culture **204**
   2.1 Cultural studies and social class **205**
   2.2 Political economy and social class **206**
   2.3 The sociology of culture, cultural sociology, and social class **207**
   2.4 Decline and revival **208**

3. Milestones in the representation of social class in film **209**
   3.1 *Metropolis* **211**
   3.2 *Ladri di biciclette* **213**
   3.3 *All That Heaven Allows* **215**

4. Making sense of class representations on television **217**
   4.1 The upper classes **218**
   4.2 Poor and homeless persons **220**
   4.3 The working classes **221**
   4.4 The middle classes **225**

EPILOGUE **228**

ACKNOWLEDGEMENTS **232**

REFERENCES **233**

INDEX **252**

Introduction

Rarely has a television adaptation been anticipated as much as *The Last of Us* (HBO, 2023–present), based on the post-apocalyptic and dystopian video game with the same name from 2013. The American series is set in a world coping with the consequences of a deadly pandemic caused by an infection of a Cordyceps fungus. To manage the pandemic, the United States has been turned into a police state with uninfected people living in quarantine zones across the country. The series recounts the story of Joel (Pedro Pascal), a middle-aged man, and Ellie (Bella Ramsey), a teenage girl. Joel is tasked with bringing Ellie safely to a faction of Fireflies, a revolutionary anti-government group. Since Ellie is the only person known to be immune to the infection, she is seen as the key to developing a vaccine. Besides being lauded by critics and fans, the series succeeded in drawing domestic and international audiences, becoming "the most-viewed title ever on HBO's subscription streaming service in Europe" (Vivarelli, 2023).

The series also made headlines with 'Long, Long Time' (season 1, episode 3). Television critics hailed the idiosyncratic episode, describing it as "groundbreaking" (Chilton, 2023a), "absolutely magical television" (Welch, 2023), and "tout simplement miraculeux" [simply miraculous] (Bordages, 2023). Although the series is a fairly faithful adaptation of the video game, the series creators took their liberties with this particular episode. Largely a stand-alone episode, it narrates the backstory of Bill, a side character in the video game. Thanks to his mistrust of governments, Bill (Nick Offerman) survived a government-organised mass execution of his fellow villagers of Lincoln, Massachusetts. Living in a self-barricaded neighbourhood surrounded by booby traps, he managed to create a safe area inaccessible to uninfected or infected humans. One day, a man named Frank (Murray Bartlett) accidentally falls into one of his pits and convinces Bill to allow him some food before continuing his trip to Boston. What starts with a dinner of rabbit stew, paired wines, and a heartfelt moment around the piano turns into sex and romance (see figure 1). The episode stands out for its decision to depict key moments in Bill and Frank's sixteen-year-long relationship. The scenes range from everyday moments of bliss (e.g. growing strawberries), episodes of intense stress (e.g. Bill getting shot in the stomach), and celebrations of their love for one another (e.g. by getting married in an alternate world where Massachusetts had not recognised same-sex marriage) to the moment Frank's degenerative neuromuscular disorder becomes insupportable and he has to ask Bill to help him die.

The decision to create a stand-alone episode that sidelined the series' main characters in favour of a compelling romance between middle-aged men can rightfully be considered groundbreaking in the history of LGBTQ representation on the small screen. Although historical analyses have revealed how television in Western society featured references to LGBTQ culture from the start, albeit coded, stereotypical, or used for humoristic purposes (Fejes & Petrich, 1993; Tropiano, 2002), it has been a slow process toward diverse representations of LGBTQ people on mainstream television. Only since the 1990s, mirroring the implementation of progressive policies and a broader social recognition of LGBTQ people, has Western television increasingly provided well-developed characters who identified as lesbian or gay and, to a lesser extent, bisexual (Kooijman, 2019; Porfido, 2009; Streitmatter, 2009). As most of these depictions have (for a long time) been rather bland, modest, heteronormative, and limited to soap operas, sitcoms, drama series, or lifestyle formats (Battles & Hilton-Morrow, 2002; Ng, 2013; Shugart, 2003), any series that took LGBTQ identities seriously and challenged genre-related expectations (e.g. by introducing LGBTQ heroes in science fiction or police procedurals) contributed to a diversified range of LGBTQ characters on the small screen. Especially the first two decades of the twenty-first century have brought us series that revolve around an LGBTQ character (e.g. *La Théorie du Y* [The Theory of Y] (RTBF, 2016–2022), *Please Like Me* (ABC/ABC2, 2013–2016)) or take place within LGBTQ communities (e.g. *The L-Word* (Showtime, 2004–2009), *Queer as Folk* (Showtime, 2000–2005)), the mainstreaming of drag queens thanks to RuPaul and the Drag Race franchise, and well-rounded trans characters performed by trans actors in *Orange is the New Black* (Netflix, 2013–2019), *Euphoria* (HBO, 2019–present) and *The Politician* (Netflix, 2019–present).

And yet, despite this progress in terms of representation, the simple matter of depicting two men in love in *The Last of Us* led to an online backlash. This was most apparent in the audience ratings that appeared on IMDB (Internet Movie Database), an online film and television database that collects information about audiovisual products such as cast, producers, and directors, and allows audiences to rate films and series. As media critic Louis Chilton (2023b) pointed out, the episode received twice as many votes as the other episodes, resulting in the second-lowest rating (8.1/10). He suspected the episode fell victim to 'review bombing', an online practice whereby users rate popular culture products exceptionally low to voice discontent. Acknowledging the often large number of votes posted in a relatively brief time span, it is likely that these review bombings may have been purposively organised (e.g. through online forums or blogs).

Figure 1. On-set photograph from *The Last of Us* (2023–present). Bill (Nick Offerman) plays the piano for Frank (Murray Bartlett). Photo credit: PlayStation Productions/Sony Pictures Television/Album, © Imageselect/Alamy.

This act of review bombing should not be seen as an isolated incident. It is part of a tangled web of events that revolve around identity, sociocultural diversity, and popular media culture. Also part of this web is the effort made by several Western European public service media to produce and programme content more tailored to the increasingly diverse society they are expected to represent. A commonly used strategy is 'mainstreaming of diversity', which refers to the inclusion of characters from sociocultural minoritised groups into popular programmes like soap operas or sitcoms (Saha, 2018; see Chapter 3). Another strategy concerns the practice of reconsidering content that public service media produced and/or distributed in the past. For instance, the British BBC and Belgian VRT experienced a public backlash over the decision to remove episodes of popular sitcoms – respectively *Fawlty Towers* (BBC, 1975–1979) and *FC De Kampioenen* [FC The Champions] (VRT, 1990–2020) – from their online platforms due to the inclusion of racial slurs and harmful stereotypes. Under pressure from vocal fans online – who found the removal among other things an act of censorship and 'cancel culture', an attack on freedom of speech, and a misunderstanding of how humour works – the episodes were reinstated albeit with the display of a disclaimer warning for outdated language and views (Bonneure, 2020; *Fawlty Towers*, 2020; Lion & Dhaenens, 2023).

What these examples illustrate is a heightened sensitivity toward the role of popular media culture in shaping and/or challenging perceptions and beliefs about minoritised identities in contemporary Western society. For instance, minoritised groups and engaged citizens have turned to social media to demand fair and balanced representation in film and television content and called out celebrities for publicly voicing opinions deemed offensive and/or prejudiced. Furthermore, there is an increased awareness of not only racism and sexism, but also homophobia, classism, or disablism. The increased use and understanding of terms once considered academic and/or activist, such as 'heteronormativity', 'patriarchy', 'white privilege', or 'ableism', has resulted in a socially shared vocabulary enabling media critics and engaged citizens to more precisely address their concerns over the content they experience as offensive or discriminatory. At the same time, the terms have been mocked and rejected by social conservative critics and people who consider themselves average Joes, stressing that the pendulum has swung too far. This is particularly apparent with the concept of 'woke'. In the early twentieth century in the United States, 'woke' emerged as an African American vernacular word that reminded fellow black Americans to remain alert to everyday racism. Yet, at the beginning of the twenty-first century, 'woke' transformed into an internationally used, ambiguous, and contradictory term. For minoritised groups and socially engaged activists, 'woke' encompasses actions that attract mainstream attention to acts of social injustice. Moderate and social conservatives, on the other hand, use 'woke' as a shorthand for framing demands by minoritised groups as excessive forms of political correctness (Cammaerts, 2022; Romano, 2020; see Chapter 1). Consequently, debates over 'woke' and identity politics are increasingly experienced and/or framed as heated and heavily polarised.

It would be tempting to consider these debates a sign of the times, fabricated by social media and a globalised media culture in which moral outcries and backlashes have become trans- and international. Although social media certainly plays a crucial role in the acceleration of time needed for news to spread and reach transnational audiences, so-called 'culture wars' have been fought since the establishment of democratic nation-states throughout the nineteenth century in Europe. At stake in these culture wars was the position of religion in a modern state and, more broadly, which norms and values were considered representative of modern life. Whether it concerned the organisation of education, politics, marriage, or the press, Catholics and anticlerical entities took positions that were diametrically opposed (Clark & Kaiser, 2003). As early as this, these culture wars were "primarily fought through the cultural media: the spoken and printed word, the image, the symbol" (Clark & Kaiser, 2003, p. 5). Although the causes changed in the twentieth century (e.g. reproductive rights, same-sex marriage, anti-discrimination policies), heavily mediated conflicts about identity and culture have continued to divide public opinion.

People may roll their eyes over 'yet another' uproar about artists and celebrities using an ableist slur, making classist remarks, or being accused of sexually transgressive behaviour. They may find these outrages banal and insignificant compared to their personal worries or to 'bigger' concerns of a geopolitical nature. However, for many people with minoritised identities, these uproars and backlashes can impact their everyday lives since it is difficult to detach or distance oneself from these mediated culture wars if one shares the same (or another) minoritised identity. Recent history has shown us how, on the one hand, women, LGBTQ people, people with a diasporic background, or disabled persons have been granted forms of legal protection (e.g. anti-discrimination legislation) and/or legal rights (e.g. abortion rights, interracial marriage, same-sex marriage and adoption laws, the right to fully participate in society as a person with a disability). Similarly, certain policies implemented by public institutions and commercial enterprises (e.g. a school's policies on reporting sexually transgressive behaviour, a company's anti-discrimination charter) have also helped achieve a more inclusive society. At the same time, many countries have become stricter on who is allowed to participate in society and how (e.g. stringent immigration policies, same-sex marriage bans, anti-abortion legislations) and tolerate the discrimination of cultural minorities (e.g. not questioning social and cultural rituals or professional practices that are heteronormative, patriarchal, or racist). What is more, rights for minoritised people often feel conditional and temporary and at constant risk of being reversed. For instance, American women in a dozen states have lost their constitutional right to abortion due to the decision by the U.S. Supreme Court in 2022 to officially reverse the Roe v. Wade ruling from 1973, which stipulated that women were protected by the constitution to have an abortion (Dwyer, 2022). Such legal setbacks tend to reverberate in society, granting people indirectly the 'right' to discriminate against minoritised groups. Witnessing how hard-fought legal gains have come under pressure once again may help understand why activists and audiences also scrutinise to what extent popular media culture has advanced and/or hampered the living conditions of sociocultural minoritised groups.

Even though the impact of media on people has, at times, been overestimated (Gauntlett, 2008; Hermes, 2024), scholars in media and cultural studies agree that media and popular culture have played a vital role in how identity and sociocultural diversity are experienced in (Western) societies (Ang, 1996; Buckingham, 1993; Fiske, 1987; Hall, 2005). Representation matters. To those who rarely see themselves in society, representation in popular media culture – if done in a fair and well-rounded manner – feels like an act of recognition. For those who grow up without any role models, media and popular culture may even be a crucial source for making sense of oneself. Think of LGBTQ people growing up in a heterosexual and cisgender family context, or people with a disability surrounded by able-bodied peers and family members. It can also debunk stereotypes that majority audiences may hold about minoritised groups. Already in the early twentieth century, German doctor Magnus Hirschfeld hoped to address a large audience about his scientific knowledge of homosexuality. Making *Anders als die Andern* [Different from the Others] (Richard Oswald, 1919) together with Austrian director Richard Oswald allowed him to use a fictitious story about two men in love to represent homosexuality as a natural variation (Dyer, 2003; see Chapter 3). Similarly, the film movement of Italian neorealism in the 1940s and early 1950s was able to represent the hardships poor and working-class people endured in post-war Italy in a manner that defied a naïve and romantic approach (Ben-Ghiat, 2001; Cook, 1996; see Chapter 6). Lastly, in music genres like soul in the 1960s and hip-hop in the 1970s, black Americans were able to express their everyday lived experiences, worries, and frustrations with racism and discrimination as well as foster a community through messages of hope and unity (Iwamoto, 2003; Maultsby, 1983; Watkins, 2006; see Chapter 4).

Politicians and policymakers too are quite aware of the powerful, symbolic role media and popular culture can adopt in the culture wars that are waged. Censoring or even banning content that revolves around minoritised identities and/or questions power dynamics among sociocultural groups is gaining momentum once more. The Hungarian government adopted a law in 2021 that forbids the 'promotion' of LGBTQ people and themes in educational content, fiction, or advertisements available to minors (Kovács, 2021), while American parent-led groups and state legislators succeeded in banning an increasing number of books about people of colour, gender identity, and sexual diversity in public school libraries and classrooms (Meehan & Friedman, 2023). Some may argue that the banning of LGBTQ-themed content or books about people of colour is not that different from the call to 'cancel' sitcom episodes with so-called 'outdated' humour. Such a standpoint, however, ignores that the first type of content is concerned with the empowerment of minorities and the fostering of a diverse and inclusive society, while the second type of content features humour that is hurtful, racist, and offensive and that reaffirms prejudices majority audiences may have against minoritised groups (Lion & Dhaenens, 2023). This book aims to provide these and other insights in the hope that nuanced and thoughtful thinking about identity and popular culture will counteract polarised and populist rhetoric that tends to hog all the attention.

Aim and approach

Even though knowledge about identity, sociocultural diversity, and popular media culture in society and academia has increased, many students, scholars, and engaged citizens are seeking out historical and theoretical insights to be better equipped to talk and think about these themes. For instance, some may have a basic understanding of what 'woke' means but lack a historical awareness of the transformation of the term. Similarly, some may desire to understand why some television programmes have been argued to be 'heteronormative', 'classist', or 'ableist'. This book aims to provide readers with comprehensible, tangible, and nuanced insights into the relationship between popular media culture and sociocultural diversity in Western society.

To do so, this book's approach is threefold. First, starting from the belief that historical knowledge is essential to better grasp contemporary debates and practices about sociocultural diversity in popular media culture, the book sheds light on a selection of historical contexts and milestones. Attention is paid to changing insights concerning the different axes of identity at stake, to the development of research into sociocultural diversity in media and popular culture, and to remarkable transformations and trends in the history of representing minoritised groups. Second, the book explores a selection of key theoretical concepts, developed by scholars of communication sciences, media and cultural studies, and social theory, which help better understand the diverse ways popular media culture has engaged with sociocultural diversity, particularly about aspects of production and representation. Third, the book offers reflections on contemporary trends, transformations, and challenges.

To define the scope more closely, I continue by highlighting what this book covers and what it does not. First, rather than focusing on a single axis of identity (e.g. gender), this book covers five different axes of identity, namely 'gender', 'sexual orientation', 'race, ethnicity, and diaspora', 'dis/ability', and 'social class'. As such, I aim to contribute to a series of excellent works that have highlighted the relationship between one particular sociocultural identity axis and media (e.g. Krijnen & Van Bauwel, 2022; Saha, 2018) and edited volumes that have focused on a (selection of) identity categories at stake in this book (e.g. Lind, 2023; Yousman et al., 2020). I underscore that although each chapter revolves around one axis of identity, meaningful intersections with other minoritised identity categories are also explored. Last, minoritised identity groups are the book's main concern, but 'majority' identity categories (e.g. men and masculinity, whiteness, heterosexuality) receive their fair share of attention.

Second, although research from different traditions and disciplines is discussed, the book mainly focuses on scholars from media and cultural studies. In this book, 'media and cultural studies' is treated as an interdisciplinary field with a shared set of theories, methods, and attitudes toward the role of knowledge in society, especially concerning sociocultural diversity. There are valid arguments to consider 'media studies' distinct from 'cultural studies'. For instance, whereas media studies has its roots in (post-)positivist communication sciences (see Chapter 1), cultural studies was inspired by culturalist, structuralist, and Marxist thinking (see Chapters 1 and 6) (Erni, 2001). At the same time, the Birmingham Centre for Contemporary Cultural Studies, a key institution in the development of cultural studies, has consistently studied media culture, which encouraged media scholars to look into cultural studies approaches and adapt them. As several university programmes, journals (e.g. *Continuum: Journal of Media & Cultural Studies*), and (hand)books on 'media and cultural studies' (e.g. Durham & Kellner, 2006; Hammer & Kellner, 2009; Turner, 2019) illustrate, many treat both 'traditions' as one interdisciplinary and heterogeneous field today. Some scholars also speak of a 'media and cultural studies approach' to study the relationship between society and popular media culture (Buckingham, 1993; Wood, 2024). Such an approach assumes that (media) culture does not simply *reflect* society, but *co-constructs* it. In studying cultural media texts, such as soaps, films, or songs, scholars in media and cultural studies aim to demonstrate how and to what extent media and popular culture reiterate social inequalities and/or advance the causes of minoritised groups (Kellner, 1995; Turner, 2003; Wood, 2024; see Chapter 1).

Third, this book is particularly interested in popular media culture. Aware of the different ways to define popular culture (see Storey, 2021), this book describes 'popular media culture' as the practices, discourses, and experiences relating to the production, distribution, and consumption of mediated content that is intended to attract a relatively large set of audiences. To delineate the scope a bit more, this book focuses on three major cultural industries, namely film, television, and popular music. People remain invested in consuming music, film, and television. For instance, the annual global music report published by IFPI (International Federation of the Phonographic Industry), the organisation that represents over 8,000 record company members, demonstrated how the global recorded music industry is thriving. After years of decline, the recorded music industry revived around 2015 and saw its revenues increase each year. In 2023, it amounted to a market value of more than 28 billion American dollars (IFPI, 2024). Further, despite having suffered significantly from the COVID-19 pandemic, the film industry is slowly recuperating. An annual report on world film-market trends published by the European Audiovisual Observatory, a European public service organisation that provides information and aid to the European audiovisual industry, highlighted how the global gross box office revenue of 2022 was 25.9 billion American dollars, an increase of 21.8% compared to 2021. It also stressed how, for instance, film production in Europe had resumed its pre-pandemic growth (Kanzler & Simone, 2023). Likewise, people still watch television – interpreted here as referring to a variety of audiovisual content consumed live or on demand on a variety of 'small screens', such as a television or a smartphone. To illustrate, European consumers increasingly paid for video-on-demand services, resulting in a revenue of 19.8 billion euros in 2022 (Ene et al., 2024). Although film, television, and popular music make up most of the content, other media (e.g. magazines, news media, social media) will also be touched upon when relevant.

It should be noted that the book limits itself to popular media culture produced and consumed in Western capitalist economies and democratic countries. Many of these societies present themselves as inclusive and concerned with human rights although, in reality, we can find systemic and banal practices of exclusion and discrimination. This is taken as a background when exploring how Western film, television, and popular music engage with matters of diversity and inclusivity. At this point, I want to highlight that many examples in this book come from Anglophone countries. First, this has to do with the fact that scholars essential to the development of research into sociocultural diversity and popular media culture (e.g. Elizabeth Ellcessor, Richard Dyer, Stuart Hall, bell hooks, Anamik Saha) (have) lived and worked in Anglophone countries. Second, although non-Anglophone Western audiences appreciate popular culture products from diverse countries, including national content, they do consume a sizable proportion of American and, to a lesser extent, British film, television, and popular music (De Bens & De Smaele, 2001; Kuipers, 2011; Verboord & Brandellero, 2018). Consequently, when a famous American artist like Lil Nas X comes out as gay, his words reverberate far beyond the United States. That is why this book pays quite some attention to media professionals, artists, and popular culture products from Anglophone countries, as their symbolic role in contemporary debates over sociocultural diversity in Western society cannot be underestimated. At the same time, this book aims to challenge this hegemony of Anglophone popular culture by discussing lesser-known examples from non-Anglophone countries. Being a Belgian media scholar, I introduce you to a few Belgian examples and invite you to see the similarities and differences between content and practices from other countries. Last, as an able-bodied, gay, white cisman, and part of the upper middle class, I am conscious that my positionality has undoubtedly shaped my writings, reflections, and the selection of topics and cases this book discusses, despite my efforts to be reflexive about this. I take responsibility for any biases and shortcomings, and I welcome feedback from readers.

Chapter breakdown

The book features six chapters. To understand how sociocultural diversity has been engaged with in past and contemporary popular media culture, an understanding of key concepts, debates, and approaches is needed. That is why the first chapter serves as a general introduction to the central themes of this book. The chapter begins with a section that provides tangible conceptualisations of 'identity' and 'sociocultural diversity' and explains why the book predominantly relies on a social constructionist framework. It continues with an elaboration on the political and ideological aspects of identity by focusing on 'identity politics', 'intersectionality', 'wokeness', and 'cancel culture'. The second part tackles the divergent paradigmatic approaches to studying sociocultural diversity in popular media culture while distinguishing approaches within communication sciences from approaches within media and cultural studies. The third section of the chapter zooms in on aspects that relate to media representation and sociocultural diversity, namely 'politics of representation', 'stereotyping', and 'trans-coding strategies'.

The second chapter explores gender and popular media culture. The chapter starts with an introduction to ways of making sense of 'sex', 'gender', 'masculinities', and 'femininities' while emphasising the role feminisms have played in thinking about gender and patriarchy. The chapter continues with an introduction to the research on gender and popular media culture and distinguishes a communication scientific approach to gender from a media and cultural studies approach. The chapter also deepens the media and cultural studies approach with an exploration of practices of gendering in the music industry. Besides, it tackles pornography and illustrates how the much-debated phenomenon led to oppositional views among feminist scholars. Last, the chapter introduces you to the emerging field of trans media studies, with a discussion of trans(gender) representation in news media and audiovisual fiction.

In the third chapter, the attention shifts toward sexual orientation and popular media culture. The chapter begins by conceptualising 'sexuality', 'sexual orientation', 'sexual behaviour', and 'sexual identity', and providing a historical outline of how discourses on nonheterosexuality changed from the end of the nineteenth century onward. In the second part, the chapter tackles two divergent traditions that studied sexual diversity and popular media culture: cultivation-theory-informed studies in communication sciences and queer-theory-informed studies in media and cultural studies. Turning toward matters of representation, the chapter recounts the history of representing sexual diversity in film and television. Last, the chapter turns to fan audiences and introduces you to the queer practices of 'slash fiction' and 'queer reading'.

The fourth chapter starts with a discussion of the concepts of 'race', 'ethnicity', and 'diaspora', elaborating on the various ways these concepts have been interpreted, used, and contested. Next, it broaches different strands of research into racial and ethnic diversity and popular media culture, with attention to postcolonial studies, Orientalism, and framing theory. Following this, the chapter turns to matters of production, offering reflections on the impact of capitalism on representing racial and ethnic diversity, the policies and initiatives that have been taken to address diversity in the workplace and in media content, and the pitfalls and pressures that come with it. Last, the chapter explores the ramifications of the 'racialisation' of popular culture by briefly recounting the history of American black popular music.

In the fifth chapter, the relations between disability, ability, and popular media culture are explored. Concepts such as 'disability', 'dis/ability', 'impairment', 'disablism', and 'ableism' are discussed. Further, it pays attention to how changing discourses in thinking about impairment and disability led to different models of disability. The chapter also introduces you to the small but burgeoning field of research on dis/ability and popular media culture. Next, it explores the many disablist stereotypes that have been used to represent disabled people. Besides, attention is paid to ableist modes of representation and well-developed and critical representations of disability. The chapter ends by arguing why media accessibility is essential for disabled people and touching upon the challenges that disabled media professionals experience when trying to access the media industry.

The last chapter draws attention to social class and popular media culture. It starts with a discussion of modern and contemporary theories of social class, broaching concepts such as 'class consciousness', 'forms of capital', 'tokenism', and 'classism'. The midsection demonstrates how different traditions of research have been important to the study of social class in popular media culture (i.e. 'cultural studies', 'political economy', and the sociological traditions of 'sociology of culture' and 'cultural sociology'), while also reflecting on the decreased interest in studying social class and popular media culture. In the last part, the chapter explores how various social classes have been represented. The first section provides insights into three historical milestones in the history of cinema, while the second section explores modes of representing social classes in contemporary television content.

CHAPTER 1

CONCEPTS, DEBATES, AND APPROACHES

1. IDENTITY AND DIVERSITY IN WESTERN SOCIETY

1.1. About identity

Identity is ubiquitous in people's everyday lives. People use several markers or labels of identity to make sense of who they are and how to present themselves to others. For instance, they may see themselves as 'male', 'bisexual', 'black', and/or 'Hindu'. Some of these terms were attributed to people. Think of how many persons were described as 'boy' or 'girl' when born, solely based on their sex characteristics. In other instances, people may use certain identity categories for self-identification. When, for example, a man experiences sexual desires for people of the same sex or gender, this person may identify as 'gay' or 'bisexual'. The instances illustrate how bodily traits (e.g. skin colour, biological sex characteristics, sexual desire, capabilities, age) have been used as a basis for identity categories. Similarly, sociocultural features (e.g. nationality, religion, social class) have also led to identity markers (e.g. Dutch, Muslim, working class). For instance, when someone is raised in a blue-collar community[1] and a household with little to no discretionary income, the person can be seen as part of the working class.

The examples outlined above reveal how identification works. According to sociologist Richard Jenkins (2014), identification is "the systematic establishment and signification, between individuals, between collectivities and between individuals and collectivities, of relationships of similarity and difference" (p. 19). As a result, identity "denotes the ways in which individuals and collectivities are distinguished in their relations with other individuals and collectivities" (p. 19). For instance, a person may self-identify as gay because he experiences his sexual desires as *similar* to how people who are described and/or who identify as gay, homosexual, or queer experience sexuality, and as *different* from how people who are described and/or who identify as heterosexual experience sexuality. Besides, Jenkins stressed that individual and collective identities "are as much an interactional product of 'external' identification by others, as they are of 'internal' self-identification" (p. 204). For instance, a person may self-identify as a woman because she has been repeatedly identified by others as a woman and has learned about being a woman since the day she was born. However, ideas about womanhood, which inform the process of identification, do not emerge out of thin air.

---

1   Blue-collar worker is a term that refers to someone within the working class who generally performs manual, physical labour.

As Jenkins underscored, identification is also shaped by and dependent on culture. It is in culture, which encompasses cultural artefacts (e.g. books, clothing), practices (e.g. rituals, habits), and norms and values (e.g. proper behaviour), where people encounter discourses and representations of identities.

These cultural discourses and representations about identity are central to this book, as they are being produced and reproduced in popular media culture. On the one hand, they are valuable as they may help people make sense of who they are as a person. They provide stability, clarity, and coherence. Moreover, they also create a sense of belonging when one learns about others who share the same identity. On the other hand, identity labels may hamper people's lives as they also engender normative assumptions about people (Hall, 1996; Moya, 2000; Nicholson, 2010). For instance, when born with male sex characteristics, you will likely be raised a boy and expected to act, walk, talk, and dress 'like a man', even when you feel you want to act or walk differently than what is considered 'normal' or 'idealised' masculine behaviour within a given cultural context (see Chapter 2). Note that these cultural discourses and representations are context-specific and vary widely depending on time and place.

1.2. *Social constructionist perspective*

The postulation that cultural discourses and representations about identity categories differ from one cultural context to another should be understood as a social constructionist argument. Even though identity has been discussed in plenty of academic disciplines, such as (social) psychology, law, or economics, this book relies on the work of social and cultural theorists who reflected on identity from a social constructionist perspective. Social constructionism is a theory of knowledge that has become a dominant approach to thinking about identity from the 1970s on. Social constructionism does not dismiss that there is an objective reality (which refers to its ontological position) but argues that how we make sense of that reality is socially constructed (which refers to its epistemological position). Even though many traditions of social constructionism (e.g. historicism, symbolic interactionism, materialist feminism) exist, they all postulate that identities are socially constructed and vary culturally and historically (Brickell, 2006).

Social constructionist thought challenges essentialist thinking. Essentialism is a philosophical doctrine, which assumes that certain identities (e.g. being a woman) are natural, biological, ahistorical, and exist before the birth of a person. Second, it makes the universalist claim that persons with the same identity all share the same feelings and experiences. For instance, if you are a woman, you share certain feelings and experiences with all women, throughout history and across the globe. Third, it considers men and women "inherently different beings who belong to separate categories" (Milestone & Meyer, 2012, p. 12). In contrast, social constructionism, which is informed by non-essentialist philosophy, argues that how a person makes sense of their identities depends on how, within a given time and place, people make sense of aspects that relate to those identities. Put differently, a social constructionist perspective of gender does not dismiss that there are differences between men and women, but stresses that these differences should be seen as the outcome of *social processes* and *cultural practices* (Jenkins, 2014; Milestone & Meyer, 2012).

1.3. Sociocultural diversity, inequality, and identity politics

In contemporary Western society, the concept of sociocultural diversity is often used as an umbrella term to refer to the coexistence of people who differ by, for instance, gender, sexual orientation, racial, ethnic, or diasporic identity, social class, or dis/ability. Simply put, sociocultural diversity includes "all kinds of differences between individuals and groups" (Arnesen & Allan, 2009, p. 11). At times, 'sociocultural diversity' has been used as a neutral term to imply that there are myriad ways of being and identifying oneself in society and that everyone is treated equally. In this book, however, I demonstrate how discourses about diversity are deeply political and caught up in power dynamics and highly contested sets of norms and values.

To this day, certain identity categories have been discursively constructed in Western society as 'normal', 'mainstream', or 'superior', while other identities have been constructed as 'abnormal', 'deviant', or 'inferior'. Think about how in daily conversations, politics, or popular literature, identities have been discussed in binary, oppositional, and, in many cases, hierarchical terms. For instance, men and women are seen as two very distinct categories of people, in which men are granted more power than women. Another discursive practice is the creation of cultural discourses that limit the diversity within certain identity categories. For instance, even though there are many ways to be black or to be a man, only a limited set of behaviours, attitudes, and expressions is considered normal or appropriate for each identity category. By repeatedly articulating these binary, hierarchical, and normative assumptions about people's identities, Western society embeds, normalises, and obfuscates structural inequalities[2] in institutions (e.g. education, justice, politics), culture, and everyday life practices.

---

2   An example of structural inequality is occupational segregation based on gender, as it often results in gender pay inequality. Gendered discourses stipulating which occupations should be practised by women and which ones by men contribute to occupational segregation (Hegewisch & Hartmann, 2014).

That is why people have felt the need to unite with others who share the same identity to make visible, question, and overthrow structural and discursive forms of oppression. In these moments, people with the same minoritised identity have formed a group and engaged in identity politics. Chris Barker (2012) defined identity politics as follows: "The forging of 'new languages' of identity combined with acting to change social practices, usually through the formation of coalitions where at least some values are shared" (p. 504). However, some standpoints in identity politics have been criticised. Take, for instance, the emergence of social movements organised around gender or race. Among them, there were feminist movements (e.g. radical feminists) and civil rights movements (e.g. Black Power) that aimed to unite women by emphasising a shared women's culture, and black people by celebrating a shared black culture, respectively (Nicholson, 2010). Poststructuralist and social constructionist scholars, however, pointed out that this shared culture was presented as homogenous and essentialist (Bernstein, 2005; Moya, 2000; Nicholson, 2010). As Paula M. L. Moya (2000) underscored, several social movements ignored or downplayed the "instability and internal heterogeneity of identity categories" (p. 3). As such, they disregarded how the intersections with other axes of identity (e.g. dis/ability, gender, race) can lead to experiences not included in the cultural discourses or representations of social movements.

At the same time, Mary Bernstein (2005) pointed out that emphasising a shared identity and culture could also be seen as strategic as it facilitates the formation of a social collective and a clear and delineated set of political and cultural goals. Her ideas echo Gayatri Chakravorty Spivak's reflections on strategic essentialism, which Spivak formulated in an interview with Elizabeth Grosz (1984/85). Spivak argued that one does not have to be an essentialist to make use of essentialism from time to time to achieve common goals: "You pick up the universal that will give you the power to fight against the other side" (p. 184). Bernstein and Spivak's strategic essentialism does not imply that these coalitions or collectives organised around a shared signifier or identity (e.g. 'woman') should ignore the diversity within those coalitions. Yet, as the examples above illustrate, some of these temporary collectives have failed to avoid the trap of essentialism and participated in the discursive and material exclusion of people who may share the 'common' identity label but differ by other minoritised identities.

Focus on the #MeToo movement

A good example of a social movement engaged in identity politics is the #MeToo movement. It was initially set up as an activist group in 2006 by Tarana Burke, named 'me too' Movement (see figure 2). The goal was to support survivors of sexual violence and other forms of systemic abuse of power, who were mainly young women of colour. Besides, the movement tried to interrupt sexual violence through advocacy and to campaign for policies and laws to prevent these forms of violence and abuse. In 2017, the phrase went viral after Hollywood actress Alyssa Milano used it as a hashtag to call out sexual abuse and to encourage other survivors to make visible the magnitude of sexual abuse. In participating and sharing their experiences on social media, women joined forces to interrupt sexual assault, sexual harassment, and abuse of power and to demand policy changes (Brockes, 2018; metoomvmt.org).

The fact that the abuse reported by chiefly white Hollywood actresses received much more media attention than the young women of colour Burke was concerned with demonstrates the differences among women. One reason for this was that the actresses,

Figure 2. Portrait of Tarana Burke taken in 2018.
Photo credit: Sven Hoppe/dpa/Alamy Live News. © Imageselect/Alamy.

like other privileged high-profile celebrities, hold celebrity capital. With this concept, Olivier Driessens (2013) fleshed out a form of capital different from the forms of capital Pierre Bourdieu had described to discuss social divisions in society (see Chapter 6). Celebrity capital refers to "accumulated media visibility through recurrent media representations" (p. 13), which, in this case, the actresses were able to use to call out sexual harassment. The actresses reported being aware of their privileged position and wanting to use their capital to raise awareness, spark debate, and use their privileges to serve others who do not own the means to do so. On the other hand, it cannot undo the fact that women of colour working in precarious positions do not dispose of the same symbolic or material means to call out men in powerful positions as high-profile women do. It also illustrates why it is important to acknowledge the diversity and disparities among women because of other intersecting identities. These forms of inequalities and discrimination have been the subject of Kimberlé Crenshaw's work, which led to the theory of intersectionality.

1.4. *Intersectionality*

In 1991, Kimberlé Crenshaw coined and interpreted the concept of intersectionality. Crenshaw is a scholar in law, critical race theory, and civil rights. Her article on violence against women of colour had the ambition to advance the knowledge on the topic by exploring the racial and gender dimensions of such violence. This exploration had a particular set-up. She wanted to challenge the way identity politics were practised. On the one hand, she valued that identity politics exposed practices of oppression as social and systemic instead of isolated and individual, something that often happened in the framing of violence against women. Further, she found identity politics to be a source of "strength, community, and intellectual development" (Crenshaw, 1991, p. 1242) and able to unite people around a shared identity and cause. Yet, she took issue with how identity politics did not take seriously intra-group differences. The discourses used in identity politics were focused on challenging either racism or sexism but rarely acknowledged the intersectionality between both minoritised identity categories. Consequently, to tackle the issue of violence against women of colour effectively, she argued that this issue had to be understood as "the product of intersecting patterns of both sexism and racism" (p. 1243).

In her article on intersectionality, she described three forms: structural intersectionality, political intersectionality, and representational intersectionality. Structural intersectionality refers to "the ways in which the location of women of color at the intersection of race and gender makes [their] actual experience of domestic violence, rape, and remedial reform qualitatively different than that of white women" (p. 1245). She pointed out that legislation and policies aiming to challenge gender-based violence have often started from white women's experiences, thereby ignoring structural hindrances women of colour may experience (e.g. different ideas about family honour, refugee women risking deportation). Political intersectionality is about ensuring that structural intersectionality is acknowledged when conducting politics. In demanding this, Crenshaw challenged the identity politics of feminist movements and anti-racist movements that have unintentionally contributed to marginalising the violence against women of colour. Crenshaw made us attentive to the fact that women of colour who wanted to fight oppression have often been forced to split their energy between two formations (i.e. 'black men' and 'white women'), which have not experienced double subordination. As a result, anti-racist identity politics have led to anti-racist discourses that dismiss questions about gender and sexism. Similarly, feminist identity politics have resulted in anti-sexist discourses that fail to take into account race and racism.

The third form of intersectionality is representational intersectionality, which refers to the cultural construction of women of colour. For the scope of this book, an understanding of this form is pivotal. It concerns the practice of looking at cultural representations from an intersectional lens and asking questions about the sociocultural implications of these representations. To make her case, Crenshaw offered reflections on an American lawsuit against the members of 2 Live Crew, a hip-hop collective whose members were arrested and charged under a Florida obscenity statute for their performance in a sex club in Florida in June 1990. In other words, their performance was considered offensive and obscene. The arrest came two days after a federal court judge ruled that the sexually explicit lyrics in *As Nasty as They Wanna Be* (1989), the band's third album, were legally obscene. The judge stated that the album was "an appeal directed to 'dirty' *thoughts* and the loins, not to the intellect and the mind" (Campbell, 1991, p. 190, emphasis in original). The album was considered to lack serious literary, artistic, or political value while being offensive as defined by state law. Regarding the live performance, the members were acquitted in October 1990. Yet, the federal court's decision that the album was obscene was upheld, which meant that record stores in several counties in Florida were not allowed to sell the album. In 1992, the federal court ruling was eventually overturned on the basis that the federal judge had been unable to demonstrate why the album lacked artistic value.

Crenshaw was interested in the public debate that ensued. In particular, she was interested in what was being said about the representation of black women. Two oppositional positions dominated the public debate. On one side, you had the feminist position, which Crenshaw associated with the writings of a political columnist named George Will. He argued that the music was 'misogynistic filth', and engaged in objectifying black women and condoning sexual violence against women. This position was substantiated by referring to the lyrics of the hip-hop collective. The lyrics are not only sexually explicit but also co-construct black women as 'bitches', 'cunts', and 'hos' [sic], whose prime role is to please the men and their 'almighty dicks'. Looking at the album of 2 Live Crew through a feminist prism, it is obvious why this work qualifies as misogynistic. Yet, an exclusively feminist lens fails to acknowledge how this case was also shaped by race. Plenty of other (white) rock bands have written sexist and misogynist lyrics but were never prosecuted for obscenity. Moreover, the federal court used forms of racism to call out 2 Live Crew's use of sexism. The court made use of stereotypes of black men to depict the collective as violent, hypermasculine, hypersexual, and aggressive. Another racist attitude can be discerned in the federal court's position toward the cultural roots of African American hip-hop culture. Particular practices and musical conventions that subvert mainstream white pop music were denied having artistic value.

On the other side, you had the anti-racist position embodied by Henry Louis Gates, a leading scholar in African American culture. He took on the defence of 2 Live Crew. He argued that the collective's lyrics and mode of address should not be thought of as misogynist but as exaggerations intended to expose the ridiculousness of stereotypes of black masculinity.[3] For Gates, this practice may have had a political and cultural motivation. The political argument entailed that 2 Live Crew wanted to advance the black anti-racist agenda by liberating black men from these stereotypes. The cultural argument entailed that the hip-hop collective used these modes of address and words simply to be funny – they were not intended to cause women pain and for that reason could not be seen as injurious. Such a position, however, dismissed the power relations in certain sociocultural contexts. Were the 'comedians' punching up (i.e. mocking people with economic and/or symbolic power, who are part of majorities) or punching down (i.e. targeting minoritised groups or groups lacking power) (Pérez, 2013; Lion & Dhaenens, 2023)? The anti-racist prism dismissed the material and symbolic power of men in society, even when they were part of a minoritised group. Hence, despite the fact it concerned intra-group humour (black people joking about black people), it cannot be ignored that it was men mocking women as a means to bond with other men. Crenshaw (1991) rephrased it as follows: "Humor in which women are objec-

---

3   This practice has also been described as 'hyperstereotyping', a practice discussed in Chapter 2.

tified as packages of bodily parts to serve whatever male-bonding/male-competition needs [...] subordinates women in much the same way that racist humour subordinates African Americans" (p. 1293).

To conclude, Crenshaw suggested that taking on an intersectional approach implies that categories of identities are still valuable (e.g. 'women', 'people of colour') if they factor in intersectional experiences, which have often been marginalised. Since coining the concept, intersectionality has become a key lens for scholars who understand its value in studying contemporary forms of oppression. Even though there is discord within academia and activist organisations about the reach of intersectionality,[4] Crenshaw and her research centre (Center for Intersectionality and Social Policy Studies) clarified that intersectionality:

> [...] starts from the premise that people have multiple identities, and being members of more than one "group," they can simultaneously experience oppression and privilege. Intersectionality sheds light on the unique experiences that are produced when various forms of discrimination intersect with these converging identities. It is a dynamic strategy for linking the grounds of discrimination (e.g. race, gender, class, sexual identity, etc.) to historical, social, economic, political, and legal contexts and norms that intertwine to create structures of oppression and privilege. (https://intersectionality.law.columbia.edu/)

Following this description, I consider the term 'intersectionality' also helpful in exploring various forms of discrimination (e.g. understanding the ramifications of being a disabled person of colour).

1.5. And what about woke and cancel culture?

Since the late 2010s, debates over identity and sociocultural diversity have often been framed as debates over wokeness. Heated and polarised discussions about sociocultural minorities are certainly nothing new, but what typifies these contemporary debates in Western society is the way divergent opinions and arguments about distinct identity-related issues are all labelled as 'woke'. To better understand contemporary interpretations of wokeness, a brief history of the term is needed. Already in the early twentieth century, the term circulated in

---

[4] For instance, should the concept of intersectionality only be used for studies that consider the experiences of women of colour? Can it help us to think about all kinds of intersecting identities, including minority and majority identities?

African American communities as a reminder to be vigilant and stay alert, since black Americans continued to be the target of discrimination and oppression (Cammaerts, 2022; Romano, 2020). The term was introduced to mainstream American society in 1962, when William Melvin Kelley, a young black novelist, wrote an article for the *New York Times*. 'Woke' was prominently featured in the title of the piece, 'If You're Woke You Dig It'. The article demonstrated how the language used by beatnik culture – an anti-materialist and nonconforming American subculture – came from black American vernacular and, presumably deliberately, he refrained from explaining what woke meant (Rhodes, 2022; Romano, 2020). According to Aja Romano (2020), however, the article allowed us to indirectly understand the meaning of woke, which is "[...] to be a socially conscious Black American, someone aware of the ephemeral nature of Black vernacular, who might actively be shifting that vernacular away from white people who would exploit it or change its meaning." African American words such as 'hip' had been appropriated and commodified by white Americans, and therefore Kelley may have feared the same would happen to 'woke'.

Throughout the twentieth century, the term took on different meanings (e.g. knowing your partner might be cheating on you), but the idea of being aware of systemic and social injustice persisted as, for instance, expressed in the song 'Master Teacher' (2008) by Erykah Badu (Romano, 2020). However, the 2014 Ferguson unrest in Missouri is considered a pivotal moment as #StayWoke became one of the key political slogans used in the streets and on social media. The protests, in response to the killing of Michael Brown, an 18-year-old African American man, by a police officer, were intended to bring back attention to race-related inequalities and oppression. 'Woke' was also appropriated by Black Lives Matter. This social movement emerged in 2013 as a response to the killing of unarmed black Americans. Using social media and protests in major cities, the different chapters of the movement protested against police abuse, racial injustice, and other systemic practices of devaluing the lives of black and brown people in the United States (Clayton, 2018; Whiteout, 2018). For people involved in Black Lives Matter, 'woke' was a way of warning others about police brutality (Romano, 2020).

From here on, the term has also been increasingly used to draw attention to other forms of discrimination and social injustice (Cammaerts, 2022; Whiteout, 2018), which, in turn, resulted in mainstream and international attention to 'wokeness'. One of the first outcomes of this increased knowledge about woke has been the coexistence of the activist interpretation of woke with the emergence of 'corporate wokeness' (Kanai & Gill, 2020; Rhodes, 2022). Corporate wokeness refers to "the apparent championing of identity politics" (Kanai & Gill, 2020, p. 11) by corporations like Nike, Inc. and The Coca-Cola Company. Dubbed 'woke-washing', these corporations often engage in the superficial act of window dressing, as their promotional and marketing discourses rarely coincide with a true commitment to social justice. Francesca Sobande (2019) highlighted that marketing managers should understand that the inclusion of minoritised identities does not:

> equate [...] with activism or indication of a strong socio-political stance. [...] Thus, brands that are seriously invested in aiding efforts to address social injustices cannot simply do so in the form of marketing content, and instead, must assess their approaches to issues including the principles underpinning their in-house labour practices, production methods and sources and uses of profit. (p. 2740)

Another outcome has been the international resignification of 'woke'. For instance, in the Netherlands and Belgium, news media only started using the English term in 2017. The initial coverage focused on what the word meant in the United States. Gradually, journalists and public figures started using 'woke' as a lens to look at local identity politics and social injustice. Akin to the way #MeToo was appropriated by local activists, 'woke' became a word to draw attention to local forms of structural inequality and social injustice. Remarkably, moderate and social conservative critics were rather quick in transforming the activist meaning of woke into signifying what they consider to be an excessive form of political correctness. They have used the term in a derogatory manner to signpost a series of practices they found to be an attack on traditional norms and values, established cultural practices, or freedom of speech. Examples of practices include the demand for inclusivity on management boards, the request to address someone with their correct pronouns, the inclusion of a third pronoun in a dictionary, or the demand to change the Dutch word 'blank' to 'wit' – which, in English, both translate to 'white' but have different political connotations (Kanobana, 2021).

In the United States and other Western European countries, woke has also been associated with cancel culture. The concept originates from the demand by activists for accountability of high-profile persons or organisations with prestige, standing, and power in a variety of fields (e.g. politics, business, celebrity culture) engaged in (systemic) wrongdoing. The activists are often part of communities that have been discriminated against or marginalised based on their minoritised identity. This demand for accountability is what has been dubbed or framed as cancel culture, as demands to address and rectify misconduct or oppression are being amplified by requesting "the withdrawal of any kind of support (viewership, social media follows, purchases of products endorsed by the person, etc.) for those who are assessed to have said or done something unacceptable or highly problematic, generally from a social justice perspective especially alert to sexism, heterosexism, homophobia, racism, bullying, and related issues" (Ng, 2020, p. 623). Eve Ng (2020) stressed that "content circulation via digital platforms facilitates fast, large-scale responses to acts deemed problematic, often empowering traditionally marginalised groups in the moment, but it also highlights the dearth of considered assessments and debate" (p. 625). She argued that the attributes of social media do not create room for nuance, contemplation, and debate. Similarly, Judith Butler (2020, in Ferber), among others, stressed the importance of confrontation and slow and thoughtful debate, as well as acknowledging that people make mistakes and can learn from those mistakes. However, Butler also drew our attention to the fact that these debates over the alleged dangers of cancel culture tend to obfuscate and dismiss the issues (e.g. forms of institutional racism) that underlie media uproars about wokeness and cancel culture.

Therefore, it remains important to understand the role of media and popular culture in these debates. For instance, are journalists discussing the underlying issues thoroughly or are they using a social media backlash over the removal of an episode on Netflix as clickbait? Are representations that feature identity-based stereotypes intended to hurt people or are they used to mock and expose the stereotypes? To what extent are media producers of talent shows aware of their role in perpetuating a climate where sexual harassment is minimised or ignored? These and other questions are not new. Scholars in media and cultural studies were studying these issues long before they were considered 'woke'. Rather, the identity-related debates point out that social inequalities in Western society persist. Media and cultural scholars can play an important role by exploring and studying how and to what extent media and popular culture have contributed to preserving societal hierarchies (e.g. by reiterating stereotypical representations) or challenging them (e.g. by creating an inclusive newsroom).

2. RESEARCHING DIVERSITY AND POPULAR MEDIA CULTURE

2.1. *Divergent paradigmatic perspectives*

Since the second half of the twentieth century, scholars have started studying the relationship between sociocultural diversity and popular media culture. Although they share an interest in the same research topic, their approaches differ significantly. For the scope of this book, I distinguish the field of 'communication sciences' from the field of 'media and cultural studies'. While in some academic contexts communication sciences is treated as an expansive field that encompasses all research on media and communication, including post-positivist mass communication research and critical media studies (see below), 'communication sciences' and 'media and cultural studies' are generally seen as fields that each rely on a different paradigmatic perspective. This does not imply that each field is homogenous. In communication sciences, for instance, its sociological traditions offer different concepts and ideas on media use than its psychological traditions. Second, to consider 'communication sciences' and 'media and cultural studies' as completely distinct from one another would violate the truth since they show some overlap (e.g. similar methods), have been inspired by one another (e.g. adopting each other's theories or concepts), and often present results that are complementary.

Nonetheless, for the scope of this book, it is relevant to point out that scholars in communication sciences and media and cultural studies generally differ from one another regarding the philosophical assumptions shaping their research. These paradigmatic assumptions concern, among others, questions of ontology (i.e. what is the nature of reality), epistemology (i.e. how can we acquire knowledge about reality), and axiology (i.e. what is the role and value of theory and knowledge) (Guba & Lincoln, 1994; Miller, 2005; Stevens, 2022). Whereas a post-positivist perspective is common within communication sciences, an interpretative and critical perspective characterises media and cultural studies.

Researchers adopting a post-positivist perspective aim to explain, predict, and control phenomena (Guba & Lincoln, 1994). The approach emerged out of positivism, with which it shares the same research objectives and the belief that there is an objective reality. However, *post*-positivist researchers argue that reality can only be partially observed and apprehended. This position is often described as a critical-realist ontology (Guba & Lincoln, 1994). Further, they stress that full objectivity cannot be achieved, as the researcher will always somehow interfere in the research (e.g. personal biases). Nonetheless, they believe that by rigorously following scientific procedures, they can find regularities and causal relationships and/or make predictions about certain phenomena (Guba & Lincoln, 1994; Stevens, 2022). Further, certain scientific criteria (e.g. reliability, validity) must be met to minimise the researcher's biases and potential impact on the results (Miller, 2005).

Scholars adopting an interpretative perspective (sometimes referred to as a constructivist perspective) aim to understand and reconstruct how people in divergent contexts make sense of the world (Guba & Lincoln, 1994). In contrast to (post-)positivism, an interpretative perspective is informed by social constructionism and argues that people experience reality differently. Hence, interpretative scholars argue that it is impossible to make generalisations or predictions about reality or to establish causal relationships. Instead, they explore the different sense-making processes of people and/or explore similarities and differences in how people experience certain phenomena. Since this approach starts from a subjective epistemology, it is not concerned with objectivity. Instead, to achieve their research goals, interpretative scholars immerse themselves in specific social contexts and get as close as possible to the research subject(s). Knowledge is acquired through social interaction and carefully reconstructing the subjective experiences of others (Guba & Lincoln, 1994; Miller, 2005).

Last, scholars adopting a critical perspective want to critique and transform "the social, political, cultural, economic, ethnic, and gender structures that constrain and exploit humankind, by engagement in confrontation, even conflict" (Guba & Lincoln, 1994, p. 113). Although there are critical scholars that start from a critical-realist ontology, many adhere to social constructionism (Miller, 2005; Stevens, 2022). This is apparent in their argument that the aforementioned structures may appear natural and unchangeable but are, in fact, socially constructed. Crucially, critical scholars argue that these structures (which include beliefs about reality and society) only appear unchangeable because ideologies have presented them as a natural order in society, even when they are structures of inequality. That is why critical scholars assume an explicit emancipatory position in their work and believe their research can and should help change structures of inequality in society (Guba & Lincoln, 1994; Miller, 2005).

2.2. Communication sciences: Realism and socialisation

As stressed in the introduction, this book predominantly relies on media and cultural studies. Yet, many trailblazing ideas about sociocultural diversity and popular media culture have been shaped by scholars within communication sciences. Communication sciences – also labelled as 'communication research', 'communication studies', or 'mass communication research' – is known for adopting a (post-)positivist perspective, a logical consequence of the fact that (post-)positivist assumptions guided researchers and schools of thought that made communication sciences in the 1950s and 1960s a discipline in its own right (Joye & Loisen, 2017). As I discuss some of its theories and findings in later chapters, I want to introduce two aspects that informed its view on studying sociocultural diversity and popular media culture.

First, there is the assumption that media can and should reflect the real world or, in other words, act as a mirror for society (Barker, 2012; Gill, 2007). This translates into an adherence to realism, as post-positivist scholars believe that representations of minoritised identities have to be 'realistic' and 'accurate'. Informed by a (critical) realist ontology, communication researchers assume that certain methods (e.g. quantitative content analysis) and protocols (e.g. measuring reliability), for instance, can capture how women are depicted in media, enable comparison between these images and women in the real world, and facilitate an assessment of how distorted the media images are compared to the real world (Van Zoonen, 1994). Take note that the ontological and epistemological foundations of this type of research are mainly post-positivist, but its axiological position gravitates toward the critical approach as this type of research aims to criticise the role of media in sustaining structures of social inequality.

Second, there is the assumption that media play an important role in the process of socialisation. A recurring objective among communication scholars, for instance, is to establish the impact of stereotypical images of minoritised groups on the perceptions and attitudes of people. Inspired by social psychology, some communication scholars have used experimental designs to determine short-term cognitive or behavioural effects (Van Zoonen, 1994). Other scholars who have been more interested in studying the long-term and latent impact of media on people turned to cultivation theory (Joye & Loisen, 2017). This theory, developed in the late 1960s, draws on the cultivation hypothesis of communication scholar George Gerbner (1998). Gerbner argued that the increased centrality of television has started to dominate people's 'symbolic environment', thus influencing audiences' perception of reality. He assumed that television audiences would steadily come to understand social reality as constructed on television. Cultivation theory thus implies that "representation in the fictional world signifies social existence;

absence means symbolic annihilation" (Gerbner & Gross, 1976, p. 182). Put differently, even though different minoritised groups are an integral part of the real world, not representing them in media implies that they do not matter symbolically. It also means that what is being represented is equally important to look at, as television is considered able to cultivate assumptions "about the facts, norms, and values of society" (p. 182). For instance, concerning images of women, Gerbner referred to a wide range of studies that demonstrated that heavy viewers were more likely to hold sexist or gender-stereotypical opinions or to attribute a narrower set of roles and activities to women (Gerbner, 1998).[5]

Communication researchers who emphasised the importance of realistic images, however, have been criticised for dismissing that all media images are cultural constructions, even the 'seemingly' realistic ones. As scholars in media and cultural studies argue, to understand the meaning of media images one has to interpret these images in relation to the contexts in which they are produced and consumed (Barker, 2012; Gill, 2007; Van Zoonen, 1994). For instance, if you want to assess whether a newspaper article or sitcom episode has the intention to discriminate against somebody through stereotyping, you also need to consider the logic and conventions of the medium (e.g. the structure of a newspaper article) and type of texts (e.g. the genre conventions and narrative structures of a sitcom) (Dyer 1984/2006, 1993; Van Zoonen, 1994). Furthermore, whose 'reality' is considered realistic or accurate? As should be clear by now, people may share the same disabled or ethnic identity, but that does not mean that they share the same values, norms, life goals, or interests. Besides, in their reliance on quantitative content analyses, communication researchers have mainly focused on manifest content. Even though quantitative research can reveal disparities and trends (e.g. a systematic underrepresentation of music artists of colour in the programming of music festivals), qualitative research into latent meanings of a text can reveal ingrained prejudices and less conspicuous stereotypes (Dhaenens & Van Bauwel, 2022; Gill, 2007). Last, some scholars within this tradition have overemphasised the effects of mass media on audiences, discrediting the myriads of ways audiences are able to decode images (Gauntlett, 2008; Hall, 1980; Hermes, 2024; Van Zoonen, 1994) (see below).

---

5   To illustrate how cultivation theory has been used to study the representation of women, I refer to Gaye Tuchman's work in Chapter 2. Concerning the representation of nonheterosexual people, I refer to Larry Gross's work in Chapter 3.

2.3. Media and cultural studies: Ideology and sense-making practices

Another approach to studying media, communication, and popular culture was developed in the field of media and cultural studies, which is characterised by research that adopts a critical and/or interpretative perspective. Media and cultural studies is indebted to the British cultural studies tradition, which fully matured with the establishment of the Birmingham Centre for Contemporary Cultural Studies (CCCS) in 1964. Founded by scholars within English literary studies, noteworthy Richard Hoggart, the centre aimed to (initially) study the everyday life practices of the British working class (Kellner, 1995; Turner, 2003). From the 1950s on, Hoggart and his contemporaries Raymond Williams and E. P. Thompson were already concerned with preserving and valorising the culture of the working class while being critical of capitalist structures and popular culture (Kellner, 2023; Turner, 2003).

Many scholars affiliated with the CCCS have found inspiration in Marxism (see Chapter 6). Marxist thought allowed them to see how culture, conceptualised as "the texts and practices of everyday life" (Storey, 1996, p. 2), co-constitutes society and history. They argue that culture does not simply reflect society but takes on a vital role in co-constructing which ideologies become and remain hegemonic in society. Following Teun van Dijk (2006), ideologies should be thought of as belief systems, including ideas, norms, and values, which are socially shared and shape the social identity of a group. They are fundamental in the sense that they "control and organize other socially shared beliefs" (p. 116). For instance, feminist ideologies shape ideas about abortion, the gender pay gap, and access to education. Last, they are something that people gradually acquire, making them relatively stable and thereby invisible and experienced as normal. However, they are not set in stone: they can be questioned and challenged, and over time disintegrate (Van Dijk, 2006). They should be thought of as 'hegemonic', an idea based on Antonio Gramsci's (1971) concept of hegemony. Hegemony refers to a situation in which a ruling class or group can maintain its power and authority because it exercises a "moral and intellectual leadership", which is able to make subordinate groups or classes believe that the ruling classes' belief systems are for the benefit of all (Jones, 2006, p. 55). Yet, the notion of hegemony also implies that a hegemonic ideology can be challenged and resisted. Scholars in media and cultural studies argue that media and popular culture can play a pivotal role in both sustaining certain ideologies *as* hegemonic as well as resisting and challenging their hegemonic position (see below). In other words, media and cultural scholars who adopt a critical perspective aim to unveil the ideological dimensions of media and popular culture texts and practices (Storey, 2021; Turner, 2003). Furthermore, many research projects within media and cultural studies use theories on ideology and hegemony to understand how sociocultural diversity and inequality are dealt with in popular media culture. Although the CCCS was chiefly concerned with class-related issues in the 1960s, it broadened its scope from the 1970s onward to issues that relate to gender, race and ethnicity, and sexual diversity. A recurrent objective in these studies was the exploration of "the ways that cultural forms served either to further social domination, or to enable people to resist and struggle against domination" (Kellner, 1995, p. 31).

Social and cultural theorist Stuart Hall, who directed the CCCS from 1968 to 1979, also shaped the field by questioning the linear model of mass communication. He formulated his ideas in his seminal essay 'Encoding/decoding' (1980). He argued that mediated communication could be seen as "a structure produced and sustained through the articulation of linked but distinctive moments – production, circulation, distribution/consumption, reproduction" (p. 128). In this process, meaning has to be encoded into a discursive form (e.g. recounting an event as a written news article) and circulated (e.g. distribution via newspapers). The process of communication is only 'successful' if someone decodes the mediated text into something that makes sense to the decoder. This article brought to our awareness that, first, 'encoders' and 'decoders' are shaped by ideology and probably draw from those ideological frameworks when encoding messages (as producers of media) and decoding messages (as audiences/consumers of media). Second, there is not one way to decode a message, meaning that there are numerous ways to make sense of the same message. Media producers may hope for a preferred reading, which implies that audiences make sense of the text as it was intended by the producers. In this case, the encoding and decoding parties share the same ideologies and do not question the ideas, norms, and values expressed in the text. In the case of a negotiated reading, audiences chiefly agree with the preferred meaning of a text but disagree with elements or arguments that conflict with some of their own ideas, norms, and values. Last, an oppositional or resistant reading refers to a situation where audiences interpret the text in a way that defies the intended meaning because the audience members hold different ideas, norms, and values and/or deliberately object and resist the ideologies embedded in the text (Hall, 1980). Such oppositional or resistant reading practices have been referred to as acts of cultural resistance. They can express alternatives and counter-discourses to hegemonic ideologies and contribute to social change (Duncombe, 2002). In Chapter 3, I illustrate how fan practices such as slash fiction and queer reading can act as practices of cultural resistance and challenge the hegemony of heteronormativity.

Hall's work has informed plenty of audience and reception studies in media and cultural studies that inquired into how people make sense of media and/or receive the images they see on screen (During, 2005; Turner, 2003). In contrast to studies relying on cultivation theory, these studies adopted an interpretative perspective as the goal was to explore the sense-making practices of audiences. For studies on sociocultural diversity, this gave way to reception studies that explored how people with minoritised identities have made sense of series or films that intended to represent them or to audience studies that focused on the role media and popular culture assume in how minoritised people make sense of their identities. For instance, Fien Adriaens (2014) invited Turkish Belgian girls to create a collage of a fictional television programme they would like to see. Using various ethnographic methods, Adriaens assessed how diaspora girls in Flanders, Belgium, made sense of their identities. She found that what these girls shared most was a concern with figuring out which femininities are appropriate. Their diasporic identity was important to them, as it was represented in many pitched programmes, but the role it assumed differed between the girls. The study highlighted how people have different intersecting identities (age, gender, ethnicity) and how youngsters shift between those subject positions, depending on the context they are in.

Even though the CCCS and its scholars have played a formative role in the field, various centres and divergent approaches emerged within and outside the United Kingdom (During, 2005). Notwithstanding the diversity of theoretical frameworks (e.g. Marxism, structuralism, poststructuralism, feminisms) and methods (textual analysis, ethnographic methods) they use, the interpretative and critical perspectives remain the main approaches to studying the intricate relations between society and media and culture. Some adopted the term 'cultural studies' to describe their research, while others introduced a cultural studies approach in existing disciplines and programmes such as sociology, history, or literature. As I have mentioned before, some scholars within departments of communication sciences also started researching media from a cultural studies approach. These scholars often situate themselves within 'media studies' as a way to distinguish themselves from communication sciences. Because of the overlap in theoretical perspectives, methodological approaches, and interests, these research traditions are grouped in this book under the denominator of 'media and cultural studies'.

Scholars in media and cultural studies have often been criticised by fellow scholars. Some of these criticisms are addressed in later chapters, but I already want to highlight a few. For instance, the first wave of British cultural studies was criticised by scholars interested in audience studies for overly relying on textual analysis and critical readings of cultural texts, without analysing how audiences made sense of these cultural texts. Then again, media and cultural scholars engaging with actual audiences through ethnographic research or interviews were criticised for an overly celebratory attitude toward 'resistant' reading practices by audiences. Such criticism came from scholars informed by political economy who addressed the need to study the production context of popular media culture (Kellner, 1995; see also Chapter 6). Nonetheless, as Simon During (2005) highlighted, the field of media and cultural studies is also known for its self-reflexivity and ability to examine its history and, when needed, adjust its objectives, methods, and theoretical standpoints. Especially when the objectives are to understand how minoritised identities have been represented in popular media culture and to use that knowledge to challenge social inequalities and make societies more inclusive, media and cultural studies has proven to be a well-suited and well-equipped field.

3. REPRESENTATION

3.1. Politics of representation

In a book called *Represent!*, it should come as no surprise that most of the studies and authors discussed here are concerned with representation. Since culture and language are crucial in the process of how people make sense of themselves, it is only logical scholars are interested in studying *how* identities are described, discussed, and represented. Drawing on Stuart Hall (1997), representation can be understood as "the production of meaning through language" (p. 28). In Hall's work, we can recognise a social constructionist positionality, as he argued that the meaning of things, subjects, or concepts depends on the temporal and spatial context to which they belong.

Hall (1997) directed our attention to cultural representations in popular media culture and stressed that these representations are not per se trivial, innocent, or value-free. Instead, they are political in the broadest sense of the word. This means that any popular culture text (e.g. a television show, a stand-up comedy performance, a YouTube channel, or a TikTok profile), deliberately or not, articulates a set of ideas, norms, and values, favouring certain practices over others, or including and privileging groups of people over other groups. These practices of representation can be seen as a form of *politics*, which, according to Hall, implies that these representations can maintain a sociocultural status quo. In other words, they are ideological and, in many instances, reiterate social and cultural disparities. At the same time, Hall (2005) argued that popular culture cannot be regarded as only affirming hegemonic ideologies (see above). Because of its ability to act as a site where production, text, and reception interact and meaning is constantly renegotiated, popular media culture can be part of a struggle *for* and *against* hegemonic ideas and beliefs about society. Put simply, audiences may come across film or television content that stereotypes and discriminates, but they may also find resistant, critical, and inclusive representations of minoritised groups.

Furthermore, contrary to what some might expect, we not only encounter critical and/or inclusive representations of minoritised identities in content produced by independent filmmakers but also in content produced by international mainstream media companies. Series produced and/or distributed by HBO and Netflix have been lauded by media critics, civil society actors, and (minoritised) audiences for their inclusion and depiction of minoritised identities. For instance, HBO's police series *The Wire* (2002–2008) has been praised for its authentic but bleak representation of inner-city life in Baltimore (Haynes, 2016; Thompson, 2012). Even though the series focuses on the city's drug trade, it uses the crime narrative to demonstrate how bureaucratic structures of organisation, political self-interest, and capitalist logic limit and hamper social and political institutions (e.g. law, politics, education, media) to engender social change and justice. It should be noted that these popular media texts are often ambiguous and subject to interpretation. For instance, some scholars and critics found the series reiterating stereotypes about poverty among black Americans (Haynes, 2016). Kecia Driver Thompson (2012), on the other hand, found the naturalist approach toward representing black and working-poor characters focused on highlighting the complexity and humanity of these characters. She argued that "[r]ather than perpetuating stereotypes, *The Wire* systematically deconstructs and undermines them, even as it holds public institutions responsible for the damage they inflict on individuals" (p. 110).

It is not always easy to figure out why independent or mainstream media companies invest in representations that are diverse and/or inclusive. As argued before, the inclusion of diversity may be an act of window dressing or woke-washing but can also be an act of true commitment to social change. For instance, many organisers of identity-based film festivals (e.g. Festival du film franco-arabe de Noisy-le-Sec, Superfest International Disability Film Festival, Oslo/Fusion International Film Festival (see figure 3) believe their festivals, first, demonstrate work about minoritised identities that have been structurally ignored in mainstream media and, second, forge connections between minoritised audiences attending and watching these films. At the same time, identity-based festivals have looked for ways to become profitable and/or stay commercially viable. Skadi Loist (2012), for instance, pointed out how certain LGBTQ film festivals increasingly catered "to a mainstream, homonormative, sponsorship-friendly group – an imagined white,

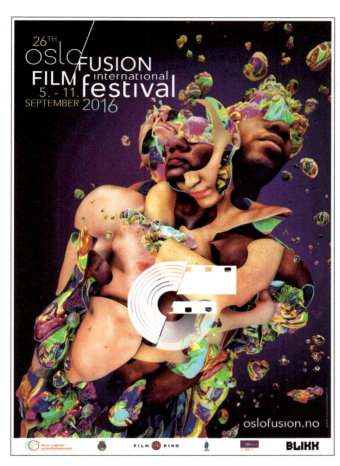

Figure 3. Poster of the 2016 Oslo/Fusion Film Festival. The Norwegian festival, founded in 1990, showcases films representing gender and sexual diversity or made by LGBTQ directors. Courtesy of Oslo/Fusion Film Festival, design Marion Habringer.

affluent homosexual (male) middle-class" (p. 164). Even though the festivals' communication may be focused on being inclusive and emancipatory, it is crucial to compare a festival's marketing with what it actually does; How is the non-profit organisation running the festival organised? Which films are selected and when and where are they programmed? Do the films represent who the festival claims to represent (e.g. mainly programming gay male-themed films or including films with diverse LGBTQ identities)? Is there a balance between identity politics and entertainment?

Even though less surprising, mainstream media companies too claimed to bring groundbreaking representations of diversity but failed to live up to their promise after delivering the actual content. For instance, the live-action remake *Beauty and the Beast* (Bill Condon, 2017) was teased and promoted as featuring Disney's first-ever openly gay character. However, many LGBTQ audiences felt betrayed after having seen the film. The homosexuality of LeFou (Josh Gad) – a side character implied to harbour a crush on Gaston (Luke Evans), the film's main antagonist – is barely explored in the film and mostly deployed for comic relief.[6]

3.2. *Stereotyping*

A key tool in the politics of representation is stereotyping. The practice of stereotyping has been studied from a variety of academic disciplines and traditions (e.g. social psychology, law, communication sciences), which has resulted in distinct approaches and definitions. Yet, many of these definitions drew inspiration from writer Walter Lippmann's conceptualisation of stereotyping. In his renowned work *Public Opinion* (1922), a book concerned with understanding mass media and its potential effects on public opinion, he discussed the concept of stereotyping as being part of the process of social categorisation. He explained that "[i]n the great blooming, buzzing confusion of the outer world we pick out what our culture has already defined for us, and we tend to perceive that which we have picked out in the form stereotyped for us by our culture" (p. 55). In other words, he stressed that people were using what they had learned (including identity categories) to make sense of the world and people around them. He argued that humans were doing this out of necessity:

> There is economy in this. For the attempt to see all things freshly and in detail, rather than as types and generalities, is exhausting, and among busy affairs practically out of the question. In a circle of friends, and in relation to close associates or competitors, there is no shortcut through, and no substitute for, an individualised understanding. Those whom we love and admire most are the men and women whose consciousness is peopled thickly with persons rather than with types, who know us rather than the classification into which we might fit. For even without phrasing it to ourselves, we feel intuitively that all classification is in relation to some purpose not necessarily our own. (p. 59)

Lippmann explained that the modern world had become increasingly complex and exhausting to decode, forcing people to rely on stereotypes to make sense of the world in a fairly quick and economic manner. Lippmann lamented the loss of time to get to know one another because the modern world forced people to seek out specific traits to "fill in the rest of the picture by means of the stereotypes we carry about in our heads" (p. 59).

---

6   This practice is dubbed 'queerbaiting', which is explored in Chapter 3.

Lippmann's theory also became a basis for thinking about stereotyping in media and cultural studies. To explore this, I turn to film and popular culture scholar Richard Dyer, a former member of the CCCS. Dyer (1993) revisited Lippmann's work to develop his own theory on stereotyping. He criticised the fact that Lippmann presented stereotyping as only having a social function (i.e. social categorisation), whereas Dyer emphasised that it also has an ideological function (i.e. the consolidation of social hierarchies). In other words, he agreed with Lippmann that stereotyping is a process of ordering but reminded us that power is unequally distributed among groups of people in society. This means that those with political, economic, or cultural power are able to create and maintain a social hierarchy and represent that social order as fixed, absolute, and 'normal'. Similarly, Lippmann's notion of stereotype as a shortcut – which refers to the practice of someone picking up cues to make assumptions about that person – is bound to power dynamics in society, as these 'cues' are not necessarily neutral or objective. Dyer pointed out that many of these assumptions are based on partial truths, false impressions, and rigid conceptions about groups of people. Especially marginalised and oppressed groups of people, the 'out-groups' in society, are faced with misguided and baseless ideas about their identities. Stereotypes about the out-groups are created and controlled by people who make up the majority in society (i.e. the in-group) and are a means to express the in-group's values and norms. Dyer (1984/2006, 1993) stressed that these stereotypes circulate widely in society (e.g. in the way we talk about each other, policy documents, or school regulations) and are part of the fabric of cultural products, such as film and television.

Focusing on how people in popular fiction are represented, Dyer (1984/2006, 1993) highlighted that they are often represented as types. A type refers to "any simple, vivid, memorable, easily grasped and widely recognised characterisation in which a few traits are foregrounded and change or 'development' is kept to a minimum" (1984/2006, p. 355). Yet, a distinction is made among types. There are social types, "which indicate those who live by the rules of society", and stereotypes, which refer to "those whom the rules are designed to exclude" (p. 355). Social types are often represented as more multidimensional and flexible in their characterisation (e.g. charming clichés about the in-group), whereas stereotypes are one-dimensional, clear-cut, unalterable, and harmful (e.g. unfounded dangerous traits attributed to the out-group).

Dyer (1984/2006) also drew our attention to two modes of stereotyping in audiovisual content: stereotyping through iconography and stereotyping through structure. Writing about homosexuality, he described the practice of stereotyping through iconography as follows: the "[u]se of a certain set of visual and aural signs which immediately bespeak homosexuality and connote the qualities associated, stereotypically, with it" (p. 357). The practice corresponds to Lippmann's shortcut.

Such representations are often the result of economic considerations. For films or series with little time to introduce new characters, iconographic stereotypes are considered an effective means to inform the audience that a character is, for instance, Jewish, part of the working class, or disabled. However, as a consequence, representations are created that reiterate clichés, half-truths, and lies about people.

Second, stereotyping through structure is the result of the function of the character in the audiovisual text's structures. Structures encompass static structures, which refer to dominant ideologies and material conditions of the film or series' imagined world, or dynamic structures, which refer to plot developments throughout a film or a series (Dyer, 1984/2006). Regarding stereotyping through static structures, we may think of the representation of a lesbian couple in which one woman is represented as more 'masculine' and the other woman as more 'feminine' and is shown to be mimicking (obsolete) heterosexual patterns (e.g. gendered household and occupational roles). This form of stereotyping starts from a heteronormative outlook on relationships (see Chapter 3). It should be stressed that these static structures, such as heteronormativity, can be found in fictional content about worlds and contexts that resemble reality as well as in fiction about imagined worlds. For example, although science-fiction films may take place in imaginary worlds, they often resemble Western patriarchal societies.

Besides, regarding stereotyping through dynamic structures, we may think of a plot in which a female politician is represented as a woman who is unable to be both a good politician and a good mother and wife, ultimately failing in her parental and family duties. Other deeply problematic examples include the stereotypes of a gay male character turning out to be a predator and a Muslim character turning out to be a terrorist. A more subtle example is representing a disabled person as a supercrip. The supercrip trope figures people with disabilities as "remarkable achievers [...] who against all odds, triumph over the tragedy of their condition" (Harnett, 2000, p. 22). It implies that disabled people are not 'normal' and should figure out a way to rise above their disability – become extraordinary – if they want to be accepted or celebrated in an able-bodied society (see Chapter 5).

3.3. Trans-coding strategies

Besides understanding stereotyping, scholars in media and cultural studies also explored how dominant modes of representation (including the use of stereotypes) can be and have been exposed, challenged, and changed. Stuart Hall (1997) discussed a few practices that he dubbed trans-coding, which he defined as "taking an existing meaning and re-appropriating it for new meanings" (p. 270). Put differently, trans-coding strategies are about shifting the meanings of certain words and images in such a way that they no longer discriminate and harm another person or sustain material or symbolic forms of inequality. Hall discussed these counterstrategies by way of racialised representations of black persons in mainstream popular media culture but underscored that his arguments could be applied to other dimensions of difference, such as gender, social class, disability, or sexuality.

Hall (1997) dubbed the first trans-coding strategy 'reversing the stereotypes'. Hall elaborated on this practice by discussing a range of American Blaxploitation movies, such as *Sweet Sweetback's Baadasssss Song* (Melvin Peebles, 1971), made in the early 1970s, which depicted black male characters as the films' main heroes (see figure 4). The genre was important as it reversed how Hollywood films represented black Americans. Whereas Hollywood tended to represent black characters as dependent, subservient, and side characters, Blaxploitation films represented black characters as main characters with agency and symbolic power. Moreover, while Hollywood used certain negative stereotypes to discredit black male characters, such as representing them as hypersexual and hypermasculine, Blaxploitation films claimed these traits as positive qualities and celebrated them. Even though Hall understood the appeal to black audiences, as these films felt like forms of revenge, he warned that extreme stereotypes (being poor, being subservient) were reversed into other extremes (e.g. being motivated by money, indulging in crime and sex). Such reversals did not challenge the continuation of representing black people as 'other'.

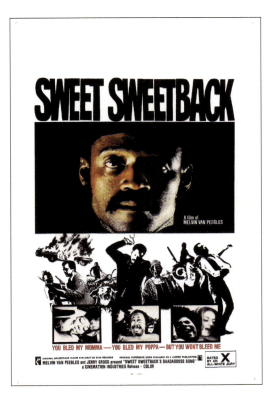

Figure 4. Film poster of *Sweet Sweetback's Baadasssss Song* (1971). Photo credit: Employee(s) of Cinemation Industries, public domain via Wikimedia commons.

A second strategy concerns the inclusion of 'positive images' where we used to see negative images or no images at all. What is crucial here is that this strategy is not concerned with reversing stereotypes (which would lead to 'new' stereotypes) but with representing difference and diversity as a positive thing. The strategy led to the creation of slogans that affirmed people's racial and ethnic minoritised identity (e.g. 'Black is Beautiful') and emphasised sameness and equality (e.g. the well-known United Colors of Benetton advertisements with models from different ethnic identities) (see figure 5). Hall, however, wondered whether the intentions behind these images were emancipatory and critical or whether they simply commodified 'difference'. Neither did they actively undermine the range of negative stereotypes that persist because the images and content evade difficult questions that revolve around structural inequalities (Hall, 1997). A sitcom like *The Cosby Show* (NBC, 1984–1992), featuring an upper-class black family, was revolutionary because of its positive representation of a successful black family but was equally criticised for its deliberate avoidance of addressing race- and class-related issues. By not tackling ongoing forms of discrimination against black people in the United States, the series implied that racism had become a thing of the past (Nelson & George, 1995).

Figure 5. Italian fashion company Benetton Group is widely known for its advertisements that emphasize diversity and inclusivity. Following a successful campaign in 1984 that celebrated 'all the colours of the world', the company renamed its brand 'United Colors of Benetton'. Photo credit: A/I 1984, 'Tutti I colori del mondo', Oliviero Toscani.

Figure 6. Film still from *If Beale Street Could Talk* (2018). Tish (KiKi Layne) visits Fonny (Stephan James) in prison. Photo credit: Landmark Media, © Imageselect/Alamy.

The third strategy Hall (1997) discussed is dubbed 'through the eye of representation', which seems to be his preferred strategy. Hall stressed that this practice "locates itself within the complexities and ambivalences of representation itself, and tries to contest it from within" (p. 274). Rather than introducing new content, the practice focuses on the *formal* capacities of media content. It acknowledges the polysemy of signs (such as language and imagery), which means that words and images may mean different things to different people. As such, it rather tries to *play* with the *struggle* over representation than reverse it or replace it with new words and images. In a way, this strategy can be seen as a subversive strategy. It does not intend to be oppositional or blunt in its tactics to challenge stereotypical meanings attached to specific images but rather uses established conventions, language, or modes of representing to erode and change meanings from within. A good example is *If Beale Street Could Talk* (Barry Jenkins, 2018), an adaptation of James Baldwin's novel by the same name from 1974 (see figure 6). The film is set in New York in the 1970s and focuses on Tish (KiKi Layne) and Fonny (Stephan James), two young black Americans who fall in love with each other and whose happiness ends abruptly when Fonny is indicated as the rapist of Victoria (Emily Rios), a Puerto Rican woman. The film is narrated in a nonlinear manner, making audiences question and reexamine initial presumptions about the main characters. As the film unfolds, it becomes clear that a white officer had coerced Victoria to identify Fonny as her rapist. As an audience, we are nudged to feel anger at the forms of social injustice that befall black Americans while, gradually, also feeling conflicted over Victoria as she must deal with the trauma of rape and being forced to accuse someone of being her rapist. The film reveals how systemic racism and misogyny are related and how social and structural hierarchies significantly impact the everyday lives of people with minoritised identities. As such, the film also works as a good illustration of Crenshaw's concept of structural intersectionality (see above). Last, the film challenges one-dimensional images of black American families, as the unplanned pregnancy of Tish evokes conflicting responses from her and Fonny's family members. What should be remembered from this example is that this strategy enables content creators to represent characters with individual traits, both positive and negative, and to allow them to change over time.

Focus on *This is America*

To conclude this chapter, I invite you to watch Childish Gambino's music video *This is America* (Hiro Murai, 2018) (see figure 7). Childish Gambino is the stage name of American artist and actor Donald Glover, whose video became a viral hit and an object of discussion and debate. Many music critics, media and cultural scholars, and fans have tried to untangle the meaning of the music video since the images and the lyrics are ambiguous and demand audiences to actively engage with the video's content. Importantly, the song and video speak to two distinct audiences. First, it addresses black audiences, in particular black American audiences, who know, feel, and share the subjectivities represented on screen, grounded in their historical and contemporary knowledge and lived experiences. The video also addresses white (American) audiences, showing them the state of the country and the role the United States and its citizens assume in upholding structural and racial hierarchies.

The video allows us to explore the use of trans-coding strategies as part of the video's politics of representation. Even though the video may feature equivocal imagery, its politics is focused on revealing what it means to be black in the United States today. To this end, Childish Gambino looks at the United States and black American culture through the eye of representation. The video emphasises the ambivalence of representation itself. One way of doing this is by including both positive and negative images of black Americans and exaggerating both. The negative ones relate to associations with violence or with some of the worst stereotypes of black people, most noteworthy the Jim Crow stereotype that Childish Gambino impersonates. Jim Crow refers to a white actor, Thomas Dartmouth Rice, who travelled the United States with a minstrel show in the early nineteenth century. He performed in blackface a character named Jim Crow, an elderly black enslaved man dressed in rags. The name 'Jim Crow' became an offensive slur used against black Americans and was later associated with Jim Crow laws in the southern states of America, which enforced racial segregation (Tischauser, 2012). For Clinton Yates (2018), Childish Gambino's embodiment of all these stereotypes is a way to express the inability to escape the past – as black Americans carry the fear and hate with them ever since and are always 'seen' to still embody the stereotype, as looters or harassers. Think, for instance, of news reports on Black Lives Matter demonstrations.

These negative images are brought up in a constant dialogue with positive images of black American culture (e.g. dancing scenes, gospel choir, the guitar player at the beginning of the music video). Yet, these images – like the negative ones – should also be seen as exaggerations and carry an ideological critique. In the United States, there has been a tendency to celebrate black Americans' contributions to popular culture, while dismissing or minimising their demands to address and end police violence and perpetual racism. This is highlighted in the scenes where people are worshipping guns while lives lost to gun violence are being ignored. The video, for instance, features a reference to the deadly Charleston Church Shooting from 2018.

Figure 7. Still from *This Is America* (2018), with Childish Gambino miming the loading of a gun. Photo credit: Landmark Media, © Imageselect/Alamy.

To conclude, the music video shows us the United States in limbo. On the one hand, there is an increased awareness of racial oppression, thanks to civil society organisations and activists, and an increased use of digital media to record forms of oppression and harassment (as is referenced in the video with youngsters using their mobile phones to record acts of violence). On the other hand, structural changes or major actions seem to be lagging. The ending of the video, with Gambino running away from a mob chasing him, imagines the consequences of not addressing racism earnestly.

CHAPTER 2

GENDER

Setting the scene: Miranda

To start this chapter, I invite you to watch the episode 'The New Me' (season 2, episode 1) from the popular British sitcom *Miranda* (BBC, 2009-2015). The sitcom, created by comedian Miranda Hart, is about a woman who used her inheritance to buy a joke shop. Hart had already performed the semi-autobiographical character during her stand-up comedy shows in 2005. After a successful pitch to the BBC, the British public service broadcaster, Hart was allowed to produce the sitcom as a radio show in 2009, *Miranda Hart's Joke Shop*. The radio show was a success, which opened the door for a television adaptation in 2009 (Ellis-Petersen, 2017; *Miranda starts filming*, 2009).

Figure 8. Still from *Miranda* (2009–2015), with Miranda (Miranda Hart) and her friends at the sushi parlour. © BBC Archive.

Miranda was created and promoted as an 'old-fashioned' British sitcom. It had a limited cast of characters, fixed locations, and narratives revolving around misunderstandings. Besides, it was filmed in a studio in front of a live audience. The sitcom narrates the everyday life of Miranda (Miranda Hart), a single woman living in a flat above her joke shop. She is socially awkward and clumsy, partly attributed to actress Miranda Hart being taller than an average woman. Among the main cast of characters, there is her overbearing mother Penny (Patricia Hodge), her best friend Stevie (Sarah Hadland), and her male friend Gary (Tom Ellis), with whom she is madly in love.

In the first episode of the second season, 'The New Me', Miranda decides that she must become a 'different woman'. Among the reasons for this change is her desire to fit in with her two female friends from high school, nicknamed 'Tilly' (Sally Phillips) and 'Stinky' (Belinda Stewart-Wilson), and to impress her mother. In this episode, Miranda meets her friends from school for lunch in a sushi parlour. Two scenes are worth discussing. In a scene that precedes her lunch date, she describes to Stevie what kind of woman she aspires to be:

> Today I have begun the new me [...] I'm gonna be the kind of woman that just leaps out of bed, and just does that [Miranda shakes her head] and their hair looks perfect. They then grab a homemade muffin out of their caskets and polka-dot biscuit tin, and head to work wearing trainers at the bottom of their skirt-suit to show off they have power-walked in. They have pot plants that don't die on them. Their fruit bowl isn't full of three-week-old rotting pears because they actually eat the fruit. [...] They just grab a wheat germ smoothie in between work because that's enough to keep them going even though at lunchtime they jogged and enjoyed it because they don't have flesh that moves independently to their mainframe [...] you know, I'm gonna be that kind of woman.

Equally important is how she delivers the monologue. Exaggerated gestures and facial expressions underline how Miranda considers this idealised femininity unachievable, disconnected from the everyday experiences of many women, and composed of contradictory norms, values, and expectations. This idealised form of femininity, described in this chapter as 'emphasised femininity' or 'hegemonic femininity' (see below), nonetheless continues to dictate how women should look, behave, and express themselves, and what women should aspire to in life. Miranda too decides to give it a go. Upon leaving the shop to see her friends from high school, she proclaims to Stevie that she will succeed in becoming a new person: "Look at her, forming before your very own eyes." To accentuate her new performance of femininity, she grabs one of the large trinket necklaces she sells in her shop.

The necklace is an essential prop for the scene set in the sushi parlour (see figure 8). Miranda, sitting next to her two friends at the sushi conveyor belt, mimics the gendered, upper-middle-class expressions of her friends. The scene highlights the pressure women feel to emulate this idealised form of femininity but also debunks those ideals. On the one hand, there are Miranda's ridiculous attempts at performing this kind of femininity. On the other hand, the actresses performing Tilly and Stinky also exaggerate their 'feminine' gestures and speech to equally make fun of an idealised femininity. To put an end to the idea of aspiring to this type of femininity, the scene finishes with a remarkable act of slapstick humour. Miranda's new necklace ends up getting stuck in the sushi conveyor belt. Unable to free it, she knocks over her friends, glasses, and food, and, eventually, has to climb onto the sushi belt. In doing so, Miranda Hart uses her body not only to make people laugh but also to challenge outdated stereotypes about how women should look and behave.

According to Ellie Tomsett (2018), this kind of self-deprecating humour performed by female comedians should be understood as intrinsically ambiguous. Self-deprecating humour is used when "comedians target themselves in their jokes, disparaging and depreciating their perceived cultural value" (p. 6). On the one hand, this type of humour has been experienced as a way to liberate oneself from gender stereotypes and to validate 'real' women instead of idealised performances of femininity. Furthermore, these strategies can also be seen as practices of hyperstereotyping. In discussing the identity-based stereotypes in the adult animated sitcom *The Simpsons* (Fox, 1989-present), Jonathan Gray (2006) argued that exaggerated stereotyping (often cramming all stereotypes into one character) has been used "to make the process of stereotyping the target, rather than the people themselves" (p. 64). Gray, however, acknowledged how hyperstereotyping may also backfire as not all audiences may decode the images as a critique of stereotypes. For many, self-deprecating humour may thus come across as devaluing women as it echoes a tradition of male comedy in which women and their bodies have been the butt of the joke. Does it really challenge patriarchal ideas about women and their bodies if it is a woman making fun of her own body?

In the end, much depends on the audiences' sense-making practices. Do they read the use of this self-deprecating humour as intended (i.e. to question gender stereotypes) or do they interpret it as affirming traditional ideas about women (i.e. laughing *at* women with unruly bodies)? At the same time, this ambiguity cannot simply be resolved as many popular culture texts are open to contradictory interpretations. Rather than dismissing all forms of self-deprecating humour out of fear of constraining and devaluing women, several humour scholars (Tomsett, 2018; Russell, 2002) argued to understand this type of humour as a cultural practice that is simultaneously emancipatory and restrictive.

1. SEX, GENDER, AND FEMINISMS

1.1. Disentangling sex from gender

A discussion of gender and popular media culture should inevitably start with a conceptualisation of the identity categories at stake. Even though 'gender' is the core concept of this chapter, it needs to be understood in relation to 'sex' – which is related to gender but not the same. Sex is generally understood as the biochemical and genetic structures that differentiate 'male' human beings from 'female' human beings in terms of one's reproductive system and secondary sex characteristics (e.g. beard, breast development). Although it is generally referred to in binary terms (i.e. either 'male' or 'female'), scientists and scholars continue to debate whether we should conceive of sex as a continuum (see Fausto-Sterling, 1993) or a dichotomy (see Sax, 2002). At the heart of this debate are intersex conditions, which refer to "variations in sexual biology [...] that do not fit into binary definitions of male or female" (Morrison et al., 2021, p. 2713). Although the debate continues to be waged, it is a fact that intersex persons have to navigate life in a society that starts from a dichotomous perspective on sex.

Gender refers to the social construction of gender categories (e.g. male/masculine, female/feminine, nonbinary) and "the socially imposed attributes and behaviours which are assigned to these categories" (Milestone & Meyer, 2012, p. 12). It refers to how people make sense of their bodies, feelings, and desires in terms of traits, norms, and values that are gendered. The (self-)identification with a particular gender category (e.g. male, female, nonbinary) refers to a person's gender identity. Gender categories are often assumed to be congruent with a person's sex as assigned at birth. For instance, when your sex is assigned 'male', your gender will be identified as 'male', and you will be nudged and expected to experience particular attributes and behaviour as 'male' and think of yourself as a boy/man. People who experience their gender as congruent with their sex and gender assigned at birth are generally described as cisgender persons. People who experience their gender as different from the sex and gender assigned at birth are generally described as transgender or trans persons (Morrison et al., 2021). A related identity category is nonbinary, used by people who embrace "a diversity of expressions, moving beyond and not confined exclusively to the man/woman, masculine/feminine gender binary categorization" (Morrison et al., 2021, p. 2713).

1.2. Masculinities and femininities

People have been socialised to not only make sense of their own gender identity but also of someone else's gender identity. They base themselves on cultural repertoires (which often include stereotypes) to categorise and attribute a gender identity to a person. To do so, they rely on a person's gender expression, which refers to the presentation of the self that expresses a gender identity or gender role, which may or may not correspond to how one experiences their gender. Think about clothing, hairstyles, habits, but also behaviour. The fact that people link certain clothing styles to either men or women has to do with their understanding of how masculinity and femininity are defined in a given society. 'Masculinity' and 'femininity' refer to cultural repertoires that stipulate which expectations, roles, discourses, behaviour, and expressions are considered masculine and which are considered feminine.

This cultural knowledge for constructing a self-identity or making assumptions about another person's gender identity has also been instrumental in the establishment of a hegemonic gender order. To explore this, we turn to sociologist Raewyn Connell. She, among others, argued that there is no such thing as one 'masculinity' or 'femininity', as diverse gendered cultural repertoires result in different patterns of masculinity and femininity. Crucially, these 'masculinities' and 'femininities' should not be seen as fixed or essentialist character types but as temporary and context-dependent configurations that are the result of gender relations among men (Connell, 2005). In her research, she mostly focused on understanding masculinities in Western society. Based on studies conducted in high schools, she started to understand why a gender order was being preserved (Connell, 2014). She postulated that a gender hierarchy, in institutions like schools but also in society at large, is composed of four different patterns of masculinity interacting with one another: hegemony, complicity, subordination, and marginalisation (Connell, 2005). In this gender hierarchy, there is one pattern of masculinity that is "most honoured, which occupies the position of centrality in a structure of gender relations, and whose privileged position helps to stabilise the gender order as a whole, especially the social subordination of women" (2014, p. 8). Connell described this pattern as hegemonic masculinity. The expressions, norms, values, or ideals associated with this pattern are culturally specific but are generally expressed by men who embody the cultural ideal and possess institutional power and authority (Connell, 2005).

At the same time, Connell (2005) pointed out that the "number of men rigorously practising the hegemonic pattern in its entirety may be quite small" (p. 79). To understand then why this pattern of masculinity is rarely challenged and remains 'hegemonic', we need to look at the other patterns of masculinity. Complicity, or complicit masculinity, refers to the pattern embodied and expressed by men who benefit from supporting a patriarchal gender order and the subordination of women, "without the tensions or risks of being the frontline troops of patriarchy" (p. 79). Put differently, although they do not embody the cultural ideal of masculinity and/or hold institutional power, they do not (publicly) question the patriarchal gender order. Some of them may aspire to embody hegemonic masculinity one day. Others merely emulate hegemonic masculine behaviour in public for personal gains. Think of men who publicly mimic the behaviours of other men (e.g. refraining from showing emotions, or making sexist jokes) to form homosocial ties, while they may act and think differently in private. In any case, complicit masculinity contributes to the legitimacy of hegemonic masculinity.

The success of hegemonic masculinity also depends on how it is contrasted with patterns of masculinity that are viewed as inferior in the gender order, often accompanied by symbolic practices of discrimination (e.g. shouting slurs, stereotyping) and material practices of exclusion (e.g. not granting equal rights). First, the pattern of subordinated masculinity refers to masculinities that deviate from what is considered 'normal' and 'ideal' ways of acting like a man. In contemporary Western society, this refers to masculinities embodied by nonheterosexual men, transmen, and heterosexual men whose gender expressions are considered 'feminine' or 'effeminate' (Connell, 2005, p. 80). Second, the pattern of marginalised masculinity refers to masculinities embodied by men who are discriminated against because of their racial, ethnic, and/or class identity. Think, for instance, of men whose gender expression resembles hegemonic masculine ideals but who are still considered inferior because they are a person of colour and/or part of the working class.[7]

---

[7] Connell's theory on hegemonic masculinity has been a frequent target of criticism. Connell and Messerschmidt (2005) addressed some of these criticisms at length in an article presenting a revised theory on hegemonic masculinity. For instance, they created more room for the agency of women and acknowledged the diverse dynamics existing between patterns of masculinity expressed at global, regional, and local levels. For instance, patterns of hegemonic masculinity expressed at the global level may impact regional or local patterns of hegemonic masculinity and vice versa. At the same time, some have misunderstood the theory and treated 'hegemonic masculinity' as a concept that presupposes fixed traits (e.g. being aggressive, sexist) or assumed that it referred to dominant types of men and masculinity (e.g. common forms of masculinity). Such reflections ignore that hegemonic masculinity refers to a discursive political ideal that guarantees the continuation of a patriarchal gender order. As such, instead of presuming fixed traits, it should be seen as dynamic and depending on the specific sociocultural context in which it is expressed. Second, rather than seeking out which groups of men are dominant in a given society, it is about figuring out which ideal of masculinity is legitimised to subordinate women and masculinities that do not live up to this ideal (Beasley, 2008; Messerschmidt, 2019).

Where does that leave femininities? For Connell, the term 'hegemonic femininity' seemed difficult as she found at the time of writing that there was no femininity that had the same hegemonic power as any pattern of masculinity could have. She argued that we can discern a pattern of femininity in a given society that is dominant, but it does not exercise institutional or structural power like hegemonic masculinity. She described it as a form of femininity that "is defined around compliance with this subordination and is oriented to accommodating the interests and desires of men. I will call this 'emphasized femininity'" (Connell, 1997, p. 23, my emphasis). She did allow room for other femininities: "Others are defined centrally by strategies of resistance or forms of non-compliance. Others again are defined by complex strategic combinations of compliance, resistance and co-operation" (p. 23). Since she was chiefly interested in studying masculinities, she did not explore these other forms of femininities in detail.

Mimi Schippers (2007) took on the challenge to rethink and complement Connell's work on masculinity, femininity, and hegemony. She argued that there is room for hegemonic femininity that coexists with hegemonic masculinity: "Hegemonic femininity consists of the characteristics defined as womanly that establish and legitimate a hierarchical and complementary relationship to hegemonic masculinity and that, by doing so, guarantee the dominant position of men and the subordination of women" (p. 94). Hegemonic femininity is discursively constructed as inferior to all masculinities, but also superior to other femininities. A related concept is pariah femininity. This refers to the practice and embodiment of features associated with hegemonic masculinity by women. As Schippers argued, it "is precisely because women often embody and practice these features of hegemonic masculinity, and because this challenges the hegemonic relationship between masculinity and femininity, that these characteristics, when embodied by women, are stigmatized and sanctioned. [...] I propose calling this set of characteristics pariah femininities instead of subordinate femininities because they are deemed, not so much inferior, as contaminating to the relationship between masculinity and femininity" (p. 95). Last, she also hinted at the existence of alternative femininities and masculinities, where people actively reject hegemonic femininity and masculinity and defy/challenge the idea of "a complementary relation of dominance and subordination between women and men" (p. 98).

1.3. Feminism(s)

Besides social constructionism (see Chapter 1), feminisms played an important role in the process of disentangling sex from gender and in the creation of multiple theoretical lenses to better understand and tackle any form of political, social, cultural, legal, or economic inequality between men and women. Feminist scholars and activists have worked side by side to advance the rights of women across the globe, although it is equally important to underscore the plurality of feminisms.

The first wave of feminism, which originated in the late 1840s, was mostly concerned with the legal struggle for equal rights for women in the public sphere, spearheaded by the suffragettes, who demanded that women be allowed to vote. The second wave of feminism, which started around the 1960s, pertained to a broader range of issues (e.g. abortion rights, sex, pornography, equal pay, fair representation of women in media) (Kelly, 2005; Stryker, 2008). Especially during the second wave, distinct strands of feminism (e.g. liberal feminism, radical feminism, socialist feminism) emerged as a response to former or other feminist formations. They differed from one another in terms of paradigmatic assumptions (e.g. essentialist versus social constructionist perspectives) and disagreed over who should be included (e.g. whether lesbian women were considered part of the movement) and how to achieve social change (e.g. overthrowing capitalist societies or changing gender disparities from within) (Barker, 2012; Gill, 2007; Milestone & Meyer, 2012). Further, although the different feminist factions agreed that the cultural construction of womanhood in media and popular culture had to be tackled as well, they held opposing opinions regarding the role of media and popular culture in preserving a patriarchal gender order. For instance, liberal feminists rooted their activism in their own experiences as white, middle- or upper-class heterosexual women. They showed little interest or awareness of the lived experiences of women who were different from them. These liberal feminist assumptions informed the early studies or critiques about the representation of women in mass media, which lacked reflections about race and class (see below) (Barker, 2012). Later in this chapter, I also explore the discord between libertarian, sex-positive feminists, and radical feminists about the role of porn in society.

Yet, such divisiveness led to a new generation of feminist thinkers and activists who wanted to adhere to a feminism that was nonjudgmental and aimed at coalition building. R. Claire Snyder (2008) described how this led to a third wave of feminism,[8] which emerged in the early 1990s. Rather than using the all-encompassing term 'woman' and professing grand narratives, third-wave feminists adopted an inclusive attitude, making room for diverse narratives that represent the

---

8 Even though the idea of a third wave of feminism has become commonly accepted, it should be noted that some issues raised by third-wave feminists were already tackled by second-wave feminists (e.g. the inclusion of nonheterosexual women, as illustrated by the work done by lesbian feminists during the 1970s and 1980s) (Kelly, 2005).

different experiences of women shaped by their racial, ethnic, sexual, and/or religious identities (Kelly, 2005; Snyder, 2008; Stryker, 2008). Such an approach demonstrates that they were guided by Kimberlé Crenshaw's theory of intersectionality (see Chapter 1) and queer theory (see Chapter 3), particularly Judith Butler's work.

Because of Butler's importance to gender theory, I briefly discuss one of their key concepts, gender performativity. Butler argued that not only gender but also sex is socially constructed. This does not imply that they denied the material differences that exist between bodies but aimed to expose and question "the very laws that seek to establish causal or expressive lines of connection among biological sex, culturally constituted genders, and the 'expression' or 'effect' of both in the manifestation of sexual desire through sexual practice" (1999, p. 22). Butler argued that these laws should be understood as hegemonic discourses that create distinct sexual and gendered identities, and nudge how people should embody and experience their bodies. It is important to understand that "[...] gender is not a performance that a prior subject elects to do, but gender is *performative* in the sense that it constitutes as an effect the very subject it appears to express" (Butler, 1993, p. 314, emphasis in original). Through "a stylized repetition of acts" (p. 191) (e.g. bodily gestures, way of talking, modes of dress), people 'become' gendered rather than express an innate gender identity. Notably, the theory was not intended to "celebrate each and every new possibility *qua* possibility" (p. 203, emphasis in original), only to make intelligible those identities that already exist (e.g. trans identities, alternative masculinities, nonbinary identities) but which have been discursively rendered unintelligible, stigmatised, and punished (see below).

It should be noted that third-wave feminists have paid a lot of attention to the role of communication, media, and popular culture. This can be attributed to the fact that from the 1990s and especially the 2000s on, people have gained more opportunities to access and interact with all sorts of media while, at the same time, they have become increasingly dependent on media and communication technologies to navigate their everyday lives (Snyder, 2008). This resulted in diverse forms of DIY feminism, which range from print and online publications of feminist critiques of popular culture products and statements from celebrities to the punk movement Riot grrrl (see below) (Karaian & Mitchell, 2009).

Yet, among third-wave feminists, there is a strand of feminism that is contested because it identifies with concepts such as 'girl power' and 'girlie culture'. It concerns women who "feel entitled to interact with men as equals, claim sexual pleasure as they desire it (heterosexual or otherwise), and actively play with femininity" (Snyder, 2008, p. 179). This strand of feminism is sometimes labelled as postfeminism. However, it should be stressed that postfeminism as a phenomenon entails more than being engaged in 'girlie culture'. According to Sarah Banet-Weiser (2018), postfeminism encompasses "a set of ideologies, strategies, and practices that marshal liberal feminist discourses such as freedom, choice, and independence, and incorporate them into a wide array of media, merchandising, and consumer participation" (p. 153). Crucially, the underlying argument is that Western society no longer needs feminism or collective feminist politics as the goals set by second-wave feminists have been achieved. Being freed from patriarchal and feminist dictates, women are now able to become whatever they want. They can choose to have a career, raise a family, or both. Yet, in emphasising discourses of choice and individualism, postfeminists tend to ignore or downplay persistent structural gender inequalities (Banet-Weiser, 2018; McRobbie, 2004b). Many scholars have noted how postfeminism became a dominant framework to represent and frame women in popular culture. Famous examples include the all-female pop act Spice Girls (see figure 9), *Bridget Jones's Diary* (Sharon Maguire, 2001), *Sex and the City* (HBO, 1998–2004), and *Ally McBeal* (Fox, 1997–2002). As nuanced readings of these cultural texts reveal, they may not have contributed to challenging structural inequalities but have articulated feminist standpoints, such as women's agency and sexual freedom (Adriaens & Van Bauwel, 2014; McRobbie, 2004b).

Figure 9. Photograph of the Spice girls promoting the Spice Cam in 1997. The pop act collaborated with Polaroid, which developed an instant camera named after the group. Photo credit: Pictorial Press, © Imageselect/Alamy.

This brief overview had no ambition to be exhaustive. Instead, it illustrated the diversity among feminisms. Second, it demonstrated how the development of (post-)feminist ideas can enter into a dialogue with popular media culture. Yet, the discussion of postfeminism and popular media culture should be seen as an appetiser as the next sections will deepen the relationship between gender and popular media culture.

2. RESEARCHING GENDER AND POPULAR MEDIA CULTURE

The second wave of feminism led to a diversification of issues of concern to feminist scholars and activists, including increased attention to the way media treated women. As Liesbet van Zoonen (1994) argued, from the second wave of feminism on, the women's movement "is not only engaged in a material struggle about equal rights and opportunities for women, but also in a symbolic conflict about definitions of femininity (and by omission masculinity)" (p. 12). For instance, feminist author and activist Betty Friedan's work *The Feminine Mystique* (1963), which is considered to be one of the impetuses of the second wave, demonstrated how media and magazines at the time established the myth of the suburban housewife whose role is to support her husband and find true fulfilment in motherhood.

Within academia, media and communication scholars started devoting their attention to gender and media, which led to a diversity of studies and perspectives. According to Van Zoonen (1994) and Tonny Krijnen and Sofie Van Bauwel (2022), three themes became dominant, which remain of central interest in gender and media studies: stereotypes, ideology, and pornography. The study of stereotypes, on the one hand, and the study of ideology, on the other hand, can be related to the two dominant approaches discussed in Chapter 1. Stereotypes have been studied by researchers within communication sciences who adopted a (post-)positivist perspective, whereas questions regarding ideology have been central to a media and cultural studies approach.[9] In this section, both approaches toward gender and popular media culture are discussed and compared. Next, the three subsequent sections serve to discuss specific topics and themes regarding gender and popular media culture, namely the gendered dimensions of popular music culture, pornography and the sex wars, and the representation of trans persons in media.

2.1. *Communication sciences: Stereotypes and cultivation*

The first studies in communication sciences that revolved around gender were studies into the absence and misrepresentation of women in mass media (Barker, 2012; Krijnen & Van Bauwel, 2022; Van Zoonen, 1994). These early feminist media studies adopted a (post-)positivist perspective. They believed that it was the role of media to show or reflect women as they are in real life (Barker, 2012; Gill, 2007). These studies, written in the 1970s and 1980s, stressed that women had been an essential part of everyday life and were increasingly becoming part of the labour force. This shift had an impact on the way public life was organised as women encountered various forms of sex discrimination (Tuchman, 1978). However, media rarely represented women in positive and well-developed roles and, instead, presented their audiences with worn-out stereotypical images of women (see below). In other words, these studies argued that images of women in media were not 'realistic' or 'accurate'. To explain why gender stereotypes in media persisted, they pointed to the gender socialisation of men working within mass media (Van Zoonen, 1994).

They also argued that processes of gender socialisation were, in turn, shaped by what people saw in mainstream media. As seen in Chapter 1, these arguments were informed by George Gerbner's cultivation theory and the power of television to cultivate assumptions about society. Gerbner (1998) himself directed our attention to a series of studies, conducted in the 1980s and 1990s. Each study highlighted how audiences who watched a lot of television were more likely to hold sexist or gender-stereotypical opinions about men and women, including assumptions about ambitions, activities, interests, and qualities.

Yet, the studies on gender and media discussed by Gerbner are preceded by the work of sociologist Gaye Tuchman. In a chapter published in 1978, 'The Symbolic

---

9   This does not mean that gender stereotypes have not been studied in media and cultural studies. Rather, as seen in Chapter 1, scholars adopting a media and cultural studies approach argue that stereotypes are able to affirm or provoke and question (gender) ideologies.

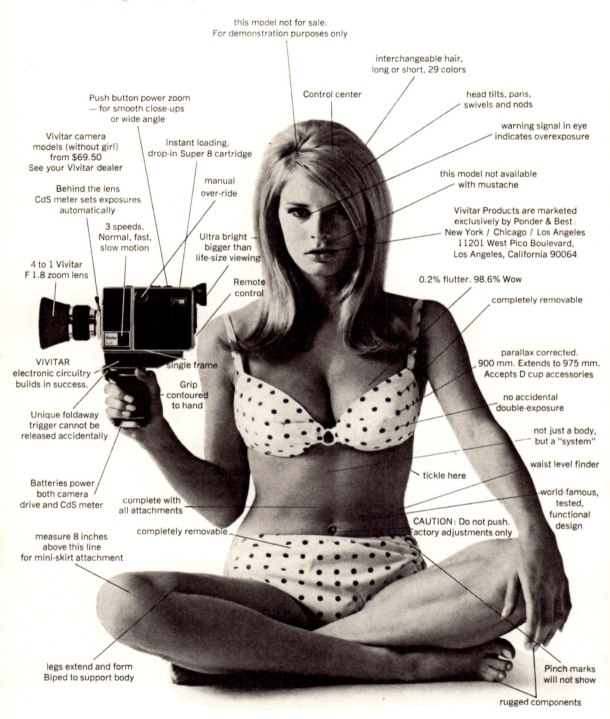

Figure 10. A 1967 advertisement for Vivitar's Super 8 Movie Camera. The ad illustrates the trivialization, objectification, and sexualisation of women. It depicts the female model as a commodity, equating her with the camera, whose 'features' are 'designed' to please the male consumer. Photo credit: Retro AdArchives, © Imageselect/Alamy.

Annihilation of Women by the Mass Media', she relied on Gerbner's theoretical framework to review, interpret, and compare the results of a series of sociological and communication scientific studies conducted by fellow scholars. These chiefly quantitative studies examined the images of women in the content and advertisements shown on television and published in women's magazines and newspapers in the United States (see figure 10). Based on her review, she postulated that mass media deployed strategies that contributed to the symbolic annihilation of women. She described the first strategy as one of *absence and omission of women* in mass media. Plenty of studies demonstrated how women were not included in an equal manner to men and were not represented in roles they did adopt in real life. For instance, up to the early 1970s, men dominated American prime-time television content (e.g. 74% of all characters in prime-time content aired in 1973 were men). Women were outnumbered despite making up half of the population. Further, when represented, women were only shown in a limited set of roles. For instance, they were rarely depicted as workers. In the few cases that they were shown as part of the labour force, they performed clerical and other pink-collar[10] jobs; "men are doctors, women are nurses; men are lawyers, women, secretaries; men work in corporations, women tend boutiques" (Tuchman, 1978, p. 13).

Second, by representing women in only a limited set of professions and roles, mass media also *trivialised* women; by not depicting women as actively participating in public life and/or practising various professions, media implied that women were only 'good' at a limited set of roles. Moreover, mass media trivialised women in roles relating to the private sphere and homemaking, traditionally considered the domain of women. Women were often represented as loving, caring, and obedient housewives. In women's magazines, "the ideal woman [...] is passive and dependent. Her fate and her happiness rest with a man, not with participation in the labor force" (p. 18). While mass media encouraged women to marry and have children, they discouraged them from pursuing education, training, or aspiring to a position of power and independence. Furthermore, the trivialisation could also be seen in images that featured women as less competent than men – both in the public and the private sphere. Think of television series in which female professionals repeatedly required help from male professionals to achieve something or in which women depended on their husbands to deal with emotional problems. These images and narratives not only reiterated the idea that women were less worthy than men but also that women were defined in terms of their relationships with men.

---

10 Pink-collar professions refer to jobs that have been stereotypically considered as women's professions, including care professions (nursing, teaching young children), secretarial work, and beauty-oriented professions.

Third, by featuring fewer images of women compared to men and by only figuring women and men in traditional roles, mass media *condemned* women to this limited set of roles. Relying on the cultivation hypothesis, Tuchman postulated that male and female audiences would come to believe these norms and views to be reflective of reality. She is not the only one who made these claims. Even today, scholars working within a (post-)positivist framework have cautioned about the potential risks of mainstream media due to their ability to cultivate people's assumptions about society and, consequently, sociocultural diversity. Importantly, in the work of these scholars, not only traditional media but also digital media (such as video games) and social media (such as Instagram) are increasingly approached as systems of cultivation (e.g. Scharrer & Warren, 2022; Stein et al., 2021).

2.2. *Media and cultural studies: Ideology*

Even though, as we will see, the field of media and cultural studies comes across as a natural habitat for studying gender and popular media culture, the tradition of cultural studies was initially not that welcoming or receptive to feminist concerns. The early years of the CCCS focused on class issues and resistance and took women and patriarchal power dynamics for granted. Female members of the CCCS felt that their concerns were ignored and questioned why gender as an axis of subordination was not incorporated into the centre's cultural analyses. To this end, the centre's Women's Studies Group decided to make a statement and in 1978 published *Women Take Issue: Aspects of Women's Subordination*, a collection of essays by CCCS members such as Charlotte Brunsdon, Dorothy Hobson, and Angela McRobbie. The essays highlighted the difficulties of conducting feminist intellectual research, while also broadening the centre's research agenda by highlighting the necessity to explore audiences' practices of consumption and pleasure (Turner, 2003).

Looking at contemporary media and cultural studies, gender and feminism have taken a central position. In comparison to communication sciences, media and cultural studies is interested in exploring the relationships between gender ideologies and popular media culture rather than assessing whether images of women are 'accurate' or 'realistic' (Barker, 2012; Gill, 2007; Krijnen & Van Bauwel, 2022). First, media and cultural studies scholars postulate that gender ideologies shape the production processes of popular culture. For instance, they argue that a film is not only the result of creative and artistic decisions made by directors and their crew. We should also wonder about whether there were women involved in the production process and, if so, whether they were taking on the role of director, writer, or producer, or whether they were employed in more traditionally gendered professions (e.g. costumes, make-up). Further, did the institutional framework in which the film was produced encourage active reflection on the politics of gender representation? For instance, were reflections on gender required to acquire funds? Did the filmmaker spontaneously tackle gender when pitching, writing, and directing a project? Finally, as we have seen with the #MeToo movement, we should be aware that gender ideologies also affect power relations between male and female professionals in media and film companies.

Second, they stress that popular culture texts (e.g. magazines, television shows, songs, memes) represent, explicitly or implicitly, ideological ideas about gender. As such, rather than assessing whether images of men or women are 'accurate', 'truthful', or 'realistic', scholars in media and cultural studies explore whether, and to what extent, gender representation is used to affirm a patriarchal gender order or to provoke or overturn gendered hierarchies in society at large. For instance, they will not exclusively focus on singling out gender stereotypes (e.g. damsel in distress, dumb blonde), but examine the role given to women in relation to the overarching plot, their interactions with male and female characters, and aspects of genre or format. In these studies, representations or expressions of masculinity and femininity are considered ideological and can be seen as tools to preserve or provoke gendered hierarchies.

Third, they argue that people – who are equally ideologically located – make sense of popular media culture by negotiating the ideas, norms, and values expressed in popular media culture texts with their own (see Hall's encoding/decoding model in Chapter 1). For instance, a comedy intended to deconstruct gender stereotypes (like *Miranda*) – whose humour regime requires some knowledge and understanding of how satire works – may be decoded in different ways. On the one hand, there may be audiences who interpret the satire or hyperstereotyping as intended. Some of them may full-heartedly agree with the comedy's critical message, while others may consider the gender critique 'too woke' and/or in conflict with their own beliefs about men and women. On the other hand, there may be audiences who fail to grasp the satirical undertones and feel offended by the content while others may see their gender beliefs affirmed on screen. In demonstrating these complex processes of negotiating meaning, the field of media and cultural studies aims to highlight the polysemy of popular media culture and elucidate why some popular culture texts may incite contradictory responses.

3. GENDER, THE MUSIC INDUSTRY, AND ROCK MUSIC[11]

Throughout the twentieth century, the diverse popular culture industries that developed were deeply gendered from the start and played an important role in sustaining a patriarchal gender order. Moreover, the established gendered patterns turned out to be resilient and hard to eradicate. Adopting a media and cultural studies approach, this section addresses the practices of gendering in the music industry, with a particular focus on rock music. Using Connell's and Schippers' theoretical lenses on masculinities and femininities, I illustrate how a large set of practices and representations have reproduced this gender hierarchy.

3.1. *The music industry and hegemonic masculinity*

First, we need to turn our gaze toward the production context of popular music and particularly to how the music industry is organised. Looking at the people and institutions who govern the music industry, it is important to point out that women are underrepresented in key professions in the music industry (e.g. producers, music publishers, A&R [artists and repertoire] representatives, record label managers, or board directors) (Cooper et al., 2017; Leonard, 2016; Mullens & Zanoni, 2019; Strong & Raine, 2019). Since the emergence of the international music industry in the early twentieth century, male music professionals have been able to set out strategies about how to run a record company, decide which artists should be signed, and which music should be produced, as well as establish everyday modes of working in the music industry. Over the years, a pattern of hegemonic masculinity has formed and taken root in the way the music industry is organised. This pattern, for instance, manifests itself in assumptions about the role of men and women in the music industry. For instance, internalised biases about gender and music genres may be used by A&R representatives when nudging male and female artists toward different music genres (see below). Similarly, the fact that the music industry is male-dominated may result in few female professionals in upper managerial roles which, in turn, may discourage other women from pursuing a career as directors or managers in the music industry. Further, plenty of professional practices in the music industry have been

---

11   This section is in part based on the following article: Dhaenens, F. (2023). "Timeless" rock masculinities: Understanding the gendered dimension of an annual Belgian radio music poll. *Feminist Media Studies*, 23(1), 154-169.

male-oriented. For instance, scouting for new talent and networking are organised outside of regular office hours (e.g. artists and musicians regularly perform late at night). For female music professionals who, for instance, combine their work with raising children, such working conditions have made it difficult to perform at a high level (Mullens & Zanoni, 2019). In general, if you want to succeed as a woman in the music business, you are forced to navigate a context where hegemonic masculine ideals have shaped how to conduct business.

Another consequence is that to be successful as a woman in the music industry, women not only need to be good at their jobs but are also expected to balance their gender performance. If they mimic qualities associated with hegemonic masculinity (e.g. being authoritative, goal-oriented, and independent), they may be perceived as enacting pariah femininity and run the risk of being treated as 'other', 'different', and a threat to the male-oriented organisation of the music industry (Schippers, 2007). If they, however, perform a femininity that is subservient to hegemonic masculinity, described by Connell (2005) as a pattern of emphasised femininity or by Schippers (2007) as hegemonic femininity, they will probably be nudged toward a limited set of professional roles in the music industry.

3.2. Female artists navigating a music culture shaped by hegemonic masculinity

Musicians and artists occupy a central position in the ecology of popular music culture. Like other female music professionals, female musicians and artists have to navigate practices and assumptions shaped by hegemonic masculinity. First, there are the material and institutional practices that make a professional music career more difficult for women than for men. Female artists have to deal with similar issues as discussed in the previous section on working in the industry. For instance, homosocial practices may hamper the ability of female artists to gain access to informal networks of music professionals to advance their careers. These networks are important as they can, for instance, result in financial support to record a demo (Bayton, 1997; Leonard, 2007). Networks are also valuable for women who desire to form or join a band. As Mary Ann Clawson (1999) illustrated, men can more easily form a band through homosocial ties. Think of how many famous all-male rock bands started as a group of male friends from high school who bonded over music.

Second, there are the widespread cultural assumptions the industry and audiences hold about popular music culture, which are also often gendered. To illustrate, I discuss the gendering of music genres and the gendering of musical instruments. Regarding music genres, it should be underscored that they continue to play a vital role in popular music culture. Roy Shuker (2012) argued that music genres can be distinguished by musical traits (e.g. sound, instruments, lyrics) and non-musical traits (e.g. record art, dress code of band members). Even though many artists have questioned the practice of inscribing oneself into a music genre, their music will nonetheless be reviewed, marketed, and experienced by audiences through the lens of genres. Genres function as frames of reference that help artists create their music, industry professionals brand their artists, festival and radio curators select acts, and audiences discover new artists within the same genre.

During the second half of the twentieth century, the period in which popular music culture came to full bloom, discourses on genres were increasingly gendered. Especially the differentiating of rock from pop music happened on the basis of gendered assumptions. Diane Railton (2002) pointed out how rock music was gendered as masculine from the 1960s on. Critics, scholars, and journalists celebrated rock music because of certain values and practices considered 'masculine'; rock musicians were considered independent because they learned to play an instrument on their own and they were politically and publicly engaged because the lyrics often tackled political themes. Other scholars (Coates, 1997; Krüger, 2021; Whiteley, 2000) highlighted how rock music was perceived as an authentic and straightforward genre: rock musicians were seen as artists who expressed their true emotions and thoughts. Consequently, rock was considered as a 'serious' genre, whereas pop music was considered 'fabricated' and 'trivial' (see below). Sheila Whiteley (2000) pointed out how, for instance, rock music was part of the British counterculture of the 1960s. Rock bands used their music to articulate progressive political standpoints and react against forms of inequality (e.g. about social class) but at the same time expressed conservative attitudes toward women. She found women to be represented as objects rather than subjects, without giving "serious thought to the individuality or, indeed, the diversity of women. There is little commentary on commitments, women's sexual desires and experiences […] Women provided a fantasy escape, a focus for easy eroticism" (pp. 40–41). Even today, male artists in rock music have, deliberately or not, participated in sustaining this pattern of hegemonic masculinity (De Boise, 2014; Warwick, 2015).

Pop music, on the other hand, became associated with all things deemed feminine. Whether it concerned the sound, instrumentation, lyrical themes, performance styles, or imagined audiences, pop music has long been discredited compared to rock music. Whereas rock became associated with acoustic and electronic instruments played live, pop music became linked with songs produced and prefabricated in studios (Coates, 1997). These prefabricated songs were not the only thing considered 'inauthentic' about pop music; a vocalist singing a song written by another person, like a professional songwriter, was considered unable to convey true and honest emotions. Furthermore, since many of these pop songs revolved around topics such as longing and romance, pop music was also considered politically inferior as it did not tackle 'real' problems as rock artists did. Whereas rock songs were assumed to make people think, pop songs were considered simple but pleasant distractions that made people dance (Coates, 1997; Railton, 2002). Unsurprisingly, rock music became dominated by male artists, while pop music became a popular genre for female artists to succeed in.

The gendered and oppositional relation between rock and pop can also be traced back to the mastery of particular musical instruments. Mavis Bayton (1997) interviewed approximately a hundred female musicians to explore the obstacles they faced in pursuing a music career. She indicated that the underrepresentation of female musicians in rock music could be attributed to specific sociocultural dynamics. One of these dynamics concerned the custom of gendering musical instruments. She stressed that "[l]ead guitarists are made, not born. The reasons for women's absence are entirely social" (p. 398). Rather, by teaching children that certain instruments are more appropriate for women or arguing that the physical reactions to playing drums (e.g. sweat) are unladylike, women have been discouraged from pursuing careers as musicians. These assumptions, for a long time, also shaped the way the music industry looked at aspiring artists, pushing women to perform as vocalists in mainstream pop genres, while encouraging men to perform as instrumentalists in rock genres.

3.3. The music press, the rock canon, and audiences

The idea that rock music is a masculine genre where male artists thrive cannot only be ascribed to the norms, values, and everyday practices in the music industry. Marion Leonard (2007) emphasised that we also need to take into account the role of the music press, the rock canon, and audiences and fans of rock music. Although many rock journalists, music historians, and audiences may not embody a hegemonic masculine ideal, they took part in practices of complicit masculinity that fortified the pattern of hegemonic masculinity in rock music culture. To explore this, I begin by stressing that there has been a continuous presence of female rock musicians since the early days of modern rock music, ranging from solo artists (e.g. Janis Joplin, Patti Smith, PJ Harvey) to mixed-gender bands (e.g. Fleetwood Mac, Skunk Anansie (see figure 11), Siouxsie and the Banshees, Roxette, The Cranberries), and vibrant feminist underground scenes (e.g. Riot grrrl, see below). Yet, they have been denied visibility or critical recognition.

To unpack this, we first turn to the rock music press. Simon Frith (1978) pointed out how the rock music press emerged out of underground magazines that celebrated rock's initial resistance to the commercial logic of pop music. Although many of these magazines, like *Rolling Stone*, developed into profitable and successful entertainment magazines, they set out and aligned themselves with the ideology of rock music, which was "valued for its politics, its freedom, its sexuality, its relationship to cultural struggles" (p. 143). Yet, as Helen Davies (2001) stressed, despite the rock press's image of being radical and liberal, they failed to take women in rock music seriously. Music journalists considered rock music a masculine genre by default, writing rock retrospectives that omitted female rock artists. Some journalists showed some awareness of the lack of attention to women in rock music but did little to investigate the material and symbolic barriers women encountered in the industry (Leonard, 2007). As a consequence, when rock critics did write about female rock musicians, they wrote in ways that turned female artists into something rare, peculiar, and not as serious or 'good' as male rock artists (Coates, 1997; Kearney, 2017; Leonard, 2007). For instance, successful bands and artists (e.g. The Breeders, Sinéad O'Connor) were considered 'exceptional', erasing the continuous presence of female rock artists and working against the normalisation of female rock artists. Davies (2001) also brought up the practice of writing about female (rock) musicians as *women* rather than musicians – a common practice among journalists writing about female politicians (D'Heer et al., 2022). Just think about questions regarding motherhood or bodily appearance that are rarely asked of male artists. Another trope was to 'masculinise' female rock artists. Leonard (2007) highlighted how artists such as Patti Smith and Janis Joplin were "referenced within the established male rock lineage" (p. 37), assessing their musical achievements by comparing them to masculine ways of performing rock music. Quite often, they were described as 'one of the boys'.

Yet, keeping the theory of pariah femininity in mind, women who have dared to threaten the pattern of hegemonic masculinity may have been punished for doing so. This became visible in the double standard used by journalists to write about the private lives of rock music artists (Berkers & Eeckelaer, 2014; Krüger, 2021; Leonard, 2007). Whereas male artists were allowed to have a lifestyle of 'sex, drugs, and rock 'n' roll',[12] and even celebrated for it, female artists were vindicated or victimised for doing the same thing. For instance, talking about Janis Joplin (see figure 12), Leonard (2007) pointed out how her "promiscuous behavior and reliance on drugs and alcohol have been popularly understood as elements in the

---

12 This phrase has been used to capture the hedonistic and countercultural vibe of rock-music culture during the 1960s and 1970s.

tragic decline of an insecure and unattractive woman" (p. 37). A recent example concerns the way British broadsheets wrote about singer-songwriter Amy Winehouse. Pauwke Berkers and Merel Eeckelaer (2014) compared how the British newspapers wrote about the so-called 'rock and roll lifestyles' of rock musician Pete Doherty and Amy Winehouse in the 2000s and found that while "Pete Doherty was predominantly framed as an artist who dares to live on the edge, many journalists interpret similar behavior in Amy Winehouse as damaging, harmful, and unhealthy, particularly for the artist herself" (p. 10).

Figure 11. Skin, the artist moniker of Deborah Anne Dyer, performing with her band Skunk Anansie at Bristol Bierkeller, United Kingdom, in 1995. The British band helped shape the sound of alternative rock music in the 1990s. Photo credit: Rob Watkins, © Imageselect/Alamy.

Figure 12. A 1960s photograph of singer-songwriter Janis Joplin. Photo credit: marka, © Imageselect/Alamy.

Another factor that needs to be discussed is the creation of the rock canon. The rock canon refers to a selection of rock bands considered by music journalists, critics, and historians as the best of their kind and, therefore, worth preserving and remembering. Leonard (2007) described the process of musical canonisation as one where artists are suggested for canonisation based on a set of quality standards, taste cultures, and commercial successes. For rock music, commercial factors certainly played a role in celebrating The Beatles and The Rolling Stones. At the same time, following Whiteley (2000), the parameters used to canonise rock musicians emphasised artistic qualities such as authenticity, emotional honesty, authorship, musical innovation (e.g. song structure, use of instruments), and originality vis-à-vis other rock acts and, most of all, mainstream pop music. Importantly, these were all qualities and traits deemed inherently masculine. Acknowledging the difficulties of female rock musicians to gain access to networks but also to media platforms (press, radio, television) and venues and festival stages – think of how many male acts outnumber female acts at music festivals today – male rock acts found themselves in a privileged position for canonisation. As a result, mostly popular white male rock artists and bands were included, such as Led Zeppelin, The Doors, and U2, since they generally received more press attention than female rock artists and faced fewer difficulties receiving airplay, record deals, or gigs. Although regional differences occur, with local non-Anglophone rock bands often achieving a similar status as Anglophone rock acts (Dhaenens, 2023), the internationally known rock acts are hard to de-canonise. As Leonard (2007) argued: "Once artists have become established as canonical, magazine and book publishers may focus on them to create other celebratory texts that both trade off their status and reinforce it" (p. 27). Moreover, aspiring rock acts have used the rock canon as their main source of inspiration, emulating the themes, sound and composition of canonised rock acts (e.g. having a bass player, lead guitarist, and drummer). Considering that the rock canon stabilised by the 1990s (Markowitsch, 2024), most canonised rock acts are all-male bands with members and songs affirming hegemonic masculinity. Articles or books that provide a different history of rock music by focusing on the contribution of women in rock failed to be anything more than alternative canons since they have not been able to truly change the hegemonic rock canon (Leonard, 2007).

This is apparent in the practices of audiences. Although people like to think their taste is deeply personal, music taste is equally the result of social and cultural dynamics (see also Chapter 6). Moreover, some studies (Dhaenens, 2023; Strong, 2010) demonstrated how audiences, including young people, have internalised international and local rock canons. This becomes visible through initiatives taken by media companies (ranging from radio broadcasters to magazines) to gauge their audiences' tastes and preferences. One of those initiatives is the organisation of a music poll, which refers to a ranking of songs or albums as decided by those who partake in the process. Polls about audiences' all-time favourite artists tend to feature rock songs performed by all-male rock bands (e.g. Queen, Led Zeppelin, The Beatles, The Rolling Stones). This was particularly apparent when looking at polls organised by radio stations that present themselves as alternative and geared toward young audiences. Both Catherine Strong's (2010) study into the Triple J Hottest 100 of All Time, organised by Australian public radio station Triple J, and my research (Dhaenens, 2023) into *De Tijdloze Honderd* [The Timeless Hundred], organised by Belgian public radio station Studio Brussel, revealed how the all-time favourite records and artists of the stations' audiences remain relatively stable although the profile of the stations has changed. Triple J and Studio Brussel may have started out as rock stations but increasingly diversified their profiles, focusing on trends within music, defying the rock-pop binary by embracing a variety of genres, and programming music performed by artists with minoritised identities. Yet, despite these transformations, the audiences favour the rock canon. Little research has been done to unpack the motivations of audiences, although some hypotheses have been formulated. Strong (2010) wondered whether the digital age has fragmented the taste of audiences to such an extent that only those artists predating the digital age in music seem to have had a huge impact. The findings in my study (2023) concurred with Leonard's (2007) argument that the hegemony of rock music has channelled the process of deliberating which music qualifies as 'timeless'. Personal preferences may differ – you may choose Nirvana over U2 – but what does not seem to be questioned by these audiences is the idea that the genre most worthy of being timeless is rock music.

3.4. *Small changes*

Although the rock canon and music polls remain relatively unchallenged, we have seen people in the music industry question and rethink the traditional gender politics in the music industry (Strong & Raine, 2019). Since the 1970s, small-scale initiatives have been taken to counter the dominance of men in the music industry: music festivals that centre female artists were organised (e.g. Michigan Womyn's Music Festival, Lilith Fair); women-run music businesses and non-profit organisations to achieve equity in the music industry (e.g. Women in Music) were established; underground movements emerged that deliberately challenged forms of hegemonic masculinity in rock music culture. Riot grrrl, for instance, is an often-cited American feminist punk movement from the early 1990s, with all-female bands Bikini Kill (see figure 13) and Bratmobile as its two most well-known bands (Krüger, 2021; Leonard, 2007). The bands appropriated punk music's resistance to mainstream politics and aesthetics to actively question the male dominance within the music industry and the roles ascribed to women in popular music culture and to instruct female artists on how to become involved in the production of music. To do so, they published free zines that addressed the lack of power of women in society and the punk scene in particular (Krüger, 2021; Radway, 2016).

Figure 13. Kathleen Hannah, lead singer of Bikini Kill, performing at music venue TJ's in Newport, United Kingdom, in 1993. Photo credit: Rob Watkins, © Imageselect/Alamy.

Second, it would be shortsighted to assume that all male rock artists, and male performers in general, articulate or aspire to embody hegemonic masculinity. Male artists who, from a hegemonic masculine perspective, embody a subordinate or marginalised masculinity, may very well take pride in their non-normative masculinities. What is more, such and other masculinities may figure as alternative masculinities, deliberately challenging masculine traits, norms, values, and practices deemed superior or the norm. Taylor Martin Houston (2012), for instance, interviewed fifteen male North American indie rock musicians and found the men engaged in practices that defied traditional practices of hegemonic masculinity among rock musicians. They ranged from expressing homosocial intimacy on and off stage to articulating femininity in their performances. Similarly, male artists like Beck and all-male bands like Radiohead released songs that debunk or provoke norms, values, and practices of hegemonic masculinity (Dhaenens, 2023; Lay, 2000).

Focus on IDLES

An all-male band that consistently challenged hegemonic masculinity is the British punk band IDLES (see figure 14). Several songs tackle aggressive forms of masculinity and misogyny (e.g. 'Mother' (2007)), while singer Joe Talbot has repeatedly spoken out against misogyny, racism, and homophobia. To illustrate, I ask you to listen to 'Samaritans' (2018). In the song, singer Joe Talbot recites orders given by a father to his son: "Man up, sit down, chin up, pipe down," "Socks up, don't cry," and "Grow some balls." The father represents male authority and hegemonic masculinity, while the son represents boys and young men who have not yet internalised the norms, values, and practices that sustain a patriarchal gender order. Talbot, impersonating the 'son', however, refuses to follow suit. He shouts: "I'm a real boy, boy, and I cry." The pre-chorus makes explicit what is at stake in this song: "The mask of masculinity is a mask, a mask that's wearing me." Put differently, Talbot exposes that what society conceives of as 'normal masculinity' is nothing more than a mask, but a powerful mask nonetheless. The mask has ruined the lives of many men who were nudged or forced to internalise rigid ideas about how to be a man, which affected their well-being, how to engage with other men and women, and how to express emotions and intimacy. Acknowledging the mental health issues men experience, IDLES deliberately named the song 'Samaritans'. Samaritans is the name of an Irish charity, also with branches in the UK, which provides help to those in emotional distress. Talbot said that he felt lucky to have a support network and how this organisation aims to provide that to people who do not (Glynn, 2018).

Figure 14. Portrait of IDLES taken in 2017. Singer Joe Talbot shares a kiss with guitar player Mark Bowen. Photo credit: Lindsay Melbourne.

Third, even though all-male rock acts still outnumber all-female rock acts, the number and symbolic presence of female rock musicians is growing. Moreover, they are increasingly programmed as headliners (e.g. Florence and the Machine, PJ Harvey) and are receiving important music awards (e.g. Alanis Morissette winning the Grammy Award for Best Rock Album in 1996, Brittany Howard winning the Grammy Award for Best Rock Song in 2021, and boygenius winning the Grammy Award for Best Rock Performance in 2024). Similarly, some audience music polls and music journalists' best-of lists follow that trend. American online music publication *Pitchfork*, an influential and authoritative website since the late 1990s, has been conscious of sociocultural diversity and popular music culture, especially from the 2010s on. This can be noted in their best-of-the-year lists as well as the music polls they organise. In 2023, *Pitchfork* staff found Lana Del Rey's 'A&W' (2023) the best song of the year, and SZA's *SOS* (2022) the best album of the year (Pitchfork, 2023a, 2023b). Although the poll was organised before the publication of Pitchfork's own favourite songs and albums, audiences too found 'A&W' the best song of the year. For the best album, audiences preferred Caroline Polachek's *Desire, I Want to Turn into You* (2023). It is worth mentioning that female artists outnumbered male artists in both the music journalists' and readers' top 10 of best albums and top 10 of best songs (Pitchfork, 2023a, 2023b, 2023c). Even though Pitchfork is only one online music website, it is praiseworthy to see music journalists and audiences celebrate and valorise music created by women. Although gender equality in the music industry has not yet been achieved, various people within and outside the music industry are attempting to accomplish that goal.

4. PORNOGRAPHY AND THE SEX WARS

In the late 1970s and early 1980s, feminist activists and scholars directed their attention to audiovisual pornography. The reason was the legalisation of the production of porn films in several Western countries. For instance, pornography was legalised in Denmark and the Netherlands in 1969 and in Sweden in 1971. In the United States, the regulation of porn was a more complex matter as federal obscenity laws, dating from 1873, prevented the production and distribution of material deemed obscene. Yet, throughout the early twentieth century, it became apparent that what qualified as obscene was open to interpretation. Subsequent laws fine-tuned what was considered obscene, facilitating the legal production of porn films in the United States (Williams, 1989). The easing of the laws led to a commercially profitable period for American porn producers in the late 1970s–early 1980s, often dubbed the golden age of porn (Paasonen & Saarenmaa, 2007). An infamous milestone is *Deep Throat* (Gerard Damiano, 1972), a film about a woman (performed by Linda Lovelace) who finds out that the reason she cannot have an orgasm has to do with the fact that her clitoris is located in her throat. The film was shown in regular film theatres and drew audiences who would normally not see a pornographic movie in a public space (see figure 15). The increased exposure and mainstream attention to pornography as well as the development of videotapes and the success of video stores where you could rent X-rated videos provoked not only moral guardians but also feminist activists (Williams, 1989).

Especially radical feminists took issue with pornography. In the United States, the anti-pornography movement was spearheaded by legal scholar Catharine MacKinnon and writer Andrea Dworkin. Besides developing theories on why pornography was harmful, they drafted a civil law to combat pornography. Their main argument was that pornography was sex discrimination, "a systematic practice of exploitation and subordination based on sex that differentially harms women. The harm of pornography includes dehumanization, sexual exploitation, forced sex, forced prostitution, physical injury, and social and sexual terrorism and inferiority presented as entertainment" (Dworkin, 1985, p. 24). In their argument, pornography hurts not only the women involved in making it, but also women in society. They argued that women were likely to encounter men who consumed porn and internalised the misogynistic representations. In other words, they argued that porn had the power to impact the attitudes and behaviour of young heterosexual men. Moral conservatives and radical feminists shared the belief that pornographic fantasies representing sexual violence would incite men to act aggressively against women (Williams, 1989).

Figure 15. One of the many protests calling for a boycott of *Deep Throat* (1972). Still from *Inside Deep Throat* (Fenton Bailey & Randy Barbato, 2005), a documentary about the production and reception of the pornographic film. Photo credit: Moviestore Collection, © Imageselect/Alamy.

Dworkin and MacKinnon underscored that their proposed law should not be seen as censorship:

> One reason that stopping pornographers and pornography is not censorship is that pornographers are more like the police in police states than they are like the writers in police states. They are the instruments of terror, not its victims [...] The pornographers are the secret police of male supremacy: keeping women subordinate through intimidation and assault. (Dworkin, 1985, p. 13)

They assumed that pornography was made with only a male audience in mind and intended as a tool to keep women subordinate to men. Furthermore, they believed that porn was able to turn male audiences into misogynists. Interestingly, the proposed civil law was drafted in such a way that it did not forbid the production of audiovisual content about sex. At the same time, it stated that if anyone found the material 'pornographic' and/or harmful to women, they could sue the producers for money as compensation for their hurt and ask for the removal of the pornographic work. Even though a handful of cities passed legislation based on the proposed law, it was later found unconstitutional on the grounds of free speech (Spongberg, 2006).

Not everyone agreed with the arguments expressed by the anti-porn movement. Even more, the debates that emerged among feminist thinkers have often been described as emotive and polarised, dubbed the feminist sex wars. Importantly, the debates were part of broader reflections on sexuality and feminism, including sex work and sadomasochism (Bracewell, 2016; Ferguson, 1984). Opposing radical feminists were libertarian, sex-positive, and anti-censorship feminists. They agreed with radical feminists about the way certain porn films represent heterosexual pleasures through a patriarchal lens but did not believe that censorship was the answer to fight patriarchy, nor did they agree with radical feminists' generalisations about pornography. First, they argued that pornography should not be seen as the root of sexism and misogyny in society but rather as a symptom. Further, assuming that all porn is invested in patriarchy is missing out on some of the diversity and cultural resistance present in pornography. It also disregards the role porn played in teaching women about female orgasms and nonheterosexual men about gay sex (Rubin, 1993). In other words, rather than dismissing all porn, a contextual understanding of each porn film or video is needed: who produced the pornographic work, where and how is the video distributed, how does the work represent sex acts, how does sex figure in the narrative of the work, who is the imagined audience? This information is needed to fully understand the pornographic texts' politics of representation (Williams, 1989). Candida Royalle, for instance, is often cited as a counterexample to patriarchal porn producers. She started as a porn actress and then became a director of porn described as feminist. She started Femme Productions in 1984, a predominantly female-led production company, and looked for modes to revise how sex had been represented. One of the prime elements that set this company apart from other porn studios was the way it represented women's desire, with attention to female fantasy and aspects of foreplay. Besides, its producers made sure to avoid the normative male gaze – which is a perspective in which only women are objectified and fragmented (see also Chapter 3) – and refrain from depicting sex from the viewpoint of the phallus (Williams, 1989).

Since the feminist sex wars of the 1980s, much has changed. Porn is no longer a subject portrayed on videotapes or in film theatres but can easily be found online and watched on a diversity of devices. Similarly, the internet has also facilitated the production of (amateur) porn as the hardware and software to make a porn video has become increasingly affordable and easy to use (Paasonen, 2014). What has not changed is the fact that porn remains taboo – in society and academia, despite an increase in academic scholars and journals working on porn. Similarly, porn continues to divide people. That is why I conclude this section with Kimberly Seida and Eran Shor's (2020) reflections on contemporary porn production and the role of research. They stressed:

> [...] that the study of pornography and the academic and public debate about the issue must not ignore or underestimate the "darker" and harmful aspects of this industry. Nor should it, however, be dedicated to the denigration of all pornography, ignoring both the ways it has changed and diversified over time and viewers' own complex and multifaceted accounts of their viewing experiences and perceptions. (p. 7)

5. TRANS REPRESENTATION IN MEDIA

A subfield of gender and media studies is the young field of trans media studies (also known as transgender media studies). It is informed by trans(gender) feminism, a strand of feminism that is part of the third wave of feminism (see above). Trans feminism shares with other forms of feminism a desire to "dismantle the structures that prop up gender as a system of oppression, but it does so without passing moral judgment on people who want to change their birth-assigned gender" (Stryker, 2008, p. 3). Since the mid 2010s, a new wave of anti-trans rhetoric has developed in Western society, presumably as a reaction to the increased visibility of trans persons in media (see below) and sociocultural and political-legal gains of trans people in some countries. Strikingly, such rhetoric is not only expressed by social conservatives but also women who identify as 'gender-critical feminists', known in public and academic speech as 'trans-exclusionary radical feminists'. As Judith Butler (2024) explained, they postulate that "sex is real and gender is constructed" (p. 136), a postulation that misunderstands how social construction works but which gender-critical feminists use to argue that trans women are not women and trans men are not men. Although they are a minority among feminists, social media and news media have amplified their opinions, which turned trans identities into an election issue and forced trans activists and trans feminists to defend themselves and counter the incorrect assumptions and data about being trans (Butler, 2024; Halberstam, 2018; Stryker & Bettcher, 2016). While countering false arguments is important, Judith Butler (2024), Jack Halberstam (2018), and Susan Stryker and Talia M. Bettcher (2016) also pointed out the necessity to demonstrate the many productive coalitions and alliances between feminist scholars/activists and trans scholars/activists that advanced the sociocultural and political-legal condition of trans people.

To be precise, not all scholars in the field of trans media studies rely on (trans) feminist and/or queer theoretical work. The field also comprises sociologists relying on post-positivist or interpretative methods (Billard & Zhang, 2022). Yet, they all share a desire to grasp better the relationship between trans people and (popular) media culture. Trans media studies tends to focus on the politics of representation (Fischer, 2018). Even though most studies have addressed fictional representations of trans people, I begin by discussing the work of communication scholar Thomas J. Billard (2016), who studied how American news media (e.g. *USA Today*, *The New York Times*) wrote about transgender themes. They focused on the twenty-five most circulated daily newspapers in the United States over a time span of ten years (2004–2013). They started from the postulation that news media are pivotal in representing communities and their political demands as legitimate. Hence, they found it essential to comprehend how news media wrote about transgender people, including their experiences and political demands. To study this, Billard conducted a quantitative content analysis, using nine self-developed 'legitimacy indicators'. For instance, the legitimacy indicator 'naming' demonstrates whether journalists used the trans person's correct name, which would be a legitimising action, or whether they used the name given at birth (also known as 'deadnaming'). Another indicator, 'pronoun usage', explores whether journalists used the person's correct pronouns, or whether they used the pronouns assigned at birth. Other indicators allowed Billard to assess whether journalists applied trans terminology (e.g. transgender, nonbinary) correctly, whether or not they deployed shock tactics (using the transgender identity as a shock reveal or a ploy to keep the reader hooked), whether or not they fixated on the trans person's genitalia, or whether or not they represented the trans person in a sexualised manner. Billard's study found that the discussion of trans themes in news media was limited, with only a handful of articles exploring trans themes. Moreover, the few articles that did engage with trans themes featured a significant amount of delegitimising language, mainly to be found in tabloid newspapers. Billard did find that the strategies of delegitimising decreased over the years. These findings partially concurred with the results of Rubén Olveira-Araujo's (2023a) study into the coverage of trans themes in Spanish digital news media from 2000 to 2020. The study revealed a decrease in delegitimising language, although it did not disappear. Olveira-Araujo's work (2023a, 2023b) did reveal a significant increase in reporting on trans themes in news media. At the same time, Olveira-Araujo (2023b) also noted how the emergence of the (inter)national anti-trans movement started to shape news coverage in conservative and progressive news outlets from 2016 onward. While progressive news media increasingly covered trans themes in an emancipatory and inclusive manner, conservative news media also increasingly published articles on trans themes, albeit in an anti-trans and delegitimising manner. The study illustrates how trans themes in Western society have become a topic of an increasingly polarised societal debate.

Regarding audiovisual fiction, the historical lack of representation in news media was not that different from the lack of representation in audiovisual fiction. As aptly illustrated in Sam Feder's documentary *Disclosure* (2020), trans people looking for self-representation in popular film and television had to try hard to find a character or actor that allowed for recognition. For a long time, they had to deal with images of cross-dressing, often used for comedy, like in *Viktor und Viktoria* (Reinhold Schünzel, 1933), *Some Like it Hot* (Billy Wilder, 1959), and *Tootsie* (Sydney Pollack, 1982). The 'alternatives' to these images were films with trans (or implied to be transgender) people who were represented as "mad, bad, and dangerous" (Halberstam, 2018, p. 92). These characters were often villains, serial killers, or deceivers (e.g. *Psycho* (Alfred Hitchcock, 1960)). In television fiction, trans persons were even more invisible until the beginning of the twenty-first century. Jamie Capuzza and Leland G. Spencer (2017) underscored that when they were represented, "depictions were more often than not based on negative stereotypes functioning in a way to ridicule this community via humor, disgust, fear, alienation, and anger" (p. 215).

Around the 1990s, independent film productions increasingly featured nuanced representations of trans characters. For instance, several films made by Spanish director Pedro Almodóvar revolve around well-developed trans characters (e.g. *La ley del deseo* [Law of Desire], 1987; *Todo sobre mi madre* [All About My Mother], 1999; *La mala educación* [Bad Education], 2004). The trans characters were often central in the narrative and given layered backstories, even though they at times adopted stereotypical roles (e.g. representing trans characters as sex workers). Similarly, Halberstam (2018) highlighted the symbolic importance of films such as *The Crying Game* (Neil Jordan, 1992) and *Boys Don't Cry* (Kimberley Peirce, 1999) in the history of trans representation, even though *The Crying Game* featured a fetishistic looking at a black trans body and *Boys Don't Cry* divided audiences over its depiction of violence against trans youth and its decision to cast Hilary Swank, a cisgender actress, as the trans teen.

Figure 16. On-set photograph of Jules (Hunter Schafer) in the pilot episode of *Euphoria* (2019–present). Photo credit: Home Box Office (HBO)/Album, © Imageselect/Alamy.

From the 2000s onward, the number of well-developed and main trans characters increased in scripted television (Capuzza & Spencer, 2017) and film (Bell-Metereau, 2019). A television series often praised for the way it has represented a trans character is the drama series *Euphoria* (HBO, 2019–present). The aestheticised series centres on Rue (Zendaya), a teen struggling with drug addiction. Rue finds comfort with another teen at school, Jules (Hunter Schafer) (see figure 16), with whom she starts a relationship. Jules figures as the other main character, making her one of the first main teen trans characters in television fiction. Besides casting a trans actress to perform the role of Jules, the series carefully crafted the character's narratives. The storylines created around her character do not use her trans identity as a source of worry or pain. Further, the fact that she is a trans teen is only mentioned in the third episode of the first season, but it is not framed as a 'shock reveal'. At the same time, her trans identity is real: there are moments when she reflects on her body, wonders about stopping hormonal treatment, and thinks about her attraction to men and women. These scenes reveal how for trans youth the experience of adolescence, which many young people go through, is also shaped by their trans identity. However, her transness does not define nor limit Jules.

Yet, contemporary audiovisual fiction still features stereotypical tropes. First, there is the tendency to only represent trans characters in narratives that focus on transitioning, with an emphasis on the biological and medical aspects of being a trans person (e.g. gender affirmation surgery, hormone therapy). Another recurring theme is assimilation, which can be seen in series where trans persons are shown who are able to 'pass' successfully (i.e. a trans person is perceived as a cisgender person). Further, the gender binary is often reproduced by predominantly representing trans men and trans women, thereby downplaying the experiences of nonbinary persons or trans people who do not think of themselves as exclusively trans masculine or trans feminine (Capuzza & Spencer, 2017; Vanlee et al., 2020). Another often-cited critique is the gender disparity on screen. Recurring reports have indicated that predominantly trans women are being represented, while trans men and nonbinary people are rarely represented on the small screen. Looking at American television content, there has been an increase in trans male characters and nonbinary characters from the television season of 2020–2021. At the same time, the total number of trans characters in American television content has decreased since the television season of 2022–2023 (GLAAD, 2021, 2024).

Last, a recurring topic of debate is whether trans roles in scripted television and fiction films should be performed by trans actors. This debate should be seen in a context where trans roles in film have often been performed by cisgender actors, while trans actors were rarely cast in these roles. Further, notwithstanding support among trans people for cisgender actors performing trans roles, trans actors are still considered able to bring more authenticity and sensitivity to the performance (Capuzza & Spencer, 2017; Van Haelter et al., 2022). On the other hand, Halberstam (2018) also reminded us of the complexities of the politics of representation of a film or series. Rather than focus on who is being cast, we should ask additional questions to assess how the film or television production has prepared itself to depict the lives of trans people. For instance, is the film or series produced, directed, and written by media professionals who identify as trans persons? What do we know about the casting process? Is the narrative used to challenge and provoke former transphobic modes of representation? Last, Capuzza and Spencer (2017) warned that it is also important to avoid typecasting or hiring transgender actors only for transgender roles, which limits the acting opportunities of trans actors.

CHAPTER 3

SEXUAL ORIENTATION

Setting the scene: Portrait de la jeune fille en feu

French period drama *Portrait de la jeune fille en feu* [Portrait of a Lady on Fire] (2019), directed by Céline Sciamma, is set in the late eighteenth century. We are introduced to Marianne (Noémie Merlant), a professional painter who is teaching a painting class to a group of girls. A student draws Marianne's attention to one of her paintings, a portrait of a girl whose skirt is on fire. The painting seems to trigger a memory and Marianne starts reminiscing. The film jumps back in time to her arrival on a small island in Brittany. She is hired by a noble family to paint the portrait of a young woman, Héloise (Adèle Haenel). Héloise is expected to marry a Milanese nobleman she has never met. The convention stipulates that a portrait must be delivered to the nobleman. A male painter failed at the job, so the mother of Héloise hopes a female painter may be able to succeed. Marianne is instructed to hide her professional identity from Héloise and to pretend to be a female companion. However, Marianne and Héloise grow fond of each other and eventually fall in love (see figure 17).

Figure 17. Still from *Portrait de la jeune fille en feu* (2019) depicting the affection between Héloise (Adèle Haenel) and Marianne (Noémie Merlant). Photo credit: Landmark Media, © Imageselect/Alamy.

Sciamma used the history of forgotten female painters from the eighteenth century as a backdrop to her love story and to write women into art history. That is why she did not make a biopic of a historical female painter, which would have resulted in a singular portrait of a woman who 'made it' in a patriarchal society. Instead, she wanted "to invent [a woman] to talk about [all women] and not have this heroic dynamic. It's not about her body of work. It's about an artist's work, her questions, her difficulties, and her success within one frame" (Sciamma in VanDerWerff, 2020). By doing so, she was able to depict the position of female painters at the time. For instance, there is a scene in which Marianne presents her work in the art gallery of the Louvre, which was only possible because she submitted it under the male name of her father. As such, the film demonstrates why and how female painters were made invisible. At the same time, by explicitly focusing on a female painter, the film re-inscribes female painters in spaces, narratives, and histories from which they had been omitted.

The film's relevance for this chapter is twofold. First, the film makes visible the existence and experience of same-sex desires in historical contexts. The film evokes the idea of situating same-sex desire in contexts historically mapped as hostile to homosexual behaviour.[13] Even though women were less targeted when it concerned same-sex behaviour (Garton, 2004), they could not socially live together. The desire and passion we see on screen is something both women experience as temporary. At the same time, the film refrains from representing that historical reality as overpowering and immobilising, and instead imagines how, within that context, nonheterosexual women expressed romantic and sexual intimacy.

Second, the film acts as a manifesto about the female gaze. To explain this, a brief discussion of the male gaze is needed, a concept coined by Laura Mulvey (1975). It concerns a gaze that is present in film (and art), which subjects women to its gaze. Consequentially, women are represented to fit a heterosexual male fantasy. They are objectified and connote 'to-be-looked-at-ness'. They figure as passive beings and are considered unable to return the gaze. Mulvey highlighted that the gaze is not only adopted by the person behind the camera or the characters on screen but also by audiences. The theory presupposes that male and female audiences are unable to resist the gaze. Mulvey's theory has allowed us to understand better the role of audiovisual parameters (e.g.

---

13 The main story arc is implied to take place in 1770, twenty years before the abolition of sodomy laws, which de-penalised homosexual behaviour among men. France was one of the first countries to do so. It should be seen as a period in which homosexual behaviour transformed from a prohibited to a stigmatised act (Pastorello, 2010).

montage, camera angle, mise-en-scène) in objectifying women, but it has also received its fair share of criticism. The theory reiterates binary and heteronormative assumptions about gender and sexuality (e.g. pitting men against women, ignoring nonheterosexual subject positions) while dismissing the complex ways people negotiate images (e.g. ironic viewing or resisting the sexist gaze) (Krijnen & Van Bauwel, 2022). Mulvey also implied that all mainstream Hollywood films produced at the time reiterated this 'male gaze', which prompted film scholars to look for counterexamples that did succeed in deconstructing the male gaze and/or adopting a female gaze.[14]

Sciamma considers *Portrait de la jeune fille en feu* a manifesto about the female gaze (VanDerWerff, 2020). She wanted to explore patriarchy without depicting men. The film demonstrates the impact of patriarchal practices on women (e.g. a woman being betrothed based on a portrait created to please the suitor; the demanding situation of a female painter to succeed) by looking at the practices from a female perspective. For example, in a side story, Sciamma depicts how women of different ranks help the family maid with her abortion. It is represented as an act of sorority that defies the patriarchal control over women's bodies. The female gaze is also present in how Sciamma, as a female, lesbian director, draws on her own experiences to imagine same-sex desire. She makes sure that the camera does not objectify the women's bodies while still acknowledging their sexual desires. To this end, the film features several scenes that demonstrate the women's erotic pleasures through gazing and touching one another. Last, it is worth pointing out that Marianne initially adopted a 'male gaze'. Her first portrait of Héloise was painted according to the male-defined characteristics and conventions of the art of painting. The portrait is a failure. However, it is only when Héloise returns her gaze while she is posing and the painter and model establish respect and understanding for one another that the painting becomes appreciated by the painter and the model. This is poignantly illustrated in a quote by Héloise when she says to Marianne: "Regardez. Si vous me regardez, qui je regarde moi? [Look. If you look at me, who do I look at?]"

---

14   Rather than coined by one scholar, the concept of the 'female gaze' appeared in several feminist writings (both inside and outside of academia).

1. SEXUALITY, SEXUAL IDENTITY, AND SEXUAL DIVERSITY

1.1. Conceptualisations

When talking about sexuality, various concepts tend to be used interchangeably. The broadest term is 'sexuality'. It serves as an umbrella term to denote a person's subjective experience and expression of sexual desires. Even though sexualities may encompass specific sexual practices and fantasies (e.g. BDSM), the term is mainly used in the context of a person's sexual orientation. Sexual orientation refers to a person's sexual and/or romantic interests (Galupo, 2018; Moser, 2016). In contemporary Western society, sexual orientation "requires a gender identity label for both self and those others to whom we are attracted" (Galupo, 2018, p. 62). It is worth stressing that many experience their sexual orientation as located on a spectrum, which implies that, for instance, some people experience either different-sex desires or same-sex desires, while others may indicate that they now and then experience sexual desires for a person of the same sex/gender (Vrangalova & Savin-Williams, 2012). Further, there are also people experiencing an enduring lack of sexual attraction to others, which is defined as an asexual orientation (Bogaert, 2015).

A related concept is 'sexual behaviour', which, according to Charles Moser (2016), refers to "what individuals actually do, whether or not their behavior is consistent with their sexual identity or their sexual interests. The sexual behavior may or may not be desired and may or may not be arousing to the individual" (p. 505). Consequently, it is incorrect to assume that, for instance, people who experience same-sex desires engage in sexual behaviours that are congruent with their sexual orientation. Men may have sex with women even though they are sexually attracted to men, while people may have sex with other people although they lack sexual attraction to others.

Last, 'sexual identity' can be defined as the social construction of and identification with a specific sexual orientation. People rely on cultural discourses about sexuality and sexual orientation that circulate in a given society to describe and make sense of their own and others' sexuality. For instance, in contemporary Western society, people only experiencing same-sex desire may likely identify as 'gay' or 'homosexual'. However, we should keep in mind that the labels or markers persons adopt (e.g. 'homosexual') "may not describe their actual sexual behavior, fantasy content, or to which sexual stimuli they respond" (p. 505). Further, even though sexual orientation is generally experienced as located on a spectrum, the sexual identity labels used in contemporary societies tend to be categorical (e.g. you are either 'heterosexual', 'bisexual', or 'homosexual') (Vrangalova & Savin-Williams, 2012). Consequently, 'bisexual' has often been treated as a term to refer to all sexual orientations that are not exclusively oriented toward either the same sex/gender or the other sex/gender. Similarly, the prevalent categories all start from the assumption that all people experience sexual attraction. To change this, new terminology has emerged to grasp better how people experience their sexuality (e.g. 'pansexual', 'queer', 'asexual'), while some people refrain from identifying with a label as they feel that labels are unable to represent their sexuality accurately (Bogaert, 2015; Galupo, 2018). Last, for matters of clarity, I use the umbrella term 'sexual diversity' to refer to the diversity among people in terms of how they experience and/or make sense of their sexuality.

Importantly, the idea of having a sexual identity should be understood as a recent phenomenon. Jeffrey Weeks (1996), a pioneer of social constructionism, argued that sexual identities are social categorisations constructed within a specific cultural and historical context. It is the society that gives meaning to both the subjective and social experience of sexual desires and acts. Focusing on sexual behaviour between people of the same sex, Weeks (1996) stressed that:

> [...] the various possibilities of same sex behavior are variously constructed in different cultures as an aspect of wider gender and sexual regulation. The physical acts might be similar, but their social implications are often profoundly different. (p. 42)

In other words, people have made sense of sexual behaviour differently, depending on time and place, and have not always assumed that certain sexual practices or sexual interests coincide with a particular sexual identity.

1.2. Changing discourses about nonheterosexuality in Western society [15]

The emergence of sexual identity labels can be situated at the end of the nineteenth century, when the concepts of heterosexuality and homosexuality were described and discussed in medical, psychiatric, or legal institutions (Katz, 1995). According to philosopher Michel Foucault (1976/1998), these discursive practices produced sexuality instead of repressing it. He meant that, by increasingly writ-

---

15 This section is based in part on my doctoral dissertation: Dhaenens, F. (2012a). *Gays on the small screen: A queer theoretical study into articulations of queer resistance in contemporary television fiction* (Doctoral dissertation, Ghent University).

ing and talking about 'homosexuality', intending to control and regulate sexuality, knowledge about homosexuality became widespread in society. In these discourses, homosexuality was no longer seen as something that people *did* but as something that people *were*: the 'homosexual' had become a distinct type of person. On the one hand, such knowledge was used to increasingly control people whose sexuality diverged from what was considered normal. It gave figures of authority and power discursive tools and concepts to diagnose, pathologise, isolate, and oppress homosexual individuals. On the other hand, the increased knowledge about homosexuality also produced a 'reverse discourse', in which the group categorised as 'homosexuals' began to use the terms associated with it (e.g. homosexuality) "to demand that its legitimacy or 'naturality' be acknowledged, often in the same vocabulary, using the same categories by which it was medically disqualified" (Foucault, 1976/1998, p. 101).

Figure 18. Still from *Anders als die Andern* (1919). Paul (Conrad Veid) holds his lover Kurt (Fritz Schulz) close. © Edition Filmmuseum, Filmmuseum München.

One of the first attempts to demand political legitimacy was made in Weimar Germany. Physician Magnus Hirschfeld, who headed the Institut für Sexualwissenschaft [Institute for Sexual Research], wanted to decriminalise homosexual relations between men. Besides giving lectures, he co-created a film that aimed to persuade lawmakers to overturn the penal code. In *Anders als die Andern* [Different from the Others] (Richard Oswald, 1919), considered one of the very first films to tackle homosexuality explicitly, a violin player named Paul (Conrad Veid) falls in love with Kurt (Fritz Schulz), a student (see figure 18). However, another man threatens to expose the violin player's homosexuality and starts blackmailing him. Remarkably, the film features scenes in which Hirschfeld himself is lecturing on homosexuality and explaining that homosexuality is a natural variation. The film's politics were focused on demonstrating that the social attitudes toward homosexual individuals were the real problem. The film was well received and a commercial success, but after one year it was banned (Dyer, 2003). Furthermore, the little progress that was made to advance the lives of nonheterosexual people was undone by the Nazi regime as the institute was raided and destroyed by fascist groups in 1933 and its publications destroyed during a public book burning (Meyenburg & Sigusch, 1977).

From the 1940s on, activist groups in several Western countries were formed that strived for tolerance and acceptance of homosexual individuals into mainstream heterosexual society. To achieve their goals, they made use of assimilationist discourses and politics. They emphasised the similarities between heterosexual and homosexual persons and downplayed the sexual aspects of being homosexual. These movements were referred to as homophile movements. In Europe, for instance, you had movements like Der Kreis in Switzerland, C.O.C. in the Netherlands, Forbundet af 1948 in Denmark, and Arcadie in France (Hekma, 1999). In the United States, you had the Mattachine Society and the Daughters of Bilitis (Bernstein, 2002; Jagose, 1996; Sullivan, 2003). Inspired by essentialist thinking, the homophile movements argued that sexuality was biologically determined and should for that reason not be punishable by law. Mary Bernstein (2002), speaking about American gay and lesbian movements, argued that the organisations were focused on self-help and seeking out (heterosexual) people with authority who could speak on their behalf. Random arrests by police kept them from protesting in the streets. Their only goal was to stress "their similarities to the majority [...], to show that they were upstanding citizens despite their homosexual "affliction" and to limit state action against them" (p. 542).

To spread the message and create a community, homophile movements relied on the publication of periodicals. One of the most successful periodicals at the time was the Swiss periodical *Der Kreis* (1942–1967) (see figure 19). The magazine had entries in three languages and catered to an international audience. During the 1940s and 1950s, it was one of the few journals in the world promoting the legal and social rights of homosexual people. It reported on scientific insights on homosexuality and tracked the legal changes implemented that advanced homosexual rights in Europe. At the same time, the journal aimed to culturally and intellectually enrich its readers. Consequentially, *Der Kreis* featured written and visual content, such as articles, fictional stories, poems, reviews, commentaries, photographs, drawings, and paintings (Kennedy, 1999).

Figure 19. *Der Kreis-Le Cercle*, issue 7, July 1947. Cover and photograph *Aufnahme Mack v. U.S.A* [Photograph of Mack from the U.S.A.]. Der Kreis 15 (1947), no. 7, p. 10-11. ETH Library Zurich, E-Periodica, https://www.e-periodica.ch.

From the mid 1960s on, the assimilationist politics of homophile movements were increasingly being questioned by nonheterosexual activists who were critical of the submissive political position of the homophile movements and the continuous surveillance and harassment by police based on public indecency laws. This led to the emergence of the gay liberation movement in the United States, Australia, and several Western European countries. The movement consisted of several grassroots organisations that publicly challenged the psychiatric discourses on homosexuality and argued that being gay was both a valid identity and a valid way of life. There was a willingness and desire to embrace their nonheterosexual identity publicly, believing that coming out as 'gay' or 'lesbian' would result in consciousness raising (Bernstein, 2002; Garton, 2004; Jagose, 1996).

Equally important were the many spontaneous protests organised by the gay liberation activists. Especially the Stonewall uprising (also known as the 'Stonewall riots') is often referred to as the protest that incited the gay liberation movement. When the police raided the Stonewall Inn, a queer bar in New York, on 27 June

1969, the bar customers – including lesbians, gay men, drag queens, and trans and queer people of colour – fought back and were joined in the nearby streets by locals and activists, which resulted in vehement demonstrations that lasted until the morning. Although similar protests had happened in other cities before the Stonewall uprising, gay activists across the United States supported commemorating the Stonewall uprising as the beginning of gay liberation, with Pride marches and Pride weeks organised in June as modes of remembrance. As such, it is better to understand the Stonewall uprising as representing the various protests that erupted across the United States and its commemoration as an achievement of the gay liberation movement (Armstrong & Crage, 2006). The American movement inspired others across Europe to form similar gay liberation collectives, such as the London Gay Liberation Front in the United Kingdom and the Front Homosexuel d'Action Révolutionnaire in France, and organise local Pride parades (Hamilton, 2020).

Then again, many gay liberation movements were criticised by women and people of colour as these organisations were generally led by middle-class, white gay men who were insensitive to issues that arose from intersections with other minoritised identities. As a result, splinter groups were formed, ranging from several lesbian feminist organisations, such as Purple September in the Netherlands, to grassroots organisations inspired by queer theory (see below) such as Queer Nation in the United States (Katz, 1995; Stein & Plummer, 1996; Sullivan, 2003). As I demonstrate later, queer theory provided activists and other academics with a poststructuralist perspective on sexuality as well as new terms (e.g. 'heteronormativity') to grasp better the way gender and sexuality are produced and regulated in a given society.

Despite their differences, these organisations did succeed in working together. For instance, during the AIDS epidemic in the 1980s, lesbian feminists provided care to people with AIDS and educated gay and lesbian communities. They set aside the divisions between lesbians and gay men (Winnow, 1992). They also succeeded in enforcing political changes (e.g. abolishing discriminatory laws and implementing same-sex marriage rights) and cultural changes (e.g. changing perceptions about LGBTQ identities in society) (Bernstein, 2002). Similarly, trans activists and gay, lesbian, and bisexual activists share a long history of collaborating (see Stonewall uprising). Besides practical advantages, they both had to cope with and challenge discourses of pathologisation and stigmatisation based on rigid sexual and gender norms (Motmans & Van der Ros, 2015). What should be remembered from this brief history is how the discourses about sexual orientation and identity have changed throughout history, and how the creation of distinct sexual identities in modern societies led to stigmatisation but also recognition, resistance, and emancipation.

2. RESEARCHING SEXUAL DIVERSITY AND POPULAR MEDIA CULTURE

For a long time, sexual diversity was ignored in communication sciences and media and cultural studies. If sexuality was mentioned, it was often implied to denote heterosexuality. Scholars writing about cultural representations of male and female homosexuality were mostly scholars in literature (e.g. Meyers, 1977; Stimpson, 1981). The very first studies that focused on representations of nonheterosexual individuals in popular media culture concerned analyses of coded and stereotypical representations in film (e.g. Dyer, 1977; Russo, 1985; Tyler, 1972). Little was said about homosexuality in television content, with the notable exception of an article by Newton E. Deiter (1976). A possible explanation for the lack of interest from scholars could be the glaring absence of homosexuality in popular media culture. Looking at the United States, which had turned into an important international provider of popular entertainment, there was little room for homosexuality. Until the end of the 1960s, homosexuality was considered a taboo subject for Hollywood films. Similarly, American commercial broadcast television networks, becoming popular in the 1950s and 1960s, avoided programming content they thought would scare away their audiences (Buxton, 1997).

This does not imply that homosexuality was completely absent. While some films portrayed gay and lesbian characters in implicit, coded, or stereotypical ways (Barrios, 2003; Doty, 1993; Russo, 1985, Streitmatter, 2009, see below), American print media and factual television discussed homosexuality in explicit but biased manners (Streitmatter, 2009; Tropiano, 2002). In several Western European countries (e.g. Belgium, the Netherlands, Ireland, West Germany) public service broadcasting companies provided a more nuanced and relatively progressive view on homosexuality. In documentary and factual formats, homosexuality was considered a legitimate topic for content that had to be handled in a de-stigmatising and 'neutral' manner, with experts offering insights into same-sex desire and anonymous testimonials from nonheterosexual individuals (Vanlee, 2019b). Still, the mediated visibility of sexual diversity in mainstream Western popular media remained rare until the 1990s and few communication, media, and cultural scholars wondered why.

Those who did explore how media represented sexual diversity were activists in gay and lesbian movements. For instance, different demonstrations were organised in the 1970s by American gay liberationists against homophobic content published in leading magazines and newspapers (e.g. *Village Voice*, *The Examiner*) (D'Emilio, 2007). Nonetheless, throughout the 1980s, a handful of scholars took the study of sexual diversity and popular media culture to heart and set out the research agenda. In communication sciences, Larry Gross introduced the topic of sexual diversity. Drawing from cultivation theory (see Chapter 1) to criticise the absence and underrepresentation of gay, lesbian, and bisexual people on television, he paved the way for cultivation-theory-informed communication research on media and sexual diversity. I discuss his work below.

Figure 20. Billboard announcing *Live and Sleazy*, a double LP by the American band Village People, circa 1979. Photo credit: Robert Landau, © Imageselect/Alamy.

In the field of media and cultural studies, Richard Dyer adopted the role of a trailblazer. In many of his essays and books, he examined sexual diversity in film, television, and music. Noteworthy is his essay 'In Defense of Disco' (1979), which challenged the idea that only rock and punk were progressive, critical, and authentic genres. Instead, he argued that disco music, with acts like Donna Summer, Grace Jones, and Village People (see figure 20), although a commodity produced by a capitalist music industry, had been appropriated by gay audiences in ways not intended by the industry or creators. In the experience of listening and dancing to disco music, gay men were able to make sense of and express their sexuality and feel part of a community. Furthermore, disco songs became gay anthems, whose lyrics and feel resonated with gay men. In a way, gay audiences 'queered' the original intention of disco music – think of Gloria Gaynor's 'I Will Survive' (1978) or Diana Ross's 'I'm Coming Out' (1980). Even though Dyer did not use the terms 'queering' or 'queer theory' in his essay, his reflections did nonetheless resonate with queer theory, a body of critical thought that developed in the 1980s and 1990s (see below). Dyer's aim of his essay, to demonstrate the sociocultural value of disco music for gay men, aligned with queer theory's intent to reveal how people have resisted hegemonic ideas about gender, sexuality, and culture at large.

Only from the 2000s onward did we notice the introduction of queer theory into the field of media and cultural studies, noteworthy in the work of Jack Halberstam (2005, 2011). Today, however, insights from queer theory underlie plenty of media and cultural studies that assess the relationship between sexual diversity and popular media culture (Dhaenens et al., 2008; McRobbie, 2011; Nylund, 2007). For that reason, the following section is devoted to outlining cultivation-theory-informed communication research and queer-theory-informed media and cultural studies, which both qualify as leading research traditions in the study of sexual diversity and popular media culture.

2.1. *Cultivation-theory-informed communication research*

Communication scholar Larry Gross, who collaborated with George Gerbner on improving cultivation theory and cultivation analysis, drew from Gerbner's theoretical and empirical insights to reflect on homosexuality in mainstream media. He started presenting and publishing on the topic in the 1980s. Since television was a very prominent medium in the period in which his work was taking shape, he mostly expressed his concerns about the power of television to cultivate audiences' assumptions about society. At the time of writing, television held a lot of symbolic power to 'inform' the audiences about the 'real' world. Gross (1991) believed that television contributed to the symbolic annihilation of sexual minorities. He pointed out that, in comparison to women and ethnic minoritised groups, nonheterosexual people, in general, were raised in households or contexts (e.g. neighbourhoods, schools) that were exclusively heterosexual. To this end, nonheterosexual youth depended on other sources to make sense of their sexual and romantic feelings, desires, and behaviour. Similarly, heterosexual people lacking personal contact with nonheterosexual people also depended on other mediated sources, such as television, to be informed about homosexuality. For Gross, television and other media in the 1970s and 1980s had failed sexual minorities. When sexual minorities were represented, which rarely happened, they were generally represented as one-dimensional and inferior to heterosexual people.

To understand Gross's concerns, it is important to keep in mind that he was writing about American media in the 1980s. In contrast to Western Europe (see above), mainstream American media had not reported on homosexuality neutrally or inclusively. Moreover, during the 1980s, mainstream media framed gay men as scapegoats. As sociologist Steven Seidman (1988) highlighted, the AIDS epidemic was used to reinvigorate anti-homosexuality politics propelled by social conservative factions in American society. Mainstream media contributed to turning gay men into society's folk devils by spreading fake assumptions about AIDS and homosexual men. Moreover, AIDS was used as a pretext to frame gay men as hypersexual, promiscuous, and uncontrolled. Especially conservative media tended to use these frames to pit homosexuality against heterosexuality: "Homosexuality is constructed as the very antithesis of the heterosexual marital ideal where sex is joined to romance, love and relational permanence and fidelity" (p. 192).

Gross (1991) was wary that nonheterosexual and heterosexual audiences would believe the stereotypical and one-sided images of homosexuality to reflect reality and internalise these biased and prejudiced images. Scholars in communication sciences, inspired by Gross and cultivation theory, agreed with Gross's postulations and the necessity of positive, accurate, and realistic representations of sexual diversity. It led to a range of studies assessing to what extent stereotypes have been used to depict nonheterosexual identities, often employing quantitative content analyses. For instance, Adrienne Ivory et al. (2009) drew from sociological research about power imbalances in heterosexual and same-sex relationships, which indicated that men in heterosexual couples possessed more power and agency than women, while the distribution of roles and tasks in same-sex couples was found to be rather balanced and fair. The researchers wanted to investigate how television fiction series represented power dynamics in heterosexual and same-sex couples. They relied on a content analysis of several American prime-time television series made in the 2000s. The sample included, for instance, *The Sopranos* (HBO, 1999–2007), *Six Feet Under* (HBO, 2001–2005), and *The L Word* (Showtime, 2004–2009). They found both heterosexual and male and female same-sex relationships to be represented as gendered, meaning that one partner adopted a 'masculine', dominant role and the other a 'feminine', submissive role. Evoking the cultivation hypothesis, they feared heterosexual and homosexual audiences watching these series would be susceptible to believing that it is normal to pursue a gendered relationship.

One of the strengths of cultivation-theory-informed and quantitative research in communication sciences has been their ability to reveal patterns and trends in representing nonheterosexual characters (e.g. Fisher et al., 2007). They allow us to assess whether there has been an increase in nonheterosexual characters in film and television content and whether the characters on screen are diversified in terms of sexual orientation and/or other axes of identity (e.g. gender, race/ethnicity, or social class). Media critics may applaud the introduction of a main gay character in a mainstream film genre (e.g. in superhero movies), but quantitative studies within communication studies can reveal whether or not such representations are rare.[16] Last, this strand of research has helped us gauge to what extent stereotypical images of LGBTQ individuals relate to the opinions and attitudes people hold of LGBTQ people (e.g. van Meer & Pollmann, 2022).

2.2. Queer-theory-informed media and cultural studies

Besides cultivation theory, queer theory became an important framework for thinking about sexual diversity in media and popular culture. Especially scholars within the field of media and cultural studies (Davis & Needham, 2009; West, 2018) increasingly adopted queer-theoretical ideas, concepts, and lenses to study how nonheterosexual identities and themes were broached in film (e.g. Doty, 2000), television (e.g. Chambers, 2009), and popular music culture (e.g. Leibetseder, 2016). Queer theory refers to a diverse set of theoretical and philosophical arguments about sexuality and gender, of which the foundational theories were written in the 1980s and 1990s by predominantly literary scholars (e.g. Judith Butler, Eve Kosofsky Sedgwick, Michael Warner). They were inspired by social constructionism, poststructuralism, and lesbian feminism (Jagose, 1996). Interestingly, they did not consider their work as 'queer theory'. This term was launched by author Teresa de Lauretis (1991), who organised a conference at the University of California, Santa Cruz, in 1990. She wanted to bring together scholars who were willing to think beyond the dominant frameworks on sexuality, which included models that pathologised and/or essentialised homosexuality and models that treated homosexuality as an optional lifestyle. She also felt that the academic field of gay and lesbian studies downplayed the diversity of nonheterosexual experiences, mainly focusing on white gay men. By naming research that wanted to re-examine histories on sexualities and question established discourses on homosexuality 'queer theory', she deliberately chose the concept of 'queer' to avoid provoking connotations attached to former terms (e.g. gay, lesbian) and to allow new ideas and perspectives to emerge.

---

16   It should be stressed that quantitative content analysis has also been used as a method in media and cultural studies. Scholars who employed this method have argued that critical and ideological analysis can equally benefit from descriptive data. For instance, Florian Vanlee et al. (2018) mapped the representation of sexual diversity in Flemish television content over a period of fifteen years (2001-2016). They found that "LGBT+ characters have had a significant habitual presence since 2001, with a noted correlation to specific 'lowbrow' genres, and a noted lack in 'quality' series" (p. 4). They concluded that, akin to international trends, "[t]he collected characters display a severe lack of diversity, with most LGBT+ characters being gay male characters, a significant majority being middle class, and few non-white LGBT+ characters" (p. 4).

The works that came to be associated with queer theory argued that scholars needed to increasingly question the essentialist and universalistic approach to sexuality, which assumed that 'gender' and 'sexuality' are biologically predetermined (Seidman, 1996; Stein & Plummer, 1996). Of concern to these works was demonstrating why gender and sexual hierarchies were so widely accepted as normal. For queer theorists, this normalisation was due to the power of heteronormativity. According to literary scholar Michael Warner (1999):

> If you are born with male genitalia, the logic goes, you will behave in masculine ways, desire women, desire feminine women, desire them exclusively, have sex in what are thought to be normally active and insertive ways and within officially sanctioned contexts, think of yourself as heterosexual, identify with other heterosexuals, trust in the superiority of heterosexuality no matter how tolerant you might wish to be, and never change any part of this package from childhood to senescence. (pp. 37–38)

Put differently, he argued that heteronormativity: is a system of norms, values, beliefs, practices, and institutions, which presupposes that sex, gender, and sexuality are fixed, biologically predetermined, and unchangeable; reiterates binary relations (e.g. using dyad terminology, such as 'heterosexual' and 'homosexual', 'men' and 'women'); reiterates oppositional relations (e.g. pitting 'masculinity' against 'femininity'); reiterates hierarchical relations (e.g. treating 'heterosexual' as superior to 'homosexual'); and normalises these assumptions by embedding them in institutions (e.g. matrimony), practices (e.g. raising children), norms, and values (e.g. monogamy).

Queerness, on the other hand, provokes and challenges heteronormativity. Eve Kosofsky Sedgwick (1993) described 'queer' as "the open mesh of possibilities, gaps, overlaps, dissonances and resonances, lapses and excesses of meaning when the constituent elements of anyone's gender, of anyone's sexuality aren't made (or *can't be* made) to signify monolithically" (p. 8, emphasis in original). Put differently, queer refers to subjectivities, embodiments, or practices that do not comply with or conform to heteronormative presumptions or logic. Even though today 'queer' is often used as an umbrella term to refer to people who identify as nonheterosexual, throughout most of the twentieth century 'queer' served as a derogatory slur for 'effeminate' men who engaged in 'deviant' sexual conduct. American queer activists in the 1980s and 1990s, however, appropriated the slur to undo it from its negative connotation. They trans-coded the term to signify empowerment and resistance against dominant, rigid, and implicitly violent sexual norms (Dyer, 2002). Although various interpretations of 'queer' circulate, within queer-theory-informed studies, it generally refers to subjectivities, embodiments, or acts of resistance that challenge heteronormative practices, norms, and values. Importantly, this does not imply that queer people or practices are questioning straight people or acts/practices associated with heterosexuality. Instead, queer-theory-informed studies are about raising awareness of how heteronormativity dictates which families are considered 'normal' or 'protected' by law and which ones are not, who is allowed to raise children and who is not, which persons are allowed to marry and which ones are not, which sex acts between consenting adults are considered 'normal' and which ones are not, and which gender expressions are allowed and which ones are not. Put differently, queer theory aims to expose how heteronormative assumptions have been used to create laws, policies, and customs that discriminate against people whose gender and/or sexual identity does not fit the heteronormative ideal. At the same time, following Judith Butler (1999, 2024, see Chapter 2), it aims to redescribe and value the people who live queerly but whose lived realities have been considered fictitious, unreal, and unintelligible.

Queer-theory-informed media and cultural studies formulates the same objectives but turns its gaze toward media and popular culture. Even though this strand chiefly focused on sexual diversity, it has broadened its scope to include matters relating to gender diversity. Today, this strand of research considers its core research subjects as 'LGBTQ people' (i.e. 'lesbian', 'gay', 'bisexual', 'trans', and 'queer/questioning'). In some cases, the acronym is made longer to include intersex or asexual people. In general, the acronym 'LGBTQ' figures as an umbrella term already inclusive of other sexual and gender minorities.[17]

The majority of studies within this strand are critical analyses[18] of films, television content, or music songs (e.g. Avila-Saavedra, 2009; Monaghan, 2021; Schoonover & Galt, 2016; Taylor, 2012). These studies are not so much concerned with assessing whether the representations are realistic or authentic. Rather, they demonstrate how popular culture texts that include LGBTQ characters or themes reinforce and/or challenge heteronormativity (West, 2018). The objects of study may consist of content that features LGBTQ characters prominently, but also work that implicitly deals with same-sex attraction, uses homo-erotic iconography, or only features characters that identify as straight/heterosexual. Later in this chapter, the discussion of the teen drama series SKAM (NRK, 2015–2017) will serve as an example of this approach.

---

17 Scholars within the field of trans media studies (e.g. Jack Halberstam) who rely on queer theory can also be seen as part of queer-theory-informed media and cultural studies.
18 Different methods have been used to conduct this research, including 'close readings', 'deconstruction/deconstructive readings', 'textual analysis', and 'critical discourse analysis'. In many cases, the methods allow for making similar arguments about the way a popular culture text explicitly or implicitly engages with hegemonic ideologies.

Most studies in the field are qualitative and critical analyses of popular culture texts and phenomena. Nonetheless, the ethnographic turn in cultural studies also affected scholars in queer-theory-informed media and cultural studies, which resulted in studies exploring media consumption and use. This led to, for instance, audience reception studies exploring how audiences make sense of television fiction with nonheterosexual characters and narratives (e.g. Dhaenens, 2012c; Kern, 2014; Scanlon & Lewis, 2017). It also encompasses studies about the relationship between digital media and LGBTQ users, which range from studies exploring how queer youth of colour navigate the heteronormative design choices of digital platforms (e.g. Cho, 2018) to studies assessing how heteronormativity shapes practices of self-representation of young queer men on social media (e.g. Cover & Prosser, 2013).

Recently, there is also a branch of queer production studies (e.g. Martin, 2018; O'Brien & Kerrigan, 2020; Vanlee, 2019a) that poses sociocultural and political questions about the interconnections between sexual diversity and the production of popular media culture. Sociocultural questions pertain to understanding how, for instance, nonheterosexual media professionals experience working in contemporary popular culture industries and to what extent they encounter homonegativity and homophobia. For instance, in the 2010s and 2020s, we have seen a surge in popular music artists (e.g. Lil Nas X, Omar Apollo, Troye Sivan, Rina Sawayama (see figure 21), girl in red, and Amaarae) disclosing their sexual orientation in song lyrics, music videos, social media, and/or in public interviews. Through in-depth interviews and theoretical reflections, queer production studies could investigate this surge by addressing a range of issues. For instance, to what extent have these artists been able to represent their sexuality on their own terms? Have they experienced pressure from journalists and audiences to 'out' themselves? How have they balanced their artist identity (e.g. writing music, conveying artistic meanings) with their private sexual identity? Do they believe they have to act as a role model for nonheterosexual fans? Have they felt 'pressured' by managers or record labels to perform a heteronormative, acceptable gay, lesbian, or bisexual identity, or have they been able to express their sexual identity freely?

Scholars within queer production studies can also ask political-economic questions (see also Chapter 6). For instance, to what extent are media production companies sincerely committed to representing sexual diversity and/or do their actions qualify as a form of queerbaiting? According to Michael McDermott (2020), queerbaiting "refers to the perceived intentional practice of 'baiting' audiences with the promise of queer representation, through marketing, or subtextual hints and gestures, but ultimately failing to meet expectations" (p. 1). LGBTQ audiences consider this practice particularly frustrating as they invest in a film like *Beauty and the Beast* (Bill Condon, 2017) (see Chapter 1) or a programme like *Bridgerton*[19] (Netflix, 2020–present) on the promise of recognition, only to feel betrayed by the content creators in the end.

Figure 21. Rina Sawayama at music venue Fabrique in Milan, Italy, in 2023. Photo credit: Marco Arici, © Imageselect/Alamy.

Queer-theory-informed media and cultural studies have offered us alternative perspectives on popular media culture, nuancing why the simple inclusion of a gay or lesbian character may not be the most progressive thing to do if that character is represented as desexualised and secondary to heterosexual characters. The tradition, however, also received its fair share of criticism. Some argue that its critical analyses of texts may result in reading too much into the images (e.g. highlighting the homoerotic tensions between superheroes denoted as being straight, see below). Similarly, arguing that certain gay or lesbian characters gravitate toward emulating heteronormativity can be a valid argument, yet it cannot undo the cultural significance of having an LGBTQ character in a context from which

---

19 The trailer of *Bridgerton's* first season suggested that the main family's second eldest son, Benedict Bridgerton, would have a gay-themed narrative. The actual gay character, an artist named Henry Granville, turned out to be a minor character with little screen time or narrative development.

LGBTQ characters were previously omitted. Last, in its reliance on qualitative methods, the research tradition has missed out on descriptive data that could provide context to a critical analysis of a series or film (see Vanlee et al., 2018).

3. REPRESENTING SEXUAL DIVERSITY IN FILM AND TELEVISION FICTION

Although I already shared some reflections on the representation of sexual diversity in popular media culture, this section deepens those insights by recounting a history of representing sexual diversity from the twentieth century onward in audiovisual fiction. While print media and factual television, in general, tackled homosexuality in a straightforward manner (see above), film and television fiction have deployed different strategies to represent sexual diversity. Rather than informing people, film and television fiction entertain, provoke, or move audiences. Further, film and television fiction is often the result of a balancing act. For instance, while film and television creators may desire to create a work that is equally art as it is engendering social impact, production companies or television broadcasters surely watch over the potential of the film or series to draw audiences into the theatres or in front of the small screen. As such, film and television creators who represented sexual diversity likely took different stakeholders into account, including the zeitgeist and local sensitivities. Keeping this in mind, this section revisits the history of film and television fiction and relies on dominant trends in the representation of sexual diversity to structure this history. Considering the transnational popularity of Hollywood throughout the twentieth century (Semati & Sotorin, 1999), and its ability to shape or challenge stereotypes and assumptions about sexual diversity, much attention is devoted to developments in the United States. At the same time, some (counter)examples from Western Europe will be highlighted.

3.1. Absent images and coded representation

Are we able to find depictions of sexual minorities in the early days of cinema, which roughly encompasses the mid-1880s to late 1920s, when film was still a silent medium? Based on the sociocultural position of sexual minorities at the time (see above), we would expect to see no images at all. But film historians were quick to point out that nonheterosexual identities and desires were represented. The representations of nonheterosexuality, however, were few and presented in a coded manner (Barrios, 2003; Doty, 1993; Russo, 1985). Having been accustomed to expressing same-sex desires in coded ways or engaging in same-sex sexual activities in secret, nonheterosexual people involved in the production of film were able to, deliberately or not, leave their mark (e.g. by expressing a certain coded gesture, see below). Some well-known filmmakers in the early days of Hollywood (e.g. gay director George Cukor, lesbian director Dorothy Arzner) were

Figure 22. American director Dorothy Arzner. She directed twenty films, including *The Wild Party* (1929), *Merrily We Go to Hell* (1932) and *Dance, Girl, Dance* (1940). © Imageselect/Alamy.

able to evoke same-sex desire or nonheterosexual identification through cinematographic and narrative choices (see figure 22). At the same time, the arts, including film culture, were considered a safer haven for nonheterosexual individuals (Doty, 1993).

In film, the most visible markers of nonheterosexuality were signified through gender expressions that subverted traditionally masculine or traditionally feminine behaviours, attitudes, or gestures. Acting and accessory codes that conveyed that a male character was gay involved a wide range of mannerisms (e.g. fluttering hands, pursed lips, a sly smile, sashaying, gazing in a certain manner at other men), having a little moustache, and the use of accessories (e.g. the way one wears a handkerchief). These characters were known as 'sissies' or 'pansies'. Franklin Pangborn was known for often playing such a character in comedies in the 1920s and 1930s. Among the attributes that implied that female characters were lesbian were cigars, monocles, jackets, ties, and slicked-back hair. Female characters using these attributes were known as 'the dyke' or a 'tough woman'. Marlene Dietrich and Greta Garbo played around with these coded qualities (Barrios, 2003). It is true that 'the sissy' or 'the dyke' would today be considered stereotypical. Yet, it is worth pointing out that the characters were not vilified or condemned in the films' narratives or that the audiences were repulsed by them. They were often considered harmless and funny. At the same time, they figured as minor characters and were often the butt of the joke (Barrios, 2003; Russo, 1985). Moreover, Richard Barrios (2003) underscored that a dramatic film such as *Anders als die Andern* (see above) would have been considered too progressive for the American audience. In fact, although still implicit, homosexual desire was much more thematised in Western European films than in American films. According to Richard Dyer (2003), the first film to our knowledge that features a love story between two men is a Swedish film called *Vingarne* [Wings] (Mauritz Stiller), created in 1916. Homoerotic desire was also present in other films produced in Weimar Germany, such as *Michael* (Carl Theodor Dreyer, 1924), *Die Büchse der Pandora* [Pandora's Box] (Georg Wilhelm Pabst, 1929), and *Mädchen in Uniform* [Girls in Uniform] (Leontine Sagan, 1931).

Throughout the 1920s and 1930s, audiences and censors rarely decoded these characters as nonheterosexual but as transgressing normative gender roles. This, however, changed when American Protestant, Catholic, and social conservative moral guardians were increasingly able to interpret these images as references to homosexuality. This also coincided with an increased knowledge about homosexuality in Western society. With Hollywood booming, they found film increasingly dangerous as the moral guardians considered film a powerful medium able to morally corrupt young people. Although the conservative lobbies mainly targeted the use of violence and sex in Hollywood films, they also found that films should refrain from depicting any reference to 'sex perversion', which implied homosexuality. To avoid state censors increasing their censoring, Hollywood studios succumbed and established a period of self-censorship. An independent institution was installed, named the Production Code Administration (1934–1968). The institution had the power to approve a film at the level of production to prevent it from being amoral (Black, 1989; Russo, 1985). Images or narratives that hinted at homosexuality were forbidden. Some directors and scriptwriters were, nonetheless, able to sneak in nonheterosexual characters or homoerotic desires (Barrios, 2003; Lugowski, 1999). Yet, these films started to represent homosexuality as something deviant and alien to mainstream Western society and potentially dangerous (Russo, 1985). Even though these films did not feature explicit expressions of same-sex intimacy or even words such as 'homosexuality', some audiences read these films as cautionary tales of homosexuality, which fortified the belief that nonheterosexual people had to be avoided or feared. Several films made by Alfred Hitchcock, for instance, figured problematic nonheterosexual characters. The female housekeeper in *Rebecca* (1940) was framed as predatory, while the implied male lovers who cover up a murder in *Rope* (1948) were represented as dangerous and amoral (Barrios, 2003) (see figure 23).

Figure 23. Photograph from *Rope* (1948). Rupert (James Stewart) figured out that his former students Brandon (John Dall) and Phillip (Farley Granger) murdered their classmate David. © Imageselect/Alamy.

3.2. Stereotyping

In the second half of the twentieth century, same-sex desires and nonheterosexual people were increasingly depicted in film and, to a lesser extent, television fiction. In a way, media and film companies responded to the demand of homophile and gay liberation movements for mainstream visibility and cultural legitimacy (Russo, 1985; Bernstein, 2002). Visibility was offered, but Hollywood and American television broadcasters refrained from helping nonheterosexual people gain cultural legitimacy. Instead, they reinforced stereotypical assumptions about nonheterosexual persons by depicting them as either vulnerable, neurotic, and self-loathing, or disturbed, psychotic, sadistic, and predatory (Dyer, 1984/2006; Gross, 1991; Russo, 1985). Hollywood and television broadcasters did not care about their nonheterosexual audiences. Instead, they created content for heterosexual audiences, showing them that nonheterosexual people were either comic relief, to be pitied, or to be feared. Similar trends could be noted in audiovisual fiction produced in Western European countries. Think of the recurrent use of having a gay character for comic relief, like in the British sitcom *'Allo 'Allo!* (BBC, 1982–1992), or the sad and self-loathing gay men in dramas such as the Belgian film *Het Sacrament* [The Sacrament] (Hugo Claus, 1989).

Focus on *The Children's Hour*

An illustration of representing a nonheterosexual character as self-loathing can be found in *The Children's Hour* (William Wyler, 1961), an adaptation from a controversial play by Lillian Hellman from 1934. The American film tells the story of Martha (Shirley MacLaine) and Karen (Audrey Hepburn). They run a successful private school for girls. Early in the film, a rumour is spread by one of the pupils. According to the rumour, both women are lovers. Even though unfounded and false, parents start pulling their children from the school, while Martha and Karen are mocked and harassed. In an emotional and tense scene toward the end of the film, a distressed Martha breaks down and discloses to Karen that the rumour may harbour some truth. While crying, she acknowledges that the pupil saw something in her that she had denied for so long. She also expresses that her love for Karen is more than the love between friends. Yet, in contrast to many contemporary coming-out scenes in film and television, this particular scene is not created to give the queer character a feeling of relief and recognition. She sobs and looks away from her best friend with whom she fell in love. Karen does not know what to say, but a close-up allows the spectator to read her expression as pitiful. Martha, on the other hand, loathes herself and exclaims: "I feel so damn sick and dirty I can't stand it anymore!" After the dramatic coming-out scene, Martha flees to her room and ends her life (see figure 24).

Figure 24. On-set photograph from *The Children's Hour* (1961). Martha (Shirley MacLaine) confesses her feelings for Karen (Audrey Hepburn) and spirals into self-loathing. Photo credit: United artists/Album, © Imageselect/Alamy.

As Russo (1985) emphasised, an extremely high number of films from this period ended with the death of the gay or lesbian character, such as *Advise and Consent* (Otto Preminger, 1962) and *Suddenly, Last Summer* (Joseph L. Mankiewicz, 1959). On the one hand, several of these films indeed were the first to feature a non-heterosexual character as the main character and, second, refrained from representing them by relying on an iconography of stereotypes (e.g. the 'dyke' or 'sissy' stereotypes). Yet, drawing from Dyer's (1984/2006) discussion of 'stereotyping through structure' (see Chapter 1), the plot development in which a prominent gay character dies by the end of the film had become a stereotype.

Toward the end of the twentieth century, the modes of representation started to diversify (see below), but the practice of stereotyping persisted. As rampant homophobia became less tolerated in Western society, more subtle forms of stereotyping emerged. For instance, rather than fearing homosexual people, heterosexual (male) characters were afraid of the idea that they could be perceived as gay. In comedy, in particular, scenes in which men expressed their gender in a nonnormative manner or shared an intimate, homosocial hug were often succeeded with scenes that explicitly dissociated these practices from homosexuality. A common way to do so was by representing heterosexual recuperation, which refers to practices where heterosexual (male) individuals underscore their heterosexuality (e.g. boasting of heterosexual successes, distancing oneself from being read as 'homosexual' through ironic remarks)[20] (McCormack & Anderson, 2010). Even though these scenes may lack actual nonheterosexual people, they perpetuate the idea that homosexuality is a form of inferior masculinity or, to draw from Connell (2005), subordinate masculinity. Plenty of sitcoms (e.g. *Friends* (NBC, 1994-2004)) and comedies (e.g. *Police Academy 2: Their First Assignment* (Jerry Paris, 1985)) have made use of this strategy. In these works, the humour derives from someone 'misinterpreting' a gesture or look of a heterosexual male character as an expression of same-sex desire. Such scenes are often followed by acts or gestures of hypermasculine behaviour that attempt to undo the impression that the heterosexual male character is gay (Dhaenens & Van Bauwel, 2017).

Besides, more subtle forms of stereotyping were introduced. Nonheterosexual characters may have been introduced in mainstream film and television as well-rounded characters with backstories and character development, but they often figured as supporting characters to the main heterosexual character. An example of such a practice is the gay best friend trope. Think of the many romantic comedies (e.g. *My Best Friend's Wedding* (PJ Hogan, 1997)), teen dramas (e.g. *Mean Girls* (Mark Waters, 2004)), or female-led drama series (*Sex and the City* (HBO, 1998-2004)) in which an openly gay character's main purpose is to serve as a sounding board to the female heterosexual lead character.

---

20 An example of how these practices of heterosexual recuperation live on can be spotted in the expression 'nohomo' in popular music culture. For instance, several male rappers have been rather quick to say 'nohomo' after public displays of homosocial intimacy. Similarly, online music fans (e.g. on Spotify) have used 'nohomo' as a tag when expressing an interest in songs that "possess certain qualities that make it socially suspicious for straight men to enjoy them" (De Smet & Dhaenens, 2024, p. 9).

3.3. Between heteronormativity and queerness

From the 1990s on, in concordance with increased tolerance and inclusive legislation toward nonheterosexual individuals, representations of gay, lesbian, and bisexual characters became more common, positive, well developed, and not intended to vilify or mock the nonheterosexual individual. Yet, a new tension arose in the way nonheterosexual characters were represented. Queer-theory-informed media scholars (Chambers, 2009; Herman, 2003; Westerfelhaus & Lacroix, 2006) argued that audiovisual storytellers, deliberately or not, represented nonheterosexual characters as gravitating toward either heteronormativity or queerness. Most mainstream content in film and television, including fictional and factual formats and content, evoked heteronormativity, resulting in nonheterosexual characters represented as homonormative. Homonormativity refers to a set of norms, values, beliefs, and practices of nonheterosexual people who seek inclusion in a heteronormative society. For instance, they aspire to be granted access to heteronormative institutions (e.g. civil marriage) without questioning the politics and societal impact of heteronormativity (Duggan, 2003). It is equally typified by a depoliticised standpoint as it presumes that all rights are acquired and protests (including Pride marches) are no longer needed.

Concretely, this meant that nonheterosexual characters were represented as gender-conforming (e.g. acting and expressing one's gender identity following traditional gender repertoires) and focused on assimilation (e.g. emphasising the similarities between them and heterosexual individuals) rather than celebrating differences or performing non-normative gender expressions. Typically, this type of content included same-sex couples that were monogamous and (if legally possible) married. Examples include Christian and Oliver in the German soap series *Verbotene Liebe* [Forbidden Love] (ARD, 1995–2015), Kevin and Scotty in the American drama series *Brothers & Sisters* (ABC, 2006–2011), and Valeria and Rita in the Italian comedy series *È arrivata la felicità* [Happiness Has Arrived] (RAI, 2015–2018). Another aspect that characterised heteronormative portrayals of nonheterosexual characters was the depiction of same-sex couples as desexualised (e.g. not depicting their sexual lives) and/or rarely having intimate scenes (e.g. kissing, hugging, holding hands), a critique that befell American sitcoms *Modern Family* (ABC, 2009–2020) and *Happy Endings* (ABC, 2011–2013). Besides, a heteronormative perspective also led to representing LGBTQ characters as detached from LGBTQ communities. Think of films, such as the Belgian film *Team Spirit* (Jan Verheyen, 2000), that featured only one or two nonheterosexual character(s) and represented them as having no LGBTQ friends and/or connection to LGBTQ-related community events (e.g. participating in Pride marches, LGBTQ parties, and protests). Last, in this type of content, homophobia and homonegativity were either ignored or treated as personal rather than related to heteronormative assumptions and expectations in society at large (Avila-Saavedra, 2009; Battles & Hilton-Morrow, 2002).

Several LGBTQ and heterosexual filmmakers, however, were frustrated with these heteronormative representations and started creating audiovisual content that was deliberately *queer*. Especially from the 1990s onward, a wave of independent films that challenged and changed heteronormative modes of representing sexual diversity were gaining critical acclaim at international film festivals. Film critics referred to the wave as 'new queer cinema'. Even though the films were quite diverse, they shared a postmodern style while representing sexual diversity unapologetically and defiantly (Aaron, 2004; Rich, 2013). New queer cinema put the spotlight on LGBTQ characters often excluded from the screen (e.g. sex workers, outlaws, drag communities, queer people of colour, and queer working-class individuals), it represented its LGBTQ characters as sexual, it defied the inferior and subordinate position ascribed to sexual minority identities, and it dared to be explicitly political. Examples include the American documentary *Paris is Burning* (Jennie Livingston, 1990), the American road movie *My Own Private Idaho* (Gus van Sant, 1991) (see figure 25), and the Hong Kong drama *Happy Together* (Wong Kar-Wai, 1997). Even though the label 'new queer cinema' became obsolete from the 2000s on, plenty of films and television series kept on interrogating the normalcy of a heteronormative order and looked for ways to represent sexual diversity differently. In practice, many popular films and series with LGBTQ themes tend to feature both heteronormative and (moderately) queer characters and tropes.

Figure 25. Photograph from *My Own Private Idaho* (1991). Scott (Keanu Reeves) and Mike (River Phoenix) are two male sex workers who embark on a road trip. Photo credit: AJ Pics, © Imageselect/Alamy.

Focus on SKAM[21]

To illustrate how a television programme balances heteronormativity with queer tropes, I zoom in on $SKAM$ (NRK, 2015-2017), a popular teen-drama series produced by Norwegian public service broadcasting company NRK. The series ran for four seasons and its huge popularity among young audiences (although older audiences watched as well) convinced production companies in other Western European countries and the United States to adapt the format and create local adaptations (e.g. $SKAM\ France$, $SKAM\ Italia$, $wtFOCK$ [Belgium], $Druck$ [Germany]). $SKAM$ and its remakes focus on the everyday lives of (mainly) middle-class teenagers. Each season is narrated from the point of view of one teenager and recounts mundane, meaningful, and impactful moments in their lives, including falling in love, maintaining friendships, and coping with heavy and traumatic experiences (e.g. sexual transgressive behaviour, Islamophobia). Although most seasons are narrated from the perspective of a female teenager, the third season directs attention to a cisgender male character, Isak (Tarjei Sandvik Moe). He is introduced in the first season as the best friend of Jonas (Marlon Valdés Langeland). The third season explores how Isak comes to terms with his same-sex desires, which are aroused after meeting Even (Henrik Holm) at a school event. Throughout ten episodes, $SKAM$ unpacks how Isak makes sense of his sexual desires and sexual identity and, second, how the boys experience their first same-sex relationship (see figure 26).

What is interesting about this season is that it acknowledges how heteronormativity is still dominant in contemporary Western society, even in a country with relatively progressive laws concerning homosexuality. Whereas many series take heteronormativity for granted, $SKAM$ exposes how heteronormativity shapes perceptions and attitudes about gender and sexuality among heterosexual and nonheterosexual teens. Plenty of scenes in the series demonstrate male and female teenagers expressing heteronormative assumptions (e.g. presuming that everyone is heterosexual)

---

21   This section draws from the following article: Dhaenens, F., Mediavilla Aboulaoula, S., & Lion, A. (2023). 'I'm just not gay-gay': Exploring same-sex desire and sexual minority identity formation in *SKAM* and its Western European remakes. *European Journal of Cultural Studies, 26*(6), 863-879.

or expectations (e.g. how to behave as a girl or a boy). Consequentially, Isak feels forced by his friends and society to perform a heterosexual identity (e.g. telling his friends which girl he finds sexy, hooking up with a girl to 'prove' his heterosexuality) and hegemonic masculinity (e.g. acting tough, making homonegative comments). At the same time, audiences already know that Isak desires Even, emphasised in shots that show Isak staring amorously at Even. In demonstrating how Isak struggles with his same-sex desires in part due to internalised heteronormative and homonegative assumptions and attitudes, the series makes audiences aware that it remains difficult to identify as LGBTQ in contemporary Western society.

Figure 26. Still from SKAM (2015–2017). An overhead shot captures the intimacy between Even (Henrik Holm) and Isak (Tarjei Sandvik Moe). Photo: NRK.

The series also features scenes that actively reject heteronormative assumptions and expectations. Toward the end of the season, Isak's heterosexual male friends start to question the idea of hegemonic masculinity by sharing their insecurities and questioning their own normative assumptions. Similarly, characters who express homonegative and benign stereotypes are rebuked. For instance, when Emma (Ruby Dagnall) says, "I love gay people. They're funny" (translated from Norwegian), Even asks her rhetorically whether that is not a superficial generalisation (season 3, episode 3). Most importantly, Isak is also made aware of his own internalised homonegativity. Halfway through the fifth episode, Isak shares with his roommate Eskild (Carl Martin Eggesbø), a gay university student, that he is in love with another boy. The scene starts as a wholesome moment, in which Isak seeks connection with Eskild, but turns awry when Isak feels the need to set himself apart from Eskild. He argues that:

> [t]here is nothing wrong with being gay, I'm just not like gay-gay [...] you know what I mean, right? You talk loudly about sucking dick, Kim Kardashian, and lavender scent...I mean, I totally respect that you take the whole 'gay package' all the way, but I'm not like that [...] Because it's not like I'll start wearing mascara or tights, or go to Gay Pride, just because I like Even. (translated from Norwegian)

Such discourse reveals how, on the one hand, Isak has internalised how aspects associated with LGBTQ culture are deemed 'inferior', 'abnormal', and 'un-masculine' in a heteronormative society, while on the other hand holding stereotypical assumptions about what it means to identify as gay. Take note that he dissociates himself from everything that he conceives of as being part of LGBTQ culture, including Eskild, and instead adopts a homonormative position.

Eskild, however, is appalled by Isak's comments:

> Let me tell you one thing about those you don't want to associate with. About those who have put on tights and mascara and gone out to fight for the right to be themselves. They're people who, throughout the years, have chosen to endure harassment. And hate. Who have been beaten up. Killed. And that's not because they're so keen on being different, but because they would rather die than pretend to be someone they're not. And that requires courage... (translated from Norwegian)

As such, Eskild challenges Isak's homonormative position by making him aware that Isak too is part of a community of people whose gender and sexual identities have been questioned and challenged time and again. In a way, Eskild reminds Isak as well as the series' heterosexual and LGBTQ audiences of the daily risks LGBTQ people run by simply expressing their gender and sexuality (especially those who are not able or willing to pass as heterosexual or gender-conforming) and pointing out how Pride marches and protests have been pivotal to advance the living conditions and rights of nonheterosexual people. In such instances, *SKAM* articulates a *queer* critique. It encourages heterosexual and LGBTQ audiences to become aware of their lingering prejudices and how heteronormative, homonegative, and stereotypical ideas still impact the process of sexual identity formation.

4. QUEER PRACTICES OF FAN AUDIENCES

To conclude this chapter, we turn to fan audiences. For a long time, academics and mainstream society perceived fans as psychologically and culturally dysfunctional, properties that can be traced back to the meaning of 'fanatic', the word from which 'fan' is derived (Jensen, 1992). Cornel Sandvoss (2005), however, stressed that in contemporary society, where new media technologies have changed the production and distribution of popular culture and cultural industries anticipate and incorporate fannishness, fandom has become part of everyday life. Even though there are fans who are rather passive in their expression of fandom, some adopt a more active attitude toward sharing and expressing their affection for a particular text or artist. Among the practices of film and television fans, I turn to the production of fan fiction. The practice emerged from the desire of fans to expand the universe of a given book, film, or television. To transform this desire into something productive, fans started creating new stories set within those universes (Hellekson & Busse, 2014; Staiger, 2005).

Of interest to this chapter is the creation of slash fiction. Slash fiction is a form of fan fiction that represents homoerotic affairs or relationships between two same-sex protagonists, in most cases male protagonists. The term 'slash' refers to the use of the forward slash that is placed between the two characters who are paired in fan fiction texts (Allington, 2007; Jenkins, 1992; Staiger, 2005). Henry Jenkins (1992), who wrote extensively about participatory culture and fandom, demonstrated how fans played an active role in shaping and changing the prevalent meanings attributed to popular culture texts. Regarding slash fiction, Jenkins discussed Kirk/Spock slash fiction, which was written by predominantly heterosexual women. Kirk/Spock reimagined James T. Kirk (William Shatner) and Spock (Leonard Nimoy), the lead characters from the science-fiction series *Star Trek* (NBC, 1965–1969), as lovers (see figure 27). Even though Kirk and Spock were implied to be heterosexual, audiences picked up on homoerotic tensions between the two leads and made that subtext the main theme of their own fiction stories (Jenkins, 1992). The stories presented the characters as more androgynous and conflicted than their original versions, while the plot revolved around the two male leads struggling with hegemonic masculinity and internalised homonegativity only to figure out that they were destined to be together (Staiger, 2005).

It was not only the authors of slash fiction who picked up on the homoerotic tensions lingering in film and television content with two male or two female leads. LGBTQ fans as well have read popular culture against the grain, a practice that has been dubbed queer reading. Queer reading is about uncovering and revealing how a popular culture text (be it a film, series, or even a character) may be understood as queer (Doty, 2000). Whether it concerns the use of homoerotic aesthetics or narratives that can be read as metaphors for being in the closet or suppressed homosexual desire, many popular culture texts are much 'queerer' than at first sight. Slash fiction can thus be understood as a specific form of queer reading. Besides LGBTQ fans, also (LGBTQ) academics and historians have produced queer readings, which has resulted in a shared canon of queer texts and icons. Included in the canon are some obvious pairings (e.g. Batman and Robin, puppets Bert and Ernie from *Sesame Street*, or fantasy heroines Xena and Gabrielle) and some more surprising queer icons, such as Mister Babadook from the horror movie *The Babadook* (Jennifer Kent, 2014). Thanks to the affordances of Web 2.0, easy access to affordable video capture and editing software, and video streaming platforms, fans have increasingly shared their queer readings, slash fiction, and other fan-created material online (Dhaenens, 2012b). These days, it has become easy to find slash videos on online video-sharing websites (such as YouTube). Some good examples are the fan-made videos in which popular films, like *Mean Girls* (Mark Waters, 2004) and *Captain America: The Winter Soldier* (Anthony and Joe Russo, 2014) have been re-edited into trailers or mash-up videos that hint at nonheterosexual love stories absent from the original films.

The appropriation of popular culture characters as queer icons should be understood as a form of cultural resistance by LGBTQ audiences that seeks out recognition in genres and contexts where LGBTQ characters are rarely represented. Not surprisingly, plenty of slash fiction has focused on science-fiction and fantasy series. For instance, Marvel's comics may feature several LGBTQ superheroes, but Marvel's Cinematic Universe has so far only represented one openly gay character, which was Phastos (Brian Tyree Henry) in *Eternals* (Chloé Zhao, 2021). Similarly, despite numerous studies demonstrating the queer subtext of plenty of horror films, like in *A Nightmare on Elm Street 2: Freddy's Revenge* (Jack Sholder,

1985), only a handful of horror texts feature an openly queer hero.²² Rather than settling for the gay best friend, LGBTQ audiences have increasingly claimed their right to representation in a myriad of roles and identities.

I can stop the pain...

Figure 27. Kirk/Spock fan-art by Patt Stall. It was published in the first issue of *Companion* (1978), a fanzine dedicated to K/S slash fiction based on *Star Trek: The Original Series* (1966–1969). Personal copy scan, *Companion*, Pat Stall, © Fanlore.

---

22   A good example is the horror television series *Chucky* (Syfy/USA Network, 2021–present), based on the *Child Play*'s film franchise. The series' main character is a fourteen-year-old boy who falls in love with another boy from school while trying to escape a murderous doll.

CHAPTER 4

RACE, ETHNICITY, AND DIASPORA

Setting the scene: Charlotte Adigéry

To kick off this chapter, I invite you to listen to the music of Charlotte Adigéry. She is a Belgian artist who started her musical career around 2016 when she was cast to perform a song in *Belgica* (Felix Van Groeningen, 2016), a film known for its vibrant soundtrack composed by Belgian band Soulwax. Since then, she has released music under the moniker WWWater and been a guest vocalist for Soulwax, Beraadgeslagen, and Baloji. On the set of *Belgica*, she met Bolis Pupul (the artist persona of Boris Zeebroek), with whom she also started making music (see figure 28). Together, they released a series of EPs, including *Charlotte Adigéry* (2017) and *Zandoli* (2019), both published under the name Charlotte Adigéry, and their debut album *Topical Dancer* (2022), officially published under both their names. Their music deliberately engages with a multitude of music genres, explores a broad range of themes and topics, such as racism, sexuality, and sexism, and critically contemplates their diasporic background/identity – Charlotte Adigéry's parents are from Martinique and Guadeloupe, and Bolis Pupul's mother was a Chinese woman born in Hong Kong.

Figure 28. Bolis Pupul and Charlotte Adigéry on stage at Best Kept Secret 2023, a music festival in The Netherlands. © Jan Van den Bulck.

Broaching political themes in music is important to the duo, something that has not escaped their record label, DEEWEE. The label announced *Topical Dancer* as follows: "Cultural appropriation and racism. Social media vanity. Postcolonialism and political correctness. These are not talking points that you'd ordinarily hear on the dancefloor but Charlotte and Bolis have ripped up the rulebook with their debut record" (DEEWEE, n.d.). This promotional description aptly summarises what the album aims to do, which tackles racism, misogyny, and sexual harassment while offering reflections on contemporary identity politics, repackaged in electronic dance songs that are intended to be danced to (Bulut, 2022; Peeters, 2022). Take, for instance, their single 'Blenda'. On the one hand, the song exposes how Western society expects people with diasporic backgrounds to assimilate into white cultural contexts and practices, something that is apparent in the song title's tongue-in-cheek reference to 'blending in'. On the other hand, it also reveals how 'assimilation' will not 'prevent' white people from being racist. To underscore this message, Charlotte Adigéry ironically appropriates an often-heard racist provocation addressed to people of colour. She sings, "Go back to your country where you belong," followed by the line, "Siri, can you tell me where I belong?" It makes palpable what it means for people of colour to grow up in a country where the majority of people are white, experiencing both the pressure to 'assimilate' while always being perceived as 'other' and 'different' and subject to explicit and implicit forms of racism. Further, in asking Apple's digital assistant Siri where she belongs, Charlotte Adigéry problematises the presumption that the sense of belonging of people with diasporic backgrounds is unequivocally bound to a singular geographical location, their so-called 'roots'.[23] Rather, the song implies that their sense of belonging is shaped by experiencing attachments to and estrangements from various places and people. The song also illustrates another tactic used to deliver their political reflections, which is the use of humour. According to Charlotte Adigéry, "[h]umour is a great way to make a point without being moralising. You can be moralising, but everything is a balance" (Bulut, 2022).

Humour is also one of the key ingredients of 'High Lights' (2019), a single from the EP *Zandoli*. For this chapter, it is worth checking out the music video, directed by Joaquim Bayle, that accompanied the song. The music video was filmed in Matonge, a neighbourhood in Brussels known as the African heart of the capital. The neighbourhood is named after a district in Kinshasa, DR Congo, since many

---

23   As Stuart Hall (1999/2019) explained, such a notion of cultural identity "cannot be 'thought' in this way" (p. 208). He argued that for many people with diasporic backgrounds, "identity is irredeemably a historical question […] Their origins are not singular but diverse." (p. 208)

Congolese migrants have settled there. Speaking about the song, Charlotte Adigéry said: "It was the first song written for the EP and it inspired me to explore my identity as a Caribbean black woman raised in Belgium. It started off as a celebration of the feminine black culture and then resulted in me writing more in Creole and translating my heritage through music" (Charlotte Adigéry & Bolis Pupul, 2019). A central topic in the song concerns hair care. Charlotte Adigéry recited that several people reproached her for changing her hairstyle too often, which, they claimed, would lead to audiences being unable to recognise her and, eventually, her 'financial ruination' (Van Steenkiste, 2019). She referenced this experience in the song's chorus: "I know I shouldn't do it but / I love synthetic wigs a lot." The line betrays a sense of tension and shame, as her pleasure in wearing wigs is juxtaposed with a normative gaze that has made her feel she should refrain from wearing them. Yet, with the song and video, she defied that gaze. Featuring joyful and communal scenes in the hairdressing salon and on the streets, the video celebrates hair care and the pleasure of changing styles.

This normative gaze, however, needs to be explained by discussing the historical politicisation of black hair in Western society. Kobena Mercer (1987) demonstrated how "black people's hair has been historically devalued as the most visible stigma of blackness, second only to skin" (p. 35). From the seventeenth century on, scientific racist discourses segregated people based on 'races' (see below). As a consequence, hair had important symbolic currency. Mercer explained that "hair functions as a key 'ethnic signifier' because, compared with bodily shape or facial features, it can be changed more easily by cultural practices such as straightening" (p. 36). The politicisation of black hair may thus have nudged women to hide or straighten their natural hair. At the same time, the refusal to do so and valorise one's natural hair also became a form of resistance and "a symbol of Black Pride and Black Power" (p. 37). Yet, this does not imply that wearing wigs should be read as an act of submission. From an intersectional perspective, it can be argued that Charlotte Adigéry's lyrics explore what it means to be black and a woman. The lyrics stress her agency in deciding her look, while the music video highlights there is no such thing as only one (hair)style for black women. Moreover, she pointed out that many black women consider their hairstyle (including the wearing of wigs) as a form of self-care and self-expression (Maenhaut, 2019). Once again, humour is used as a tactic to deliver that message. For instance, when she sings, "Now I could teach a drag or two / I woke up like this, 'cause all you need is glue," she forges a bond with drag (queen) artists – who also experience harassment and for whom wigs are an essential element of style – while underscoring how effortless it can be to look amazing.

1. ON RACE, ETHNICITY, AND DIASPORA

The identity axes at stake in this chapter have resulted in a plethora of theoretical concepts, with 'race' and 'ethnicity' as the most common terms to discuss and understand processes of identification that are based on a set of physical and/or cultural similarities (Barker, 2012; Downing & Husband, 2005; Solomos, 2022). At the same time, some alternatives have been proposed that aim to grasp better specific contexts and experiences, such as 'diaspora' (Karim, 2018; Safran, 1991). This section introduces you to these concepts, which form the basis for this chapter.

1.1. *About race and racialisation*

The most prominent and problematic term is 'race'. Even though sociologist Paul Gilroy (1993) pointed out that 'race' was originally used to refer to distinct cultures, the concept became more and more associated with alleged biological differences. Especially during the nineteenth century, scientists in Western Europe and North America engaged in social Darwinism (e.g. Herbert Spencer, William Graham Sumner) "enshrined the idea of European superiority as a key feature of natural evolution and selection" (Dennis, 1995, p. 244). Social Darwinism was a strand of thinking that relied on Charles Darwin's theory of natural selection and biological evolution to understand human society. It classified human 'races' based on biological and physical traits such as skin pigmentation, hair, the shape of the nose, and the shape of eyes, as well as in terms of intelligence and capabilities (Barker, 2012; Dennis, 1995; Mercer, 1987). Social Darwinism, later dubbed a form of scientific racism, was used to justify European imperialism, colonialism, and American racial segregation and oppression (Dennis, 1995).

Scientific racism in Western society was increasingly questioned and debunked from the beginning of the twentieth century. In particular, the Second World War and the racist ideology and eugenics policies of the Nazi regime are generally seen as the tipping point of the decline of scientific racism (Thompson, 2006). Furthermore, extensive biological research refuted the idea of distinct human races, making way for understanding 'race' as a social construction (Barker, 2012; Omi & Winant, 2015). Sociologists Michael Omi and Howard Winant (2015) explained that such a postulation should not be read as arguing that 'race' is a mere illusion. They argued that even though race "is not something rooted in nature, something that reflects clear and discrete variations in human identity" (p. 106), race exists as a social category. Put differently, race is the result of a process of racial formation. They considered race "a concept that signifies and symbolises social conflicts and interests by referring to different types of human bodies"

(p. 106). They underscored that what refers to "different types of bodies" is arbitrary and context-specific; specific physical differences (e.g. skin colour, height, hair texture) have been interpreted in Western society as "manifestations of more profound differences that are situated within racially identified persons: differences in such qualities as intelligence, athletic ability, temperament, and sexuality, among other traits" (p. 111).

Omi and Winant's line of thinking echoes the work of sociologist and cultural studies scholar Paul Gilroy (1987, 1993). He emphasised that phenotypical variation (i.e. observable physical differences) has been used in science and politics to create concrete systems of social differentiation. He stressed that "'[r]ace' has to be socially and politically constructed and elaborate ideological work is done to secure and maintain the different forms of 'racialization'" (1987, p. 38). Informed by a cultural studies approach, he pointed out how the social and political meaning of race has changed over time and how the signification of race should be seen as part of an ideological struggle. He illustrated his argument by pointing out how in the 1980s in the United Kingdom, "political definitions of black based on the possibility of Afro-Asian unity [moved] towards more restricted alternative formulations which have confined the concept of blackness to people of African descent" (p. 39). With this example, he demonstrated the elasticity of racial categories, such as 'black', but also the danger of treating various discriminated groups as inherently different despite all being subjected to hatred and racism. Such categorical thinking could reinforce essentialist and biologically deterministic approaches and hamper the creation of inclusive approaches to defining blackness and/or tackling racism, which remain needed.

Although race is socially constructed, its effects on people who are marked as 'non-white' in Western society are evident (Hall, 2017). Whether it concerns the labour market, the housing market, or educational systems, people of colour have experienced more obstacles and difficulties than white people in Western society (e.g. Barker, 2012; Bourabain et al., 2023; Lancee, 2021; Quillian et al., 2020). These experiences and conditions have been described and called out throughout the twentieth century. In 1903, sociologist W. E. B. Dubois (1903/2008) wrote about the daily mental conflict black Americans experienced. He argued that white American society disabled the possibility for black Americans to develop a "true selfconsciousness" and instead nudged or forced them to "always [look] at one's self through the eyes of others, of measuring one's soul by the tape of a world that looks on in amused contempt and pity" (p. 8). He described this condition as double-consciousness to grasp how black Americans experienced the balancing act of being both 'black' (e.g. being part of the pan-African diaspora) and 'American' (e.g. identifying with white and Eurocentric culture, including racist ideologies), an experience that persists even today (Joseph & Golash-Boza, 2021; Moore,

2005). In 1952, psychiatrist and philosopher Franz Fanon shared his reflections on living in France as a black French Caribbean man in his seminal book *Peau Noire, Masques Blancs*, translated in 1967 as *Black Skin, White Masks*. Like Dubois, Fanon highlighted how the colonised subject had internalised the discourses produced by the coloniser. Yet, instead of being "confronted by the dilemma, *turn white or disappear* [the black man] should be able to take cognizance of a possibility of existence" (1952/2008, p. 75, emphasis in original). To develop such a black consciousness, Fanon argued that the social structures in Western society preserving a hierarchy between white and black/colonised subjects had to be challenged and destroyed. The work of Dubois and Fanon remains relevant in the twenty-first century as, to borrow Stuart Hall's (1997/2021) words, various *discursive* systems that have created race remain unchallenged, "the systems we use to make sense, to make human societies intelligible" (p. 364). Although a discursive system such as social Darwinism has been discredited, many new racialised discourses and practices emerged. Later in this chapter, I illustrate how racialisation has manifested in popular media culture.

1.2. About ethnicity and diaspora

Besides race, 'ethnicity' is an often-used concept to reflect on people's identities. Like race, ethnicity refers to the discursive formation of categories of difference. However, whereas race is concerned with bodily aspects of people, ethnicity refers to broader categories of cultural difference. As Stuart Hall (2017) pointed out, these discursive categories often include discourses on race but also other signifiers such as "the shared languages, traditions, religious beliefs, cultural ideas, customs, and rituals that bind together particular groups" (p. 83). Moreover, as Hall stressed, ethnicity is "a form of cultural identity that, though in fact historically and culturally constructed, is powerfully tied to a sense of place and of group origins that comes to be so unified on many levels over a long period – across generations, across shared social space, and across shared histories – that it is experienced and imagined by many not as a discursive construction but as having acquired the durability of nature itself" (p. 107). Put differently, both for people who belong to a specific ethnic group and for people who do not, specific ethnicities are perceived and experienced as inherited and stable identities, despite them being the result of historical and discursive processes. To assure people stay convinced of being inherently different, several practices (e.g. flags, customs, rituals, songs) are used to differentiate the in-group (i.e. people assumed to belong to the same ethnic formation) from the out-groups (i.e. people assumed to belong to other ethnic formations) (Barker, 2012).

Like racialised categories, ethnicities have been discursively constructed as hierarchical. In Western society, the term 'ethnicity' has been used by white people to refer to anyone who is marked as 'non-white'. This practice, first, obfuscates or denies that white people are also ethnically located (see below) and, second, compresses different figurations of cultural identity into one category of otherness (Barker, 2012; Hall, 2017). For instance, in Western popular music culture, 'ethnic music' has often been used as a label to describe and market music produced in the Global South. The use of the label 'ethnic music' (as well as 'world music') has been criticised for reinstating Western musical genres as the global norm while ignoring the complexities in and between music genres produced by non-Western artists. Producer and musician Endeguena Mulu (2015), who makes Ethiopiyawi electronic music under the name of Ethiopian Records, described ethnic and world music as terms "born from the untrue, unsaid, unexpressed thought that everything that comes from the west is the pinnacle of everything; that it is the one thing that is happening in the world that is worth taking the time to enjoy; the only way forward; the only way to the future."

Hall (1996) did not necessarily discard the concept of ethnicity but argued that it has to be deconstructed and trans-coded. He underscored that people "all speak from a particular place, out of a particular history, out of a particular experience, a particular culture, without being contained by that position as 'ethnic artists' or film-makers. We are all, in that sense, ethnically located and our ethnic identities are crucial to our subjective sense of who we are" (p. 448). What needs to be challenged are the fixed and naturalised ties between ethnicity, nation, and race, which are intended to marginalise and discriminate against other ethnicities than the unnamed white ethnic majority in Western countries. In referring to these 'ethnicities' as 'new ethnicities', Hall underscored how ethnicities are not only plural but also dynamic and heterogeneous, evolving in new formations of people. Hall, for instance, spoke of the necessity to recognise "the extraordinary diversity of subjective positions, social experiences and cultural identities which compose the category 'black'" (p. 444). He explained that this diversity not only results from a person's intersecting identities (e.g. class, gender, sexuality) but also from the fact that the black experience is "a *diaspora* experience, and the consequences which this carries for the process of unsettling, recombination, hybridization and 'cut-and-mix' – in short, the process of cultural diaspora-ization (to coin an ugly term) which it implies" (p. 448, emphasis in original).

Whereas Hall used the concept of 'diaspora' to expound on 'new ethnicities', others started to treat 'diaspora' as a concept in its own right and used it to reflect on "the mobility of peoples, commodities, capital and cultures in the context of globalisation and transnationalism" in the late twentieth century (Brah & Phoenix, 2004, p. 83). Karim H. Karim (2018) demonstrated how 'diaspora' as a social phenomenon – which literally means 'the scattering of people' – has been around forever, as human migration should be understood as a constant process throughout human history. Yet, what typifies contemporary diasporas is that "[c]urrent modes of transportation have increased travel and have accelerated the growth of diasporic communities. Contemporary technologies have also made possible regular contact between the vastly separated settlements of a group. Worldwide communication networks enable the maintenance of personal and communal linkages as well as engagement with the affairs of home countries in ways that were previously unthinkable" (p. 1). Following this, it has become easier to engage in transnational identifications, where connections are made with the 'homeland' or the nation discursively constructed as the 'nation of origin' in case there is a 'homeland' or 'nation of origin', and/or with people who are part of the same diaspora but living in other countries. This may result in "wide variations of connections and attachments that such worldwide communities have with each other. Retention of ancestral customs, language and religion, marriage patterns, and, particularly, the degree of communication between various parts of the transnational group are major factors in determining its characteristics" (p. 9).

For media and communication scholar Myria Georgiou (2005), transnational communications and (real and imagined) connections with people with the same diasporic background enable and sustain diasporic communities' "shared sense of identity" (p. 490). Yet, she stressed that diasporic populations also make sense of their identities in the context of the nation-states and local communities in which they live. These contexts feature local and national political and sociocultural discourses about participation, inclusion, and exclusion. Consequentially, people within diasporic communities make sense of their personal and social identities in heterogeneous ways (Adriaens, 2014; Barker, 2012; Georgiou, 2005; Karim, 2018). Looking, for instance, at popular media culture, we can see this manifested in the way artists and media professionals with diasporic identities negotiate these different modes of identification in their work.

Focus on Tamino

Tamino is the artist persona of Tamino-Amir Moharam Fouad. The Belgian artist studied at the Amsterdam Royal Conservatory. His first single, 'Habibi' (2017), a bare, electric guitar-driven song about (unrequited) love that derives its melancholic punch from his falsetto, made quite an impression. The song helped Tamino win a national music contest for new music talent, *De Nieuwe Lichting* [The New Generation]. In 2018, he released his debut album, *Amir*, which led to international attention and critical acclaim, and international tours including gigs in cities (e.g. Cairo, Casablanca) in the West Asia-North Africa (WANA) region in 2019 (Myers, 2020; Salfiti, 2019). His second album, *Sahar* (2022), consolidated his status as an internationally known and lauded singer-songwriter, featuring songs that are sparse and subdued and songs that are lush with swelling orchestral strings (see figure 29).

An important aspect of Tamino's music is how it articulates his diasporic background/identity. Tamino, who has an Egyptian-Lebanese diasporic background, said he felt connected with the music of his grandfather Muharram Fouad, a famous singer and actor in Egypt during the 1960s and 1970s. It encouraged Tamino to study musical traditions and practices from Egypt and the WANA region (Fenimore, 2022; Myers, 2020). For instance, he incorporates melisma (i.e. a group of notes sung to one syllable of text) in his singing and he plays instruments popular in the WANA region (e.g. the 'oud', which is a string instrument) (Salfiti, 2019). Similarly, for *Amir*, he recreated a traditional Firqa. A Firqa is an orchestra associated with the golden age of Egyptian music (1920s-1950s) and is frequently linked with the Egyptian female singer and icon Umm Kulthum. For this recreation, Tamino collaborated with the Nagham Zikrayat Orchestra. The orchestra consisted mainly of musicians from the WANA region, including refugees from Iraq and Syria. Many of them were familiar with the work of his grandfather. Typical of a Firqa is that the musicians improvised to Tamino's voice rather than rigidly following the instructions on printed music sheets (Myers, 2020).

Figure 29. Tamino, performing with a custom-made oud at music venue Alcatraz in Milan, Italy, in 2023. Photo credit: Rodolfo Sassano, © Imageselect/Alamy.

At the same time, Tamino's music cannot be reduced to a pastiche of the golden age of Egyptian music, as his work represents the experience of a contemporary young man with a diasporic background living in a Belgian-Flemish context. For instance, he does not speak Arabic and writes and performs in English rather than Dutch, a common practice among rock and pop acts based in Flanders. Similarly, his music is marked by hybridity (see below), as he brings the musical traditions and practices from the WANA region into dialogue with more Western pop and indie traditions and practices in his music. Moreover, he takes issue with media and music professionals considering his music as relevant or newsworthy only because of his diasporic background. He explained that, on the one hand, his diasporic heritage has been essential to the formation of his music but, on the other hand, he does not want to be given a forum (e.g. on a radio show, at a festival, or in a news article) simply because of that (Fenimore, 2022). In an interview, he described it as follows: "I don't want that to be the only reason why I'm invited on certain platforms. I don't want people to go, 'I don't really like his music, but it's important' – he grimaces – 'it's important to show it'" (Myers, 2020). His statement reveals sentiments shared among many diasporic artists across Europe, namely the idea that one is *just* selected or programmed based on who they are or represent (i.e. their cultural identity), often as a token and a way to check the box of diversity rather than on the basis of what they create or what their music aims to represent.

To conclude this section, we highlight that the concepts discussed in this section (i.e. 'race', 'ethnicity', 'diaspora') continue to be used to reflect on themes that relate to groups of people who, in a certain moment in time, started to be discursively constructed as a group, based on certain phenotypical traits and/or cultural aspects. Although each term has received its fair share of criticism (Barker, 2012; Brubaker, 2005; Hall, 2017), 'race', 'ethnicity', and 'diaspora' remain vital to understanding blatant and banal acts of racism and discrimination as well as complex processes of identification in the context of migration, (post)colonialism, and multiculturalism. In the following section, we explore these themes in the context of popular media culture. For the sake of clarity, I will use the umbrella term 'racial and ethnic diversity' to refer to the diversity among people in terms of race, ethnicity, and diaspora.

2. RESEARCHING RACIAL AND ETHNIC DIVERSITY AND POPULAR MEDIA CULTURE

Summarising the different strands of research about race, ethnicity, and diaspora in popular media culture into a brief section would do an injustice to the rich and diverse field of study. One of the reasons why the field is quite varied has to do with the fact that the study of racial and ethnic diversity requires a context-specific approach. Even though racial, ethnic, and diasporic identities are discursive constructions, they are real in the way they have been used to generate a sense of belonging and shared identity as much as they are real in the way they have been used to create hierarchies among people and as a basis for discrimination and exclusion. To assess the role media and popular culture have played in processes of identity formation as well as discrimination, one needs to understand the historical contexts in which culturally distinct identities have been formed. From forced displacement as part of the transatlantic slave trade and colonisation to the recruitment of labourers by European countries in the second half of the twentieth century to work in the countries' booming industries and mining (Karim, 2018), these contexts are pivotal in comprehending how people were racialised and/or came to be understood in terms of distinct ethnicities. A context-specific approach also implies comprehending the contemporary policies, laws, or cultural practices used to structurally and symbolically accommodate, restrain, and/or recognise ethnic, racial, and/or diasporic communities in a given society (Siapera, 2010) and how the production, dissemination, and consumption of media and popular culture is organised, financed, and regulated in that given society. A context-specific approach does not preclude inquiries into structural and cultural forms of racism and discrimination across several local and national contexts. Rather, it allows us to more precisely unearth the roots of racism, to empirically assess the impact of racism on minoritised people, to hold up a mirror to mainstream society, including media and cultural professionals, and to contribute to social change.

Throughout the twentieth century, several scholars and thinkers increasingly addressed the role media and popular culture assumed in producing and reiterating racialised stereotypes and a Eurocentric outlook on the world. Especially postcolonial studies, which examines the enduring economic, political, social, and cultural impact of colonialism and imperialism on decolonised and minoritised groups of people, provided key insights, approaches, and theories. The previous section introduced you to Franz Fanon, whose work is foundational to postcolonial studies. Here, I focus on Edward Said's *Orientalism* (1979). Said's work focused on the different ways Orientalism has manifested itself from the eighteenth century onward. The book detailed how, with the establishment of an academic discipline in studying the so-called 'Orient', academic, political, and cultural discourses have been produced that differentiated 'the West' from 'the East'. In these discourses, the 'West' figured as familiar and elevated and the 'East' as strange, mysterious, exotic, and backwards. These discourses served the purpose of establishing the European identity as the superior one, "in short, Orientalism as a Western style for dominating, restructuring, and having authority over the Orient" (p. 3). His work, which inspired many other postcolonial scholars, led to studies exposing how Orientalist discourses shaped the production of media and popular culture content. Crucially, as Ali Behdad (2010) pointed out, Orientalism should also be seen as a politics of aesthetics. For instance, he referred to contemporary practices of uncritically circulating and exhibiting historical photographs taken by Western photographers in the WANA region in the nineteenth century, of which the aesthetics are infused with Orientalist iconography. Following Said and Behdad, we can discern the use of Orientalist aesthetics in plenty of popular films, such as *Indiana Jones and the Temple of Doom* (Steven Spielberg, 1984) (see figure 30), *Aladdin* (John Musker and Ron Clements, 1992), and *Sex and the City 2* (Michael Patrick King, 2010). The aesthetics range from the use of music 'assumed' to sound 'Oriental' to stereotypical tropes such as depicting the 'Orient' as "a universe of extremes: full of positive possibility (magic), yet bound by negative, backward traditions/laws" (Bullock & Zhou, 2017, p. 455).

Figure 30. Film poster of *Indiana Jones and the Temple of Doom* (1984), featuring Orientalist iconography. Photo credit: Photo12/7e Art/Paramount Pictures, © Imageselect/Alamy.

Said is one of many authors who provided pivotal insights and concepts for this area of study. Looking at all the scholarly work written about racial and ethnic diversity in popular media culture, it needs to be acknowledged that American and British scholars have been credited with an authoritative position. To this end, most of the canonised authors and books focus on black diasporic identities in the United States or the United Kingdom (e.g. Gilroy, 1993; Hall, 1997; hooks, 2004), with also works exploring Asian diasporic and Indian diasporic identities in said countries (e.g. Cunningham & Sinclair, 2001; Ono & Pham, 2009; Somani & Guo, 2018). Scholars working in continental European countries have focused on diasporic communities from the WANA region and former colonies (e.g. Cervulle, 2021; Karim & Al-Rawi, 2018). Their theoretical concepts and reflections have been deployed, adapted, and reinterpreted productively in other contexts. For instance, Stuart Hall's work on stereotyping and trans-coding strategies, which focused on racialised representations of black persons in white media and popular culture (see Chapter 1), can be used as a lens to reflect on how other minoritised racial or ethnic identities have been represented. At the same time, the habit of reaching out to American and British scholars should also be seen as a limitation, as it hampers the development of innovative theories and concepts that start from non-Anglophone contexts.

Hall's writings, which provide rich and complex perspectives on representation and stereotyping, have taken on a central position in media and cultural studies. Scholars in this field have predominantly explored the politics of representation in media and popular culture, ranging from Ella Shohat and Robert Stam's (1994) deconstruction of Eurocentrism in Hollywood productions to bell hooks' (2004) analysis of black masculinity in hip-hop culture. As I already tackled Hall's reflections on representation, I refer to Chapter 1 for his insights on representation. Similarly, besides Said, other postcolonial scholars have provided critical lenses and concepts to explore historical and contemporary practices of representation. Take, for instance, Homi K. Bhabba's (1994) concept of hybridity. The concept denotes the condition of cultural practices being exchanged between the coloniser and the colonised, resulting in hybrid cultures that demonstrate the inability of the coloniser to impose its pure and fixed cultural ideas and the potential of colonised people to subvert and adapt the cultural traditions of the coloniser. I refer to the discussion of Tamino's music as an illustration of hybridity in creating diasporic popular music.

In communication sciences, two theories have been important in shaping research about racial and ethnic diversity and popular media culture: cultivation theory and framing theory. First, there is a range of studies relying on cultivation theory to assess which racial or ethnic stereotypes reoccur in media and whether audiences believe that what they see on screen is real (e.g. Coleman et al., 2020;

Khan & Bruschke, 2016). Since cultivation theory has been discussed at length in previous chapters, this section highlights the research tradition that centralises framing theory, developed by Robert M. Entman (1993). Framing theory postulates that media and gatekeepers use frames to organise and present specific events and issues, which may shape how audiences perceive and think about these events (Entman, 1993; Joye & Loisen, 2017). The studies deploy qualitative and quantitative approaches to examine how minoritised identities and communities have been framed in media (e.g. Dastgeer & Gade, 2016; Poindexter et al., 2003; Rasmussen, 2014). Framing theory tends to be mainly used for research into news media. For instance, Anne C. Kroon et al. (2016) examined which frames were used to report on Romani people in news media content in five European countries (i.e. the Netherlands, Germany, Slovakia, the Czech Republic, and the United Kingdom). They found two contradictory frames dominating the public debate in news media, namely the victim frame and the perpetrator frame. While the victim frame was used in articles focusing on the social exclusion of Romani people in European countries, the perpetrator frame was used in articles that problematised the behaviour of Romani people, often by relying on stereotypical and racist assumptions.

Even though most studies on race, ethnicity, and diaspora in media and popular culture have focused on images and representation, this chapter puts the production of media and popular culture in the spotlight. Drawing from theories and research from both communication sciences and media and cultural studies, I explore a series of aspects that relate to media and cultural industries, such as the capitalist logic of the industries and government policies, and discuss how they advance and/or hamper the inclusion of racial and ethnic diversity in popular media culture. Second, the remainder of the chapter demonstrates how certain strands within popular culture have been 'racialised' by way of the history of black popular music culture in the United States.

3. RACIAL AND ETHNIC DIVERSITY IN THE PRODUCTION OF POPULAR MEDIA CULTURE

Albeit less developed than studies about the representation of racial and ethnic diversity, there is an emerging tradition of studies investigating how the production processes and production context affect how racial and ethnic diversity is negotiated and represented in popular media culture. Media and communication scholar Anamik Saha (2018, 2021) argued that to understand the politics of representation embedded in the images or texts, we also need to explore *how* at the level of production race is made. To this end, he encouraged us to pay attention to the politics of production.

First, he stressed that we should concentrate on how capitalism, which underpins Western cultural industries, affects how aspects related to racial and ethnic diversity are dealt with (e.g. exploring how cultural commodities are racialised). Second, there is an increased awareness among media producers and governments that diverse and inclusive representation matters. As such, Saha argued that we should also investigate the formal policies and regulations at the level of the government (e.g. media regulations regarding the distribution of content that incites hatred and violence) and at the level of cultural industries and media organisations (e.g. diversity initiatives), which are created to "address the marginalization and misrepresentation of minorities in the media" (Saha, 2018, p. 84). Last, he also indicated becoming aware that daily production routines or even technologies used to create content affect how racial, ethnic, and diasporic minorities are represented. To better grasp Saha's arguments, I unpack and illustrate each argument.

3.1. *Capitalism, media and cultural industries, and racial and ethnic diversity*

To understand and illustrate the role of capitalism in the way media and cultural industries engage with racial and ethnic diversity, we turn to the production of film and television in the United States. Before discussing the commercial considerations and opportunities concerning racial and ethnic diversity, we need to acknowledge that white professionals have dominated the production of film for a long time, not only as actors on the screen but also behind the camera. Yet, there have been indications of transformation and change. To assess whether and to what extent progress has been made, descriptive data can be of help. For instance, in 2011, the Division of Social Sciences of UCLA (The University of California, Los

Angeles) started a longitudinal study that assesses the state of diversity (in terms of gender and racial/ethnic diversity) in front of and behind the camera in Hollywood. The annual study examines theatrical film releases and broadcasts of various television shows (including broadcast, cable, and digital networks). To illustrate, we look at some results in the *Hollywood Diversity Report 2021*. The report was released in two parts, with the first part focusing on the top 200 theatrical and all streaming film releases in 2020 in the United States (Hunt & Ramón, 2021a) and the second part examining 461 scripted broadcast, cable, and digital platform television shows of the 2019–2020 television season (Hunt & Ramón, 2021b). The studies were intended to describe to what extent the industry was becoming more inclusive. The researchers focused on variables such as 'racial status of lead talent', 'gender of lead talent', 'writer diversity', and 'director diversity'. The study adopted a traditional communication scientific approach, using predefined categories for coding that aimed to acknowledge the differences within racial and ethnic minority groups. The following categories were used: "White, Black, Asian, Native, Latinx, Black Latinx, Multiracial/Multiethnic [...], and MENA (Middle Eastern or North African)" (Hunt & Ramón, 2021b, p. 73), with additional explanations for each category. The reports demonstrated to what extent gains were made regarding employment (e.g. director, writer) and on-screen representation (e.g. diversity of cast). The results were also discussed vis-à-vis the proportion of racial and ethnic diversity in the United States, which has increasingly become more diverse (i.e. 57.3% of the American population in 2020 was white, while 42.7% were people of colour). The demographic data on the proportion of gender and racial/ethnic diversity in the United States enabled the researchers to assess the degree of underrepresentation. Looking a bit closer at television, lead actors of colour increased in broadcast scripted programmes from 5.1% in 2011–2012 to 23.2% in 2019–2020, in cable television from 14.7% in 2011–2012 to 33.6% in 2019–2020, and digital scripted television from 20.7% in 2012–2013 to 31% in 2019–2020. In cable and digital scripted television, the representation of people of colour was approaching proportionate representation. Even though gains were noted in other employment areas (e.g. 'cable and digital show creators', 'broadcast, cable and digital episodes directors', 'credited broadcast', 'cable and digital writers'), minority media professionals were still underrepresented.

Darnell Hunt and Ana-Christina Ramón (2021b) argued that the increase in racial and ethnic diversity could be explained by social, technological, and demographic changes. For instance, they argued that television broadcast networks in the United States – which have been funded through advertising revenue – assumed for a long time that advertisers and white audiences were unwilling to see images of cultural minorities. Consequentially, cultural minorities were either omitted or represented through a white gaze, which resulted in inferior roles and racist stereotypes (see Staples & Jones, 1985). Hunt and Ramón (2021b) argued that the popularisation of streaming-on-demand services, which target paid subscribers, changed a lot. Following the logic of narrowcasting, where content is created for 'niche' or smaller audiences, streaming-on-demand services have invested in distinct types of programmes that can attract diverse subscribers around the world. This may have facilitated "the greenlighting of television shows created by people of colour and women – projects that would not have received serious consideration within the reign of Hollywood business as usual" (p. 69). On top of that, their results indicated that the demographics of television audiences in the United States had changed. Besides the fact that American households were growing more diverse by the day, the results indicated that people of colour watched disproportionally more television than white audiences. Similarly, the results showed that a majority of audiences preferred shows that featured a cast that was not ethnically homogenous but diverse. They concluded that the data demonstrated the commercial opportunities for creative industries to invest in racial and ethnic diversity (Hunt & Ramón, 2021a, 2021b).

Figure 31. Still from *Killers of the Flower Moon* (2023), with Lily Gladstone, second from the left, as Mollie Burkhart. Martin Scorsese's film recounts the Osage murders between 1910 and 1930, with attention to how female family members of the Osage Nation may have experienced the racist murders. It is one of the recent film and television productions that centred Native Americans in contemporary and historical narratives. Photo credit: BFA/Apple Studios, © Imageselect/Alamy.

The former practices illustrate what Saha (2018) called the enabling qualities of commodification, where cultural industries invest in diversity to appeal to audiences' desire for innovation and thereby create opportunities for content that may foster solidarity among diasporic communities and deconstruct racist ideologies. At the same time, he underscored that commodification is an inherently ambiguous practice that also has constraining properties. First, media and creative industries that only rely on capitalist logic to invest in representations of racial and ethnic minorities make their decision to invest in content about specific minoritised groups based on the market value of these groups. As a consequence, racial and ethnic minorities that are not considered commercially interesting risk being ignored. This may be the reason why there is a significant underrepresentation of Native Americans in Hollywood (see figure 31), as demonstrated in the *Hollywood Diversity Report 2021*. Second, media and cultural industries, which increasingly depend on processes of rationalisation, reach for established practices of packaging, formatting, and marketing that are based on limited, distorted, and stereotypical images of racial and ethnic minorities (Saha, 2018). Think of how the successes of ethnic minority sportsmen and sportswomen are often celebrated in mainstream media, while the contributions of ethnic minority people to other public domains, such as politics and the economy, are ignored or downplayed (Barker, 2012). Despite the ambivalence inherent in commodification, Saha (2018) argued that the racialised commodities produced by media and cultural industries mainly had constraining effects so far.

3.2. Diversity initiatives and policies

Some actions taken by media and cultural industries, or government-imposed regulations seem to nuance or counteract these commercial and capitalist practices. First, information and communication scholar Eugenia Siapera (2010) zoomed in on a few initiatives taken by media and cultural industries. A first example concerns the development of specific vocabularies and strategies to encourage racial and ethnic minority workers to apply for particular positions. Such strategies may include language or written statements accentuating the media company's inclusive norms and values in a job announcement. Besides, as minority media workers have indicated, media environments are often unaware of the impact of a mainly white environment on racial and ethnic minority media workers. These spaces need initiatives that explicitly address, raise awareness of, and manifest (cultural) diversity in the workplace. Some media companies have organised training and mentoring schemes and/or developed and implemented a diversity policy (see below, 'Focus on VRT'). Last, unions of media professionals should be encouraged to promote diversity in the workforce and to call for proportionate distribution of racial and ethnic diversity at all levels of the profession (Siapera, 2010).

Some companies have argued that it is hard to come across information and tools to do so. Yet, such arguments dismiss the valuable work done by academics and advocacy groups. The latter encompass bottom-up initiatives that advocate better representation of diversity. Importantly, since the late 2010s, these groups have emphasised discourses of *inclusivity* rather than diversity. A good example is Represent, a Belgian campaign and organisation, created by Belgian Malian actress Aminata Demba in 2020. Represent not only addresses the need for more inclusive professional media environments but also offers tools to media professionals, such as a reflexive questionnaire that helps media professionals reflect on diversity in relation to the company's policies, the creative processes, and the everyday experiences at the workplace (De Man et al., 2024).

Second, governments can implement policies encouraging diversity and inclusivity (Saha, 2018; Siapera, 2010). For instance, cultural industries that depend (partially) on government subsidies are increasingly asked to include in their project applications how the project(s) will be mindful of racial and ethnic diversity (De Man et al., 2024). The most visible impact of governmental policies on the production of media can be seen in countries and regions with strong public service media, such as Ireland, Belgium, and the Netherlands. In these countries, governments negotiate agreements with public service media companies, which stipulate what is expected from them over a particular period of time. Importantly, public service media are expected to represent the diversity of the national community they cater for, especially those ignored by commercial media (Saha, 2018). A few governments, like the Flemish government in Belgium, also set targets for their public service media concerning the inclusion of racial and ethnic diversity.

Focus on VRT

To illustrate some of the practices outlined above, we turn to VRT, the national public service media company of the Flemish Community in Belgium. VRT is financed by the Flemish government and in return for those funds, VRT signs a management agreement, which stipulates what is expected from VRT over a period of five years. Let us take a look at the management agreement of 2021-2025. The document features key performance indicators (KPIs) that indicate which demographic groups VRT intends to reach and which groups should be represented among its staff. First, VRT is supposed to reach at least 75% of the following categories each week: men and women; diverse age categories (e.g. '12-24', '65+'), diverse levels of education attainment (e.g. 'primary school', 'high school', 'university degree'), and people that have at least one parent with roots outside of the EU-15 (a selection of European countries). Second, in the television programmes made by VRT or by Belgian production companies, the share of women should increase from 40% to 48% by 2025, the share of people that have at least one parent with roots outside of the EU-15 should increase from 7.5% to 9.5% by 2025, and the share of people with a disability should increase from 1.5% to 2% by 2025. Similar objectives are formulated concerning the broadcaster's staff. Regarding racial and ethnic diversity, it stipulates that at least 7% of the staff should be a person with roots outside of the EU-15 (VRT, 2020).

Besides, VRT has made additional efforts beyond the government requirements. For instance, it developed and published a diversity charter in 2003 that explicitly articulates its commitment to recognising the sociocultural diversity of Flanders/Belgium:

'The VRT is the broadcaster for everyone in Flanders. Every person should recognise themselves in what we make. We present society the way it is and we are accessible for everyone. The VRT respects people the way they are. We all have more than just one identity. Our viewpoint is open and we differentiate between people rather than pigeon-holing them. We show what binds us and our aim is to build bridges between individuals, groups, generations and communities. In this way we help to build a harmonious and pluralistic society in which everyone feels at home. The VRT wants to set an example. As an employer we support equal opportunities and equality. We only judge people on the basis of their talent and offer everyone a chance to develop their qualities. Diversity enhances our quality. It inspires us and helps us to improve and innovate. Diversity plays a central role in our programming and our policy. At the VRT there is no room for intimidation, exclusion and discrimination for whatever reason. The VRT assumes that anyone who works for us, accepts this vision as self-evident. (VRT, n.d.)'

The charter clearly articulates that VRT is aware that it should provide audiovisual content that allows diverse audiences to recognise themselves, facilitate and encourage inter- and intracultural dialogues, and create a work environment that is as diverse as the society it caters for. Besides, VRT has commissioned an independent research institution to conduct the annual Diversity Monitor. The Diversity Monitor is a recurring study that measures different dimensions of diversity (i.e. 'ethnic-cultural background', 'gender', 'age', 'disability') in the programmes made in-house (by VRT) or produced by Belgian production companies, which are then compared to the key performance indicators from the management agreement. I should point out that no hard consequences are formulated for not meeting the KPIs. At the same time, VRT is obliged to report annually about the progress made. Whether or not KPIs were met will certainly be taken into consideration in the negotiations of the next management agreement.

3.3. Pitfalls, pressures, and pervasive whiteness

Despite the tools, initiatives, and policies, Saha (2018) pointed out that public service media experience commercial and political pressure as they have to compete in "an increasingly commercialized, globalized and fragmented marketplace" and figure out a way to "recognize the diversity of the nation while trying to produce a coherent and concrete sense of national identity" (p. 102). One of the pitfalls is that they often gravitate toward the 'mainstreaming of diversity', which refers to the incorporation of minorities into mainstream content, instead of treating racial and ethnic minority people as separate groups that deserve content on the basis of difference. Saha (2018) underscored the ambivalence of this. On the one hand, this mainstreaming holds the risk of bringing depoliticised, post-racial, and, at times, assimilationist representations of racial and ethnic diversity (see also Malik, 2013). An example could be a comedy set in a rural village, which features a diverse cast of characters but lacks plotlines about race- or ethnicity-specific political and sociocultural issues such as racism or micro-aggressions. On the other hand, mainstreaming practices resulted in a significant increase of ethnic minority professionals on the different platforms (e.g. television, radio, digital platforms) of public service media. Even though Saha discussed the mainstreaming of diversity in the context of public service media, other (commercial) cultural industries and media organisations also deployed similar strategies to acknowledge society's increased racial and ethnic diversity without turning it into the product's main theme.

Another issue any media company or cultural industry has to take into account is what it means to be an ethnic minority worker in a predominantly white media environment. Inspired by Kobena Mercer's (1990) conceptualisation of the burden of representation, Simon Cottle (2000) and Siapera (2010) discussed and illustrated how a media professional's minoritised identity becomes laden with contradictory expectations. Mercer argued that "[a]rtists positioned in the margins of the institutional spaces of cultural production are burdened with the impossible role of speaking as 'representatives' in the sense that they are expected to 'speak for' the black communities from which they come" (p. 62). Cottle (2010), talking about black film producers, pointed out how the burden comes from both racial and ethnic minority communities as well as white media professionals with whom producers of colour have to work. On the one hand, racial and ethnic minority audiences often demand positive images and will hold a minority media professional accountable if the representation does not fully represent a community. On the other hand, white professionals may nudge the minority producer to create certain images and narratives that are 'diverse' but marketable. Siapera (2010) added that minority media professionals are primarily seen as "representatives of their group, rather than media professionals" (p. 89). In media companies, they are expected to express the minority viewpoint (e.g. black journalists being asked to write about topics that relate to racial and ethnic diversity), while being aware that they represent just one voice in communities that are internally diverse. Siapera suggested that it would become much more sustainable and just if all media workers "become equally responsible for understanding and representing fairly cultural diversity" (p. 91). She stressed the importance of initiatives that nudge media workers to acquire critical skills when reporting on and/or creating content about racial and ethnic diversity.

Focus on *We Are Lady Parts*

In this context, I invite you to watch the British comedy series *We Are Lady Parts* (Channel 4, 2021-present). The series, set in East London, follows the lives of five Muslim women. We are first introduced to Amina Hussain (Anjana Vasan), who is busy finishing her PhD in microbiology (see figure 32). Amina is represented as a woman eager to find a husband. She also loves playing guitar and teaching music to youth. Little does she know that she will become the electric guitar player of Lady Parts, an all-female Muslim punk band. The series has been argued to defy a white gaze, as it represents London through the eyes of British diasporic Muslims. In doing so, it also challenges homogenised representations of Muslim identities by representing Muslim women and men through a lens of intersectionality. Some Muslim women wear a hijab, some do not; one woman identifies as queer; another does not want to define her relationship with the man she is dating; their diasporic background differs. Besides emphasising the diversity among Muslim women, the intersectional approach also allows for representing Muslim women differently than the worn-out stereotypes of being victims, passive, exotic, or oppressed (Broos & Van den Bulck, 2012; Navarro, 2010).

Creator Nida Manzoor (2021) explained her motivation to write the series: "Frustrated by the stereotypical narratives about Muslim women in the media as oppressed victims, lacking agency and self-hood, I wanted to write something that reflects me, my friends, the world I know." She also made a stand against the polarised discourses that diasporic people encounter – recalling how she as a child felt she had to choose between being "British (us) or [...] Pakistani/Muslim (them)." The situation works as a good illustration of what Dubois referred to as double consciousness (see above). To challenge this, she created characters who are "owning and loving their mixed identity, their wonderful third culture." While writing the script, Manzoor did experience the burden of representation. She shared that she internalised the idea that she was responsible for representing marginalised voices. She was able to reconcile some of the conflicting demands (e.g. the need for only positive images) by coming to an understanding that her stories can only play their particular part: "Representation requires a multiplicity of stories, taking up space, adding richness to the landscape and I am just one voice, reflecting the world as it appears to me, filtered through my specific passions, experiences and fears."

Figure 32. On-set photograph with Anjana Vasan as Amina in *We Are Lady Parts* (2021–present). Photo credit: Working Title Television/Album, © Imageselect/Alamy.

Last, even more difficult is to undo the subtle ways whiteness has permeated the production process of popular culture (Dyer, 1997; Saha, 2018). Richard Dyer (1997) argued that for a long time, images of white people were not considered as 'racial', which implied that white people were perceived as simply human and every person of colour as not embodying that human norm. What we have witnessed throughout history is how white people have claimed to speak for the commonality of humanity while expecting people of colour to represent their 'race' (see above). The reason why white people are not aware of their whiteness has been explained by Peggy McIntosh (1988). She argued that white people are oblivious to the fact that their whiteness grants them a privileged position in Western society. She coined the concept of white privilege to refer to the advantage white people have over people of colour in Western society in renting homes, finding a job, finding representation in popular media culture, and being allowed to be complex and versatile since white persons will not be reduced to their racial or ethnic group. Hence, Dyer wanted to expose how images of white people are also 'racialised images'.

To do so, he focused on specific patterns used to represent whiteness, including specific narrative positions, rhetorical tropes, and modes of visually representing white people in film, photography, and art. One such practice concerns the representation of white skin as an explicit and implicit ideal. Within Western society, whiteness carries "the more explicit symbolic sense of moral and also aesthetic superiority" (Dyer, 1997, p. 70). It has been associated with virtue, purity, virginity, and cleanliness. Looking at photography and film, the white skin has been idealised by, for instance, the way people are represented in the mise-en-scène (e.g. positioning a white character in the centre of the frame), the practice of whitewashing (i.e. casting a white actor to portray a person of colour), or the technology that is used. To illustrate, I want to deepen how the technologies of photography and film were developed in a manner that "lend themselves to privileging white people" (p. 83).

A key aspect when taking a picture or making a film is the role of light since, as Dyer (1997) reminded us, photography and film are 'technologies of light'. Concretely, "a photographic image is the product of the effect of light on a chemically prepared surface (the stock)" (p. 85). Yet, what is important to remember is how cameras, stock, and lighting were developed with white people in mind. To start, what was ignored was that "human skin does have different colours which reflect light differently" (p. 89). Put differently, lighter skin reflects more light than darker skin. The technology, however, was attuned to white skin. As a consequence, for a long time, when a black and a white person were in the same frame, the camera would favour the white person – thereby rendering the white skin and white person as symbolically more important (Dyer, 1997).

Figure 33. Two Shirley cards, from 1966 and 1978. Image courtesy of Hermann Zschiegner, copyright by Eastman Kodak.

Similarly, in the practice of developing and printing photographs or films, white skin has been favoured. This became particularly visible with the introduction of colour film in the 1940s. To print photographs, consumers increasingly depended on professional photo labs to print their pictures. Photo labs used norm reference cards to calibrate their printers in terms of colours and contrasts. Those cards featured white ('Caucasian') female models in high-contrast dresses and were used as "a basis for measuring and calibrating the skin tones on the photograph being printed" (Roth, 2009, p. 112). The cards created by the American company Kodak became known as 'Shirley cards', named by the male industry users after the first card model (see figure 33). Photo lab technicians would make test prints based on the unexposed negatives of the Shirley cards and compare the prints with the pre-calibrated Shirley cards delivered by the company. However, due to an absence of norm reference cards representing persons with diverse skin tones, photographs of people with darker skin tones were printed with insufficient contrast and colour balance. Lorna Roth (2009) stressed that the impact of Shirley cards on the representation of non-white skin was not taken seriously for a long time. From the 1950s on, it became less easy to ignore the problem. Issues occurred with American class and graduation photographs where children with different skin tones were depicted together, resulting in images that showed details on the faces of white children while erasing contours and particularities of the faces of children with darker skin. Another often-cited impetus was that in the 1960s and 1970s manufacturers of brown furniture and chocolate were complaining about the way their products looked in photographs. Kodak eventually caved and developed 'multiracial Shirley cards' in the 1990s. With the development of digital photography, these cards became obsolete.

Yet, digital technologies did not undo the necessity of considering how people with different skin tones look in photographs and film. Other tools and practices (e.g. on-set lighting, use of make-up) continue to shape how people look on screen and, to this end, deserve to be closely scrutinised. A series such as HBO's *Insecure* (2016–2021) and films like *Selma* (Ava DuVernay, 2014) and *Moonlight* (Barry Jenkins, 2016) have been lauded for their depiction of black skin. For instance, *Insecure*'s director of photography Ava Berkofsky explained that her ideas for on-set lighting challenged the norm in sitcom production of having the same kind of brightness on set. Although *Insecure* is also a sitcom, Berkofsky employed tactics used in filmmaking, such as keeping light off the walls, providing different levels of light to the scene, and applying shiny make-up (Harding, 2017). At the same time, these tactics remind us how common practices of filming are, even today, still structurally embedded in technologies and modes of production that, often unwittingly, privilege whiteness.

4. A HISTORICAL OUTLINE OF BLACK POPULAR MUSIC

The last part of this chapter explores and illustrates the ramifications of racialisation in popular culture. To do so, we focus on one particular form of popular culture: black popular music in the United States.[24] This historical outline starts in the early twentieth century, the period considered the beginning of popular music culture. The production of popular music distinguished itself from prior mu-

---

24 Although this chapter only discusses the history of black popular music in the United States, similar histories can be told about other black diasporas, noteworthy regarding the development of ska and reggae in Jamaica (Heathcott, 2003), or the role reggae played for African Caribbean people in Britain (Hebdige, 1979).

sical traditions by its commodity form (Shuker, 2016). From the 1920s onward, the American music industry started to boom, with the emergence of different profitable styles and genres. One genre considered commercially interesting by white music professionals in the music industry was blues music, produced by African American artists. Assuming blues music would only be bought by black consumers, the music industry reorganised the market into 'mainstream' and 'marginal' genres, based on preconceived assumptions about race, style, and audience. Three categories were created: 'popular' referred to mainstream styles of which the industry assumed they chiefly attracted urban, middle- or upper-class, white audiences; 'hillbilly' referred to rural, white working-class styles; and 'race music' referred to African American styles and audiences (Brackett, 2003; Shuker, 2016). Reebee Garofalo (1994) argued that the label 'race music' was intended as a marketing strategy to capitalise on the increased interest in blues music, with artists such as Mamie Smith and Bessie Smith: "Race was a code word that identified the recording artist as African American for the record-buying public. It served to keep the music isolated from the mainstream. The term stuck and remained the official industry designation for working-class, African American musics until 1949" (p. 276).

Only in the late 1940s did white music professionals decide that a new genre label was needed. With rhythm and blues, a term was coined based on musical style rather than 'racialised' categorisation. Nonetheless, up to the 1960s, music and audiences continued to be approached in segregated terms: country and western music were marketed to regional audiences, rhythm and blues to black audiences, and pop to mainstream (white) audiences (Garofalo, 1994). At rare times, rhythm and blues songs achieved mainstream success, also known as crossover successes. Little Richard's 'Tutti Frutti' (1955) is a famous example (see figure 34). To grasp the idea of crossing over, I need to point at the authoritative role of popularity charts published by the trade journal *Billboard*. The journal published a separate chart for each musical style. The publication of the 'Harlem Hit Parade' demonstrated that the industry became aware of the commercial potential of rhythm and blues music. On the one hand, it increased the visibility of black artists as the chart urged audiences, retailers, and radio programmers to pay attention to records of African American artists (Brackett, 1994). On the other hand, it also implied that black artists were seen as only able to perform rhythm and blues, while white artists were seen as able to thrive in several music genres. Furthermore, the crossover successes meant that black artists had to first sell well in black communities before they could make it on the mainstream charts and receive mainstream attention. Garofalo (1994) concluded that it revealed how black artists were held to a higher standard than white artists.

In the early 1960s, black musicians experienced a severe setback. First, the (temporary) discontinuation of the rhythm and blues chart in *Billboard* decreased the visibility of black artists. Second, white British bands were enjoying enormous success in the United States in the wake of The Beatles, an event often dubbed 'the British Invasion'. The white British bands pushed the few black artists out of the mainstream charts. At the same time, the 1960s were also known for ushering in a new genre and approach in American black music culture; artists such as Ray Charles, Sam Cooke, and Aretha Franklin were bringing rhythm and blues into dialogue with gospel in a genre that became known as soul (Garofalo, 1994; Wall, 2013). Importantly, soul was a term coined by black artists themselves. Soul was intrinsically linked to African American culture, most noteworthy in how soul artists "drew their music ideas, vocal and instrumental styles from the gospel tradition" (Maultsby, 1983, p. 54) and reworked the tradition in songs that expressed black pride, protest, and social change. Unlike previous performers of black popular music, soul artists explicitly addressed the social and economic issues black people experienced, while expressing messages of hope and unity (Maultsby, 1983; Wall, 2013).

Figure 34. Poster announcing a concert by Little Richard in Topeka, Kansas, United States, 1957. Photo credit: Bill Waterson, © Imageselect/Alamy.

Focus on Nina Simone

A major artist in the 1960s is jazz artist Nina Simone. Her role in activism and the political power of her songs are discussed at length in the work of Ruth Feldstein (2005). Nina Simone was trained as a classical musician. Born in 1933 in North Carolina to working-class parents, her emergence to success during the 1960s challenged the narratives about jazz and high culture at the time: an African American woman, classically trained, who had to work hard to become a performer, was changing jazz music. Nina Simone was a globally known and cherished musician and a commercially successful artist. Furthermore, she was one of the most politically vocal artists of her time, using her platform to foster black freedom and full equality (Feldstein, 2005)(see figure 35).

Figure 35. Portrait of Nina Simone taken in 1965. Photo credit: Penta Springs Limited, News to Remember, © Imageselect/Alamy.

She particularly challenged the "well-mannered politics of going slow" (p. 1350), a tired trope told by white Americans to black Americans. The trope meant that social change would eventually happen, but black people had to be patient and could not expect too much progress in a short span of time. Nina Simone's decision to use her music for politics can be traced back to the late 1950s and early 1960s when she was part of an artist community in Greenwich Village and Harlem in New York City. To speak out as a black artist was a risk. She had witnessed how a fellow black jazz vocalist, Abbey Lincoln, was censored by influential jazz critics because she had been accused of being a professional activist. Yet, it did not prevent Simone from engaging in activism. She supported national civil rights organisations and performed during their benefit conferences. Yet her most important platform was her music. At the time, jazz music was rarely used for politics. This made her political activism remarkable and essential (Feldstein, 2005).

Two songs from her oeuvre stand out: 'Mississippi Goddam' (1964) and 'To Be Young, Gifted and Black' (1970). 'Mississippi Goddam' starts from two events that happened in 1963: The killing of Medgar Evers, a civil rights activist, in Mississippi, and the killing of four black children in a church in Alabama, both by white supremacists. The song is filled with anger, particularly anger directed at white people for having told black people to take it slow while being ignorant of the recurring acts of racist violence and structural racialised inequality: "Alabama's gotten me so upset / Tennessee made me lose my rest / And everybody knows about Mississippi, goddam." Or: "You don't have to live next to me / Just give me my equality." 'To Be Young, Gifted and Black' is equally political, but focuses on black pride and the importance of belonging, while giving black youth perspective, which is underscored in the following line: "In the whole world you know / There's a million boys and girls / Who are young, gifted and Black / And that's a fact!"

From the 1970s onward, we see the development of rap and hip-hop (e.g. DJ Kool Herc, The Sugarhill Gang), and contemporary R&B (e.g. Janet Jackson, Mary J. Blige). Hip-hop and contemporary R&B shared not only a cultural but also a political sensibility (Stewart, 2005). This, however, does not imply that all lyrics and representations were aimed at social change and inclusion. Especially hip-hop music received much attention and backlash regarding its lyrics and style. Hip-hop emerged at the end of the 1970s in black impoverished inner-city communities (Neal, 1997). On the one hand, the genre has been lauded for tackling sociocultural inequalities based on race and class (Iwamoto, 2003; Watkins, 2006). On the other hand, hip-hop music performed by black male artists was also criticised for being hypermasculine, hypersexual, sexist, homophobic, and/or aggressive (hooks, 2004; Jeffries, 2010; Iwamoto, 2003; Weitzer & Kubrin, 2009) (see also Crenshaw's discussion about 2 Live Crew in Chapter 1). Author bell hooks (2004) criticised the performance and idealisation of this hip-hop masculinity because it happened at the cost of all black women and black men whose masculinity and sexuality did not fit the black masculine ideal. For hooks, this form of hip-hop masculinity dismissed the history of different ways of embodying a black masculine identity, both in music and society. Male blues musicians, for instance, acknowledged their emotionality and disclosed it via music. However, she also remarked that this 'hip-hop masculinity' was equally the result of black men being part of Western society, which has favoured a hegemonic masculinity that is patriarchal. Similarly, the role of the music industry cannot be underestimated. Rather than creating room for artists embodying black masculinity as diverse, the predominantly white music professionals in the mainstream music industry and music press found the rigid form of hip-hop masculinity more profitable and more appealing to white (male) audiences. Consequentially, especially during the 1990s, black rap artists were portrayed and promoted as stereotypes (e.g. representing black rap artists as 'thugs' or 'gangstas') and spectacles of hypermasculinity (Stewart, 2005; Watkins, 2006; Weitzer & Kubrin, 2009). This serves as a good illustration of what Saha (2018) discussed as the constraining effects of racialised cultural commodities (see above). While, at first, hip-hop allowed black Americans to express themselves creatively and voice social critique, the white music industry appropriated, formatted, and marketed the genre in such a way that it tapped into and reiterated stereotypes and prejudices about black (male) music artists.

Yet, bearing in mind that Saha (2018) also highlighted the enabling properties of racialised cultural commodities, there have been artists within black popular music culture who asserted their agency and bent the industry to their will to deconstruct stereotypes, expose power imbalances, and subvert the normative modes of production. Looking at post-millennial black music culture, black male, female, and nonbinary artists have imagined their music and fandoms as spaces of inclusion and forums to challenge structural and everyday forms of racism and sexism in mainstream society. Consider, for instance, Solange, the artist persona of Solange Piaget Knowles (see figure 36). She has consistently deployed her music, videos, and performances to raise awareness about the countless ways people of colour experience racism daily. For example, she wrote 'F.U.B.U.' (2016), which means 'For Us, By Us', to address micro-aggressions. Micro-aggressions are everyday insults, benign stereotypes, or stereotypical assumptions addressed to a person with a minoritised identity: "I remember reflecting on the everyday micro-aggressions that we experience on a daily [...] That song has resonated with so many people that have heard it because it is almost an allowance to just let it out. I named it 'F.U.B.U.' because I wanted to empower, and I looked to people who have done that in their own ways" (Solange in i-D Staff & Maicki, 2016). She emphasised how even today many non-black people say the n-word, which displays ignorance of the history of the word, as it was used to dehumanise people of the black diaspora. It also reveals an ignorance of the fact that the term was reclaimed in the 1980s and 1990s (for instance in hip-hop) by black people. It "no longer was a word of inferiority but a word of brotherhood and commonality, an opportunity to connect on a struggle only a select group could understand" (Florestal, 2021). The inclusion of the n-word in 'F.U.B.U.' should be read as marking a common experience among black people as well as requesting non-black audiences not to participate in this song. It demonstrates the necessity of symbolic spaces where only black people can participate, something Solange illustrated in these particular lines: "Don't feel bad if you can't sing along / Just be glad you got the whole wide world / This us / This shit is from us."

Figure 36. Solange, performing at Norwegian music festival Piknik i Parken 2017. Photo credit: Gonzales Photo, Tord Litleskare, © Imageselect/Alamy.

Similarly, black male artists, like Lil Nas X, Kendrick Lamar, and Moses Sumney, have deconstructed hegemonic masculine ideals that circulate in different popular music cultures and Western society. In their songs, artwork, and performances, they employed strategies that hold up a mirror to (black) men who aspire to hegemonic masculinity, break a lance for non-normative masculinities and LGBTQ identities, and challenge the racism and homophobia expressed by white men. To illustrate, I turn to Frank Ocean, the artist persona of Christopher Edwin Breaux (see figure 37). He has contributed to a deconstruction of hegemonic masculinity and hip-hop masculinity through his music. As I argued elsewhere, "[t]he 'authentic' male identity often promoted in many hip-hop songs is challenged by Frank Ocean's portrayal of diverse male characters. His songs consist of men who vary from traditional, patriarchal figures over men who reevaluate their (masculine) identities to men who are comfortable with engaging in non-normative gender behaviour. By giving these diverse masculinities a stage, Frank Ocean explores the performativity of gender and questions what it means to be a real man" (Dhaenens & De Ridder, 2015, p. 290). For instance, in the songs 'There Will Be Tears' (2011) and 'Bad Religion' (2012), he sings about the difficulties of demonstrating vulnerability and emotionality but also highlights how valuable and rewarding it is when one feels able to do so. Similarly, some songs make us aware of his queer masculinity, as his artist persona and private persona at times coalesce in his music. Preceding his much-anticipated album *Channel Orange* (2012), he shared a letter on his private Tumblr page in which he addressed rumours about him. In the letter, originally intended to be included in the thank you section of the album credits, he reminisced about a young man with whom he fell in love and who made him realise that his feelings for this young man were different from the feelings he had for the women he had been with (Ocean, 2012). Frank Ocean was certainly not the first or only black musician in the United States to publicly acknowledge experiencing sexual or romantic desires for another man. Think of Sylvester, Zebra Katz, or Kalifa (formerly known as Le1f). Yet, having artists like Frank Ocean embody alternative masculinities helped pave the way for diverse representations of masculinities and sexualities within hip-hop and other musical genres.

Frank Ocean's oeuvre also allows us to grasp why we should avoid perceiving black popular music in essentialist terms. On the one hand, the label 'black music culture' has united black artists who perform in musical genres and traditions that originated from black artistic communities. For instance, it helped to build a sense of belonging among black artists and black audiences and to create a platform to express emotional and political messages, to call out racism, and to advocate social change. On the other hand, it also led to the assumption that black artists only want to, or are only capable of, creating music that corresponds to a fixed set of genres, like soul, rap, or R&B. This practice can be traced back to the creation of race-based charts, marketing strategies, and awards (e.g. Grammy Award categories 'Best R&B Song' or 'Best Rap Album'). This racialised assumption also pertains to the habit of music journalists to confine artists such as Frank

Ocean, Moses Sumney, Anjimile, and Sudan Archives to one 'black' genre, such as R&B, even though their work transcends traditional song conventions and modes of production.

As a final remark, I want to highlight that black artists in Western countries outside of the United States have had to cope with similar racialised expectations and discriminatory practices. To illustrate, the British band English Teacher has been making music indebted to a post-punk and indie-folk tradition. Yet, despite making music in the 2020s, frontwoman Lily Fontaine had to battle the prejudices she encountered in the industry. To tackle the critics head-on, she created the song 'R&B' (2024), in which she repeatedly belts the following meaningful line: "Despite appearances, I haven't got the voice for R&B." It is a vocal reminder of how stereotypes, biases, and preconceptions about racial and ethnic diversity are still deeply ingrained in the fabric of Western society.

Figure 37. Frank Ocean on the cover of *Snatch magazine*, November 2021. Courtesy of Vincent Desailly.

CHAPTER 5

DIS/ABILITY

Setting the scene: Game of Thrones

HBO did not regret the decision to greenlight the production of *Game of Thrones* (2011–2019). The American television series, created by David Benioff and D. B. Weiss, is an adaptation of the famous fantasy book series *A Song of Ice and Fire* (1996–present), by George R. R. Martin. The medieval fantasy series, which turned out to be a critical and commercial success, is set in a fictional world and an undefined historical past. The main location of the series is Westeros, a continent where seven kingdoms are united and ruled by one king who sits on the Iron Throne in King's Landing. Following the death of King Robert Baratheon, different noble families claim their right to the Iron Throne. However, plenty of

Figure 38. On-set photograph with Peter Dinklage as Tyrion in *Game of Thrones* (2011–2019). Photo credit: HBO/Album, © Imageselect/Alamy.

fantastical elements, such as dragons, white walkers, and other supernatural twists, remind audiences they are not watching a medieval historical drama.

Even though the series, deliberately or not, invites audiences to reflect on its representations of gender, sexuality, race, and ethnicity,[25] I focus on how the series represents disability. To begin with, the series features quite a few disabled characters in the series: Tyrion Lannister (Peter Dinklage), a little person who uses his intelligence to, at first, protect his family and, later, protect Westeros; Bran Stark (Isaac Hempstead-Wright), a paralysed boy who gradually acquires supernatural abilities; Lord Varys (Conleth Hill), Theon Greyjoy (Alfie Allen), and Grey Worm (Jacob Anderson), who are all castrated men; Sandor 'The Hound' Clegane (Rory McCann), a warrior with facial disfigurements due to burn wounds; Jamie Lannister (Nikolaj Coster-Waldau), a knight who loses his hand and gradually transforms from a morally corrupt to a morally good character; Shireen (Kerry Ingram), a young girl whose face is disfigured due to a fictional disease named greyscale; Aemon Targaryen (Peter Vaughan), who is blind; and Hodor (Kristian Nairn), who has an unnamed intellectual disability.

Disabled fans and activists have appreciated the way the series represents disability. Moreover, George R. R. Martin also received a Media Access Award in 2013 for creating a universe in which the experience of disability is explored and represented accurately (Ellis, 2014). Even though the Media Access Awards[26] employ realist criteria (such as assessing whether representations are 'accurate', see Chapter 1), the event's organisers also look at media through a media and cultural studies lens. They focus on, for instance, the type of roles disabled characters play in the main narrative, whether the characters are defined by their disability, and whether they are stereotyped. From this angle, Katie Ellis (2014, 2015) argued that disabled characters in *Game of Thrones* are represented as flawed heroes. They have physical or intellectual impairments that are sometimes experienced as barriers, but they are not reduced to their disabilities. Instead, the series reveals the social disablement of people with disabilities. By doing so, audiences are nudged to root for several disabled characters and their allies who question and/or attempt to change instances of unfair treatment.

---

25 Even though the series has been lauded for its depiction of disability, it has been criticised for how it deployed Orientalist tropes and stereotypes in representing 'Essos', the Eastern regions in the series. For a convincing discussion of *Game of Thrones'* reliance on Orientalism, I refer to Mat Hardy's (2019) analysis of the series.
26 The Media Access Awards is an annual event celebrating the advancements made regarding disability-related narratives in different American media, with attention to the employment of disabled media professionals and the inclusion of disability characters in media content.

Especially Tyrion Lannister is important in the history of representing little people on television (see figure 38). Performed by Peter Dinklage, a little person himself, the character defies cultural stereotypes of little persons (e.g. being depicted as clowns to laugh at, clumsy and childish characters, or mythological figures). This is achieved through, first, the way the camera is used. By filming Tyrion at eye level instead of top-down, the camera treats Tyrion as equal to average-sized characters. Second, Tyrion is written as a complex and layered character. In general, he aims to do good for his family and society, but he is not without flaws. He is shown using his intelligence and persuasion to advise various protagonists in their efforts to achieve power and/or peace. At the same time, the series avoids being utopian and depicts how Tyrion lives in a disablist society: "Tyrion faces prejudice from the society in which he lives and is constantly devalued by his father Tywin, who resents him for his disability and his mother's death in childbirth" (Ellis, 2015, p. 5). Yet, Tyrion is also represented as a character who has learned to cope with disablism and stands up for other minoritised people. For instance, after young Bran learns that he has lost his ability to walk, Tyrion visits the Stark home to offer Bran a gift. It is a design for a saddle that will allow Bran to ride a horse again, as it is not the rider but the horse that has to be adapted to accommodate the rider. Even though Tyrion is not trusted by the Stark family, he explains that he has a "tender spot in [his] heart for cripples, bastards, and broken things" (season 1, episode 4). According to Ellis (2019), the role of the scene cannot be underestimated. First, by giving Bran tools to ride a horse, he challenges Bran's defeatist attitude by showing him how his environment (rather than himself) has to change to improve his mobility. Second, by referring to Bran as a 'cripple' and himself as a 'dwarf', Tyrion claims his disabled identity rather than hiding it, and he forges connections with other disabled people. In doing so, this scene is attuned to the principles of the social model of disability. These models offer a radically different approach to thinking about disability. Rather than assuming that disabled individuals need help to adapt to their social environments (i.e. medical and psychological models of disability), the social model argues that the social environment needs to change (e.g. removing structural, material, and social barriers) so disabled people can take part in society (see below). The scenes in *Game of Thrones* illustrate how television fiction can participate in the project envisioned by the social model of disability, even if set in a medieval fantasy world.[27]

---

27 This does not imply that Game of Thrones is free from stereotyping disabled characters. Mia Harrison (2018) pointed out that the series features some harmful stereotypes and tired old tropes (e.g. the 'supercrip' trope and representing disability as a punishment).

1. ABOUT DIS/ABILITY

1.1. Terminology

Before exploring disability in popular media culture, I will introduce a few central concepts and discussions on dis/ability. To begin, it is difficult to assess how many people in the world have a disability. The WHO (World Health Organization) estimates that 16% of the global population experiences significant disability. The organisation defines 'disability' as follows: "Disability results from the interaction between individuals with a health condition, such as cerebral palsy, Down syndrome and depression, with personal and environmental factors including negative attitudes, inaccessible transportation and public buildings, and limited social support" (WHO, n.d). This description illustrates the diversity within the category of 'disability', which encompasses physical, (neuro)developmental, sensory, intellectual, learning, or neurological disabilities. Further, while some disabilities are 'visible' to people, others are considered 'invisible'. This means that other people do not perceive a person's disability. Think of people with chronic pain, posttraumatic stress disorder, chronic fatigue syndrome, or autism spectrum disorder. As N. Ann Davis (2005) noted, people who have an invisible disability may appear able-bodied but the disorder or condition they have can certainly impact their quality of life.

Yet not everyone with an impairment may consider themselves disabled. For some, the impairments do not hamper their everyday lives while, for others, certain impairments are seen (by themselves and/or by others) as symptoms of old age. Further, due to stigma and stereotyping, some may refuse to identify as disabled even though the impairments impact their everyday lives (e.g. experiencing pain, being unable to work) (Marks, 1997; Shakespeare, 2018). On top of that, disability is dynamic. As Katie Ellis and Gerard Goggin (2015) underscored, "people can be born with impairments, acquire them, have them from time to time, and, if we live long enough, we will all surely count as disabled" (p. 6). In sum, disability scholars emphasise acknowledging the variability and multidimensionality of disability (Ellis & Goggin, 2015; Marks, 1997; Shakespeare, 2018; Van Goidsenhoven, 2020).

Besides, there is an ongoing debate about whether we should speak of 'people with disabilities' or 'disabled people' (Andrews, 2019; Marks, 1997; Shakespeare, 2018). What both terms share is their avoidance of dehumanising people: the terms do not reduce an individual or a group of people to being disabled (e.g. 'the disabled') or a specific disability (e.g. 'the blind') but acknowledge that there is a person with multiple identities and diverse traits. The difference between both terms is in how they reflect on the relation between the disability and the person who has the disability. 'People with disabilities' is a term that originates from a person-first approach. This approach considers people with disabilities as persons first instead of focusing on their impairments. It challenges the medicalisation of disability as well as the stigmatisation and stereotyping of people with disabilities. 'People with disabilities' is generally the most accepted term in academia. For instance, the American Psychological Association (APA) advocates the use of this term (Andrews, 2019; Marks, 1997). However, some activists and scholars prefer 'disabled people'. They use an identity-first approach, stressing that the person-first approach diminishes the importance of disability to a person's identity. Erin E. Andrews (2019) argued that the term and approach allow disabled people to reclaim their disability, express their belonging to a community, and voice disability pride. A good example is Deaf culture – where the capital D signifies the creation of a shared culture (e.g. sign languages) and pride in belonging to the Deaf community (Andrews, 2019; Shakespeare, 2018). Deborah Marks (1997) added that the identity-first approach also aligns itself with other minoritised identities (e.g. 'a gay person' instead of 'a person with homosexual desires'). Seeing how both terms are salient and used in academia, activism, and communities formed around disabilities, both terms will be used interchangeably in this chapter (see also Shakespeare, 2018).

Last, some discussion is needed about the concept of 'dis/ability', written with a forward slash in between 'dis' and 'ability'. The term has been coined by disability studies scholar Dan Goodley, whose academic work is situated within the field of critical disability studies. He emphasised the importance of studying disability vis-à-vis ability and disablism vis-à-vis ableism (see below). He argued that the "slashed and split term denotes the complex ways in which opposites bleed into one another" (2014, p. xiii). Think, for instance, of the Diagnostic and Statistical Manual of Mental Disorders (DSM), published by the American Psychiatric Association. The first edition was published in 1951. Since then, different editions and revisions have been published, with the publication of the DSM-5-TR in 2022 as the latest edition. The history of the DSM reveals how, within psychiatry, certain conditions were diagnosed as a mental disorder and which ones were removed from the DSM as increased knowledge demonstrated that these human conditions were incorrectly considered disorders. For instance, homosexuality was no longer considered a disorder in 1973, while in 1980 posttraumatic stress disorder and borderline personality disorder were introduced as diagnostic criteria (Surís et al., 2016). These changes illustrate that what qualifies as 'ability' or 'disability' is not as clear-cut and fixed as one may think since the criteria used for diagnosis have been questioned and refined over time. Last, Dan Goodley (2018) also advised us to become aware of the fact that not only 'disabilities' are established by specific criteria, but also 'abilities'. He pointed out how in Western society able-bodiedness became increasingly defined by criteria such as autonomy, rationality, fitness, productivity, or self-sufficiency, capabilities that are particularly valued in a capitalist economy.

1.2. Changing discourses about impairment and disability

Ever since there were humans, there have been people with illnesses and physical, mental, or sensory impairments (e.g. being blind, having learning difficulties). However, depending on whether they were living in medieval, agrarian, or capitalist societies, their experiences differed significantly. In pre-modern, agrarian societies, disabled family members were not rejected. Each family member contributed to their own ability – including disabled family members (Shakespeare, 2018). Yet, when such agrarian communities became more economically productive, the population grew and a division of labour was installed, which impacted disabled people. Nonetheless, those whose impairment did not hamper them from contributing were allowed to participate (Nibert, 1995).

However, with the advent of industrial capitalism in the late eighteenth century, disabled labourers or craftspeople were deemed less productive than non-disabled people and became gradually excluded from the workforce. Their exclusion was also nudged by the way modern cities were designed and built, where the architecture of modern buildings or the organisation of public transport disregarded the experience of disabled people, creating barriers for them to fully participate in modern societies (Shakespeare, 2018; Nibert, 1995).

Furthermore, since halfway through the eighteenth century, thinking about disability has become increasingly medicalised. Disability was seen as "unchanging, pathological, rooted in individual bodies, and always in need of cure, correction, or elimination" (Rembis et al., 2018, p. 4). Oftentimes, this approach resulted in a segregated treatment of disabled people: they were not allowed to work, they had to attend a different school from non-disabled people, and they were represented as victims in need of pity and/or help from non-disabled people. As a result, in the 1960s disability movements – which consisted of disabled people and allies – emerged that advocated thinking about disability in terms of human rights and understanding that disabled people can contribute to society and have done so in the past (Rembis et al., 2018; Shakespeare, 2018). Shakespeare (2013) aptly summarised the shift as follows:

> While the problems of disabled people have been explained historically in terms of divine punishment, karma or moral failing, and post-Enlightenment in terms of biological deficit, the disability movement has focused attention onto social oppression, cultural discourse, and environmental barriers. (p. 214)

This shift became quite visible in how the terms 'impairment' and 'disability' were defined. Various disability movements, and in particular the Disabled Peoples' International,[28] advocated distinguishing impairment more clearly from disability. For the organisation, impairment refers to "the functional limitation within the individual caused by physical, mental or sensory impairment," and disability to "the loss or limitation of opportunities to take part in the normal life of the community on an equal level with others because of physical and social barriers" (Oliver, 1998, p. 1447). Whereas medicalised thinking about disability assumed that the impairment caused a person's disability (i.e. the social and economic disadvantages that prevent a disabled person from taking part in society in ways deemed 'normal' for a human being), this shift in thinking questioned this causality. Instead, it conceived of disability as a form of social oppression and exclusion (Oliver, 1990, 1998). Put differently, a person may have an impairment but whether the person experiences it as a disability depends on whether the environment has made some changes to accommodate the person (Mogk, 2013).

The disentangling of impairment from disability was part of a wider shift in thinking about disability in society. Up to the early 1970s, 'individual models of disability' were seen as the normative models to approach people with disabilities. The individual models, which comprise the medical model and psychological model of disability, focus on the individual. They are designed to enable experts to accurately diagnose the biological (i.e. the physical and cognitive functioning of the body) and/or psychological condition of a person and to develop strategies to prevent, cure, and/or take care of the impairment. This reasoning implies that the impairment is the main reason a person experiences a disability. Even though the models do not dismiss environmental factors, their focus is on the individual and aiding the person with a disability to adjust physically and psychologically to the environment (Marks, 1997; Mogk, 2013; Priestley, 2003).

From the 1970s on, disability movements and disability scholars increasingly challenged the hegemony of the individual models, which culminated in the development of the social model of disability. A key idea of the social model is the differentiation between impairment and disability, since "[t]he former is individual and private, the latter is structural and public" (Shakespeare, 2013, p. 216). The social model does not question the reality of the impairments but argues that the impairments became socially constructed as a disability because mainstream society refused to adjust or adapt to disabled people. Consequentially, governments

---

28 DPI is a global cross-disability organisation, established in 1981, that aims to promote full and equal participation of persons with disabilities (https://disabledpeoplesinternational.org/).

and other powerful institutions have maintained various structural, material, and social barriers, such as implementing discriminatory hiring practices, constructing public buildings that are inaccessible to people with disabilities, and creating cultural discourses that established 'normality' as a universal and unchangeable category vis-à-vis disabled people as 'abnormal' (Priestley, 2003). In other words, political, social, and cultural institutions should make the necessary adaptations to include disabled people rather than expect the disabled person to adapt. As Shakespeare (2013) summarised it, "[s]ocial model thinking mandates barrier removal, anti-discrimination legislation, independent living and other responses to social oppression" (p. 216). Besides, the social model of disability also advocates the involvement of disabled people in the production of knowledge and policies. As Simon Brisenden (1986) stressed, medical experts are important in terms of providing essential medication, but the medical insights are unable to reveal what everyday life is like for a disabled person who lives "in a world run by non-disabled people" (p. 173). He stressed that *"[o]ur* experiences must be expressed in *our* words and integrated into the consciousness of mainstream society, and this goes against the accumulated sediment of a social world that is steeped in the medical model of disability" (p. 174, emphasis in original).

The social model, in turn, has also received its fair share of criticism. First, by arguing that disability is a social construction, the social model seems to imply that impairments are not a problem. This, however, ignores that impairments play an important role in many disabled people's lives and impact their emotional and physical well-being. For instance, the pain some disabled persons experience is caused directly by the impairment and not the environment. As Elizabeth Ellcessor et al. (2017) argued, "some embodied phenomena are, in fact, irreducible to social constructions" (p. 9). Second, it is often difficult to assess whether the pain or discomfort a disabled person experiences can be solely ascribed to either the impairment or the environment as both social and individual factors coalesce in the everyday life experience of a disabled person (Priestley, 2003; Shakespeare, 2013). Such criticisms, however, helped strengthen and diversify the field of contemporary disability studies. The field features research that adheres to the social model of disability as well as research that gravitates toward alternative models. Two additional models are worth mentioning here.

First, we have the relational model of disability (also known as the social-relational model of disability), developed in social sciences. Scholars who start from this model aim to bridge insights from the medical and social models. While the individual/medical model ignored the impact of social and environmental aspects, the social model ignored the functional implications of physical, mental, or sensory impairment (Martin, 2013; Tøssebro, 2004). The relational model, however, acknowledges both and argues that disability needs to be understood as the relationship between internal aspects (the impairment) and external aspects such as social, cultural, or economic contexts (Van Goidsenhoven, 2020). Put differently, disability is the result of a mismatch between a person's capabilities and their environment, a "gap between individual functioning and societal/environmental demands" (Tøssebro, 2004). Starting from this understanding of disability, scholars using this model are concerned with assessing which practices of social oppression and discrimination disabled people encounter (e.g. at work, at school) and how certain contexts (e.g. work and school environments) can be adapted to meet the needs of disabled people, without disavowing that the reality of certain impairments, such as pain, fatigue, or suffering, impact the capabilities of a disabled person (Tøssebro, 2004; Van Goidsenhoven, 2020).

Second, there is the cultural model of disability. Whereas the social model and relational model were developed in social sciences, the cultural model of disability has been formed in the writings of scholars in humanities, such as in literary theory, cultural studies, and performance studies (Snyder & Mitchell, 2006; Van Goidsenhoven, 2020). Inspired by poststructuralist thinking, "this model considers impairment, disability *and* normality as effects generated by academic knowledge, mass media, and everyday discourses" (Waldschmidt, 2017, emphasis in original). The cultural model turns our attention to the role of language, culture, and ideology, and it aims to reveal how the social construction of categories (e.g. 'disability', 'impairment', 'normal') serves the preservation of a social order. Dan Goodley's concept of 'dis/ability' (see above) can be situated within this cultural model, as it illustrates how we should not only study the margins/fringes (i.e. 'disabilities') but also the centre (i.e. 'able-bodiedness'). Considering this book's focus on popular media culture, it is not surprising that many of the studies discussed in this chapter can be related to the cultural model of disability. They demonstrate which stereotypes have been used time and again and what they signify about people with disabilities. Importantly, scholars working with this model not only formulate critiques of popular media culture. They have also demonstrated how certain popular media texts (e.g. autofiction, biographies, documentaries), especially when created by people with disabilities, can act as sources, which can reveal the multiplicity of disabled experiences. They even advocate text-based research methods over more social scientific and ethnographic approaches that involve the participation of disabled research participants, since participants have reported experiencing these approaches as exhaustive (Snyder & Mitchell, 2006).

In contemporary disability studies, many more approaches and theories have been developed. While some scholars continue to hold on to the established models, others bring together concepts and methods developed by scholars associated with different models of disability. As Leni van Goidsenhoven (2020) pointed out, such a multilayered approach may bring distinct but equally valid perspectives on the lived experiences of people with disabilities. Further, breaking free from a rigid model logic allows us to acknowledge that "[d]isability is never a single experience or a generalisable phenomenon; it is always multiple, always contains contradictions, and is, at best, a political category used to group shared experiences without erasing the differences that persist" (Ellcessor et al., 2017, p. 9).

1.3. Disablism and ableism

Last, a comprehension of 'disablism' and 'ableism' is needed. Akin to racism and sexism, disablism refers to "discriminatory, oppressive or abusive behaviour arising from the belief that disabled people are inferior to others" (Miller et al., 2004, p. 28). Many will associate disablism with disablist slurs or explicit forms of rejection and exclusion based on one's status as a disabled person. Yet, activists and scholars who start from the social, relational, and cultural model of disability argue that the practice of looking at disability *only* through a medicalised and individualised gaze also qualifies as a disablist practice since it obfuscates and removes the role of social, economic, political, legal, and cultural factors in shaping disabilities (Goodley, 2014). For Goodley (2014), disablism is particularly caught up in capitalism, as he described it as "the oppressive practices of contemporary society that threaten to exclude, eradicate and neutralise those individuals, bodies, minds and community practices that fail to fit the capitalist imperative" (p. xi). For capitalism to thrive, only "rational functional bodies and minds" are deemed productive (p. 10). From a capitalist perspective, disabled people are either considered unfit for the labour market and condemned to being dependent on charity and/or welfare, or they are expected to adapt to a "competitive, aggressive, flexible, low-paying and [...] ableist labour market" (p. 10). It should be mentioned that some countries have increasingly demonstrated awareness of some of these forms of systemic disablism.[29]

---

29   For instance, a report by the European Social Policy Network that reviewed thirty-five European countries' provision of disability-specific income support and support services for people with disabilities revealed that all surveyed countries were taking tangible measures to bring their policies into line with Principle 17 of the European Pillar of Social Rights (EPSR) and Article 28 on the Convention on the Rights of Persons with Disabilities (Baptista & Marlier, 2022). The former emphasises the right to income support and services that enable participation in the labour market and society. The latter recognises the right to an adequate standard of living and social protection. At the same time, the report expresses its concern "regarding the effectiveness of social protection systems in ensuring that people with disabilities realise their rights and have the same opportunities in life as everyone else" (p. 10). Raising awareness and developing policies are important steps to challenge disablism, but effective implementation and monitoring are also crucial.

Equally important is to become aware of how disablism is but one of many sets of beliefs that uphold an idealised image of what a human should be like – which abilities are favoured in a human being and which ones are not. This is generally referred to as ableism, which Gregor Wolbring (2008) described as "a set of beliefs, processes and practices that produce – based on abilities one exhibits or values – a particular understanding of oneself, one's body and one's relationship with others of humanity, other species and the environment, and includes how one is judged by others" (pp. 252–253). In the context of disability, ableism encompasses a set of able-bodied norms that uphold a hierarchy between bodies and selves that are constructed as the human standard and bodies and selves that fail to adhere to that standard. For instance, to be considered sane, autonomous, and self-sufficient, one is expected to be socially, cognitively, and emotionally able and competent and have the ability to hear, see, or walk (Campbell, 2012; Goodley, 2014; Jenkins, 2021). Ableism has also led to historical and contemporary acts of sexism (e.g. arguing that women were more emotional and thereby unable to bear the responsibility of voting), racism (e.g. the discourses on people of colour's abilities that emerged within social Darwinism), and homophobia (e.g. stating that heterosexuality is the only normal sexuality). These examples illustrate how ableism has been able to install several identity-based normative ideals that, to this day, remain hegemonic (Goodley, 2014; Wolbring, 2008).

2. RESEARCHING DIS/ABILITY AND POPULAR MEDIA CULTURE

Turning our gaze toward dis/ability in media and popular culture, I start by pointing out how scholars in both media and cultural studies and communication sciences have, for a long time, shown little interest in studying disability (Ellcessor et al., 2017; Ellcessor & Kirkpatrick, 2019; Harnett, 2000; Mallett & Mills, 2015; Vertoont et al., 2022). It helps comprehend why the early writings on media and disability were produced by disability scholars and disability activists involved in developing the social model of disability. They demonstrated that media and culture adopted an important role in how Western society in general looked at people with disabilities and explicitly expressed concerns about the circulation of stereotypical images of disabled people (Priestley, 2003; Shakespeare, 2018). At the same time, few of these studies were exclusively devoted to describing and unpacking how disability was attended to in media and popular culture (Ellcessor et al., 2017), with a few notable exceptions (e.g. Barnes, 1992; Cumberbatch & Negrine, 1992; Donaldson, 1981).

The study of disability in media and popular culture became gradually addressed in academia from 2000 onward, although it often happened in diverse fields such as sociology, law, literature, or performance studies (Ellis et al., 2020). The attention to disability in media and communication research remained limited, despite the presence of a few scholars who contributed significantly to the development of the field, such as Gerard Goggin, Katie Ellis, Elizabeth Ellcessor, and Bill Kirkpatrick. To address the limited and peripheral attention given to disability in media, these scholars used their platforms to urge fellow scholars in media and communication research to take the study of disability as seriously as the study of gender and race in media and communication (Ellcessor & Kirkpatrick, 2019).

Ellcessor and Kirkpatrick (2019) have advocated the integration of 'disability' and 'able-bodiedness' as lenses in studying media, communication, and popular culture. They argued that it could reveal how dis/ability is entangled in the production and consumption of media and popular culture:

> A disability perspective, then, is about decentering the physically and cognitively "normal" character, the "normal" viewer, the "normal" producer, and so on; this has profound consequences for the study of media texts, industrial practices, social relations, media policies, modes of reception, and the design of technologies and spaces. It is about rethinking the stories told, the writers and actors hired, the economics of industries, the politics of access and representation, and the range of possible readings (think "cripping the text" as analogous to "queering the text"). It is about listening to new voices and engaging in new political struggles over power and privilege. (p. 140)

In referring to 'cripping the text', Ellcessor and Kirkpatrick (2019) also evoke another theoretical framework worth mentioning, namely crip theory. The term was coined by Robert McRuer (2019) to refer to a series of academic works and activist perspectives that emerged since the 1980s, centring "atypical bodies, minds, and behaviors while interrogating that which can never be contained or described neatly by an entirely historical and limited abled-disabled binary" (p. 134). Crip theory has much in common with queer theory. Akin to the reappropriation of the term 'queer', disabled activists reclaimed the derogatory slur 'crip' from those who used it to hurt and exclude people who diverged from the able-bodied norm. Inspired by queer theory, scholars in crip theory want to denaturalise the binary and hierarchical relationship between ability and disability and expose how a discourse of 'compulsory able-bodiedness' (McRuer, 2019) nudges all people to measure up to the invisible, ableist standards of what is discursively constructed as the ideal able-bodied human (Van Goidsenhoven, 2017).

Crip theory and the cultural model of disability have proven fruitful for scholars exploring the role of mainstream media, film, and television in upholding and/or resisting ableism. They revealed how mainstream movies and television series could be 'cripped'. Akin to the practice of 'queering' and 'queer reading' (see Chapter 3), cripping a film or television programme is about uncovering their "able-bodied assumptions and exclusionary effects" (Sandahl, 2003, p. 37). Similarly, they also highlighted how disabled content creators and artists, like comedians, cripped mainstream culture in their art and performances to "expose the arbitrary delineation between normal and defective and the negative social ramifications of attempts to homogenize humanity [and] disarm what is painful with wicked humor, including camp" (p. 37).

Browsing academic library catalogues and research databases allows us to see an increase in studies that examined issues that relate to disability in media, popular culture, and communication, with research addressing disability representation in news media (e.g. Baroutsis et al., 2023; Goethals et al., 2018), television (e.g. Ellis, 2019; Mallett & Mills, 2015), film (e.g. D'Souza & Rauchberg, 2020; Mogk, 2013), popular music culture (e.g. Holmes, 2020; McKay, 2013) and digital media (e.g. Burch, 2020; Foster & Pettinicchio, 2023). For the scope of this chapter, it suffices to point out that two broader topics dominate the research into dis/ability and popular media culture: representation and accessibility. Questions concerning representation have been addressed from various perspectives, as theories, methods, and concepts from both media and cultural studies and communication sciences have been deployed to quantitatively and qualitatively study how disabilities have been represented. Second, since media and communication technologies are also increasingly intertwined in the everyday lives of people with disabilities, there is a range of studies exploring to what extent media and communication technologies facilitate and/or hinder the everyday lives of disabled people. The following sections deepen and illustrate these two topics.

3. REPRESENTING DIS/ABILITY

3.1. Underrepresentation and disablist stereotypes

Researchers looking at media and diversity within communication sciences have often been concerned with assessing whether minoritised identity groups are proportionally represented. Since approximately 16% of the global population has a disability and many may experience some form of disability in old age, one would expect that disabled people would be included proportionally in media and popular culture. Yet, a significant number of quantitative studies have demonstrated the persistent underrepresentation of disabled people in popular media (Bond, 2013; Cumberbatch & Negrine, 1992; Donaldson, 1981; Saito & Ishiyama, 2005; Vertoont, 2019). For instance, in the 2021 prime-time programming of VRT, the Flemish public service media company (see also Chapter 4), only 1.9% of the characters were people with disabilities (De Swert et al., 2021). Besides providing us with figures and trends, this strand of research also brought to our attention the recurring use of disablist stereotypes (Barnes, 1992; Vertoont, 2019).

Media, cultural, and communication scholars have written extensively about recurring disablist stereotypes in popular media. Jack A. Nelson (2000) argued that many stigmatising stereotypes date back to pre-modern times. Think of how disabled people were imagined as mythological, creepy, or childlike creatures in fairytales and folk tales. Many of these pre-modern stereotypes persisted unchallenged until the mid twentieth century. Moreover, although increasingly questioned, stereotypes of disability and disabled people tend to pop up in contemporary popular media culture. To this end, it is worth revisiting the work by Colin Barnes, a prominent scholar in disability studies. In 1992, he published a widely discussed report that provided a detailed overview of common cultural stereotypes used in British media and popular culture. Concretely, I discuss five of the eleven stereotypes he described.[30] Using both historical and contemporary illustrations, I want to underscore the persistence of some of these stereotypes despite increased awareness about disablism.

---

30 I only discuss a selection of Barnes's (1992) typology of stereotypes. I recommend reading the report if you are interested in learning more about the following stereotypes: 'The Disabled Person as an Object of Violence', 'the Disabled Person as an Object of Ridicule', 'The Disabled Person as Their Own Worst and Only Enemy', 'The Disabled Person as Sexually Abnormal', and 'The Disabled Person as Incapable of Participating Fully in Community Life'.

The first stereotype is 'the Disabled Person as Pitiable and Pathetic' (Barnes, 1992), which Nelson (2000, p. 184) aptly summarised as the stereotype of 'the victim'. Media and cultural content that relies on this stereotype represent disabled people as helpless, pitiable, dependent, sick, and/or suffering (Barnes 1992; Harnett, 2000; Norden, 1990). Besides portraying disabled people as one-dimensional and dependable, this type of content also infantilises and patronises disabled people (Shakespeare, 2018). Barnes (1992) found this particularly conspicuous in the way newspapers referred to disabled people by their first name only, in contrast to able-bodied people who appeared in the newspapers with their first and last names. Charity organisations and telethons have used these images to persuade audiences to donate money, but the stereotype has also been used in news programmes, fairytales, novels, television series, or films (Barnes, 1992; Nelson, 2000; Shakespeare, 2018).

Figure 39. On-set photograph of *A Christmas Carol* (1938), with Bob Cratchit (Gene Lockhart) carrying his son Tiny Tim (Terry Kilburn). Photo credit: United Archives GmbH, IFA Film, © Imageselect/Alamy.

In many cases, the victim stereotype is embodied by disabled children. Martin Norden (1990) noted how many films – particularly during the era of the silent film – featured a disabled child who was portrayed as innocent and sweet. The disabled child characters were "polite, respectful, humble, gentle, godly, pure" and able to "bring out the protectiveness of every good-hearted able-bodied person who comes his/her way" (p. 224). The disabled-child-as-victim trope was particularly popularised by British novelist Charles Dickens's *A Christmas Carol* (1843). The novella recounts how Ebenezer Scrooge, a rich, stingy, and heartless merchant, learns to appreciate Christmas. One of the reasons for his change of heart is learning about the physical disability of Tiny Tim, the young son of his employee Bob Cratchit. The Ghost of Christmas Yet to Come shows Scrooge that his selfish behaviour will eventually lead to the death of the young boy because the Cratchits are unable to pay for medical treatment. Plenty of film adaptations have been made of the novella, with the victim trope left unchanged. Think, for instance, of *A Christmas Carol* (Edwin Marin, 1938) (see figure 39) or *Mickey's Christmas Carol* (Burny Mattinson, 1983).

A second stereotype concerns 'the Disabled Person as Burden' (Barnes, 1992). It has much in common with the victim stereotype as it also revolves around a disabled person who needs to be cared for. However, whereas the victim stereotype aims to elicit emotional responses of pity among audiences, this stereotype is invested in emphasising how much of a burden the disabled person is on other people (e.g. an able-bodied relative or friend), organisations and institutions (e.g. a school, public transport), or society in general. For Barnes (1992), this stereotype fails to see "that with appropriate support disabled people are able to achieve the same level of autonomy and independence as non-disabled people" (p. 15). The stereotype perpetuates the idea that people who adopt the role of caregiver are martyrs as the caregivers are often unpaid family members or peers who 'sacrifice' their own lives to care for the disabled person. At the same time, it ignores the fact that societal institutions are unable or even unwilling to provide the necessary care or services.

A contemporary film that was criticised for its use of the burden trope is the American-British romantic drama film *Me Before You* (Jojo Moyes, 2016). The film recounts the story of a man named Will (Sam Claflin), a successful banker, who becomes paralysed after an accident and is shown to be dependable on caregivers to assist him in living his life. Caregiver Lou (Emilia Clarke) is hired because Will's mother hopes her presence will change his demeanour (see figure 40). Lou, who grows fond of Will, finds out that he has decided to take his own life via assisted suicide in Switzerland. Lou wants to prevent that from happening by showing him how he can have a fulfilling life as a disabled person. Yet, despite falling in love, Will does not want to become a burden and thinks she should be able to live life to the fullest. Lou is unable to change his mind. Even though the trope has been used in older films as well, *Me Before You* was able to spark a backlash from disability activists who felt the film reiterated the idea that disabled lives were of 'less value' than able-bodied people.

Figure 40. Film still from *Me Before You* (2016). Will (Sam Claflin) depends on Lou (Emilia Clarke) for shaving. Courtesy Everett Collection.

The next stereotype goes by many names. It has been described by Barnes (1992) as 'the Disabled Person as Sinister and Evil', by Nelson (2000) as 'the threat', and by Norden (1990) as 'the evil avenger'. Particularly in animation, adventure, and horror films, the villain is often a disabled character. These genre films employ several narrative and cinematographic techniques to link a character's physically disfigured body or mental disability to the villain's immorality (Harnett, 2000). Examples include Darth Vader in the *Star Wars* franchise, Captain Hook in *Peter Pan* (Clyde Geronimi, Wilfred Jackson & Hamilton Luske, 1953), Scar in *The Lion King* (Rob Minkoff & Roger Allers, 1994), and Dr. Poison in *Wonder Woman* (Patty Jenkins, 2017). Notorious has been the use of disfigured or disabled villains in the James Bond franchise (e.g. *Goldeneye*'s Alec Trevelyan, *Skyfall*'s Raoul Silva). Remarkably, despite increased awareness of identity politics in terms of gender, sexuality, or race, villains remain portrayed as disabled in the James Bond universe; *No Time to Die* (Cary Joji Fukunaga, 2021) even features three villains with facial disfigurements (i.e. Blofeld, Safin, and Primo). The stereotype has been criticised, first, for implying that disabled characters are bitter and villainous because they have not been able to come to terms with their impairment and, second, to nudge the assumed able-bodied audiences to fear the villains (Shakespeare, 2018). Noting that facial disfigurement in popular culture had become a dominant trend, the charity Changing Faces felt that it had to take action. Changing Faces is a leading British charity organisation that is committed to helping anyone in the United Kingdom "who has a visible difference, a scar, mark or condition on their face or body that makes them look different." In 2022, the organisation launched 'I am not your villain', a campaign that targeted media professionals in the film industry and asked them "to stop using scars, burns or marks as a shorthand for villainy" (Changing Faces, n.d.).

The fourth stereotype may seem a bit more dated, but its impact on the public imagery of disability cannot be underestimated. The stereotype of 'the Disabled Person as Atmosphere or Curio' pertains to the practice of deploying disabled people to express a certain mood or atmosphere. Disabled characters are dehumanised as they figure as 'objects of curiosity' (Barnes, 1992). This stereotype dates back to the mid nineteenth century when in the United States and Europe so-called 'freak shows' were staged. A freak show was a "formally organised exhibition of people with alleged physical, mental, or behavioral difference at circuses, fairs, carnivals and other amusement venues" (Bogdan, 1996, p. 23). The 'freaks' included both able-bodied and disabled individuals, and they performed in a show that was promoted as 'educational' although, in practice, freak shows were commercial events. To feign that the show was scientifically sound, hosts were asked to act like 'professors' or 'doctors'. They provided pseudoscientific arguments about the people on display, using disablist, exoticised, and racist discourses; the exhibited people were argued to come from 'mysterious', 'remote', and 'primitive' locations around the world (Bogdan, 1996). For Barnes (1992), "[s]uch exhibitions represent little more than disability voyeurism because they encourage lewd fascination with impairment" (p. 12). By the mid twentieth century, the freak show practically disappeared (Bogdan, 1996), but its legacy has lived on in popular culture.

Focus on *Freaks*

Tod Browning's *Freaks* (1932), an American Hollywood film about a French travelling circus, is a good example of how popular films represented disabled people as freaks or objects of curiosity. The film narrates the story of Hans (Harry Earles), a little person, who falls in love with Cleopatra (Olga Baclanova), an able-bodied trapeze artist. Upon learning Hans is wealthy, Cleopatra joins the circus, seduces Hans, and marries him. At the same time, she has an affair with strong man Hercules (Henry Victor), with whom she plots to poison Hans (see figure 41). However, Hans finds out about the affair and decides to plot his revenge together with the other circus members, including able-bodied and disabled performers. The film turned out to be a commercial and critical fiasco; few people went to see the film, different American theatres pulled the film after only a few weeks, and it got banned in the United Kingdom. According to Robin Larsen and Beth Haller (2002), film critics at the time noted that "*Freaks* offended audiences and exhibitors in a uniquely vivid way by introducing body shapes that were 'real' rather than 'made up'" (p. 168). Larsen and Haller linked the audiences' reactions to 'aesthetic anxiety' – a concept described by Harlan Hahn (1988). It denotes "the fears engendered by persons whose appearance deviates markedly from the usual human form or includes physical traits regarded as unappealing. These fears are reflected in both the propensity to shun those with unattractive bodily attributes and the extraordinary stress that modern society devotes to its quest for supernormal standards of bodily perfection" (p. 42). Aesthetic anxiety can be considered an externalisation of ableism. It leads to reactions and actions in which people differentiate between 'normal' and 'abnormal' physical appearances, favour people whose physical appearance and behaviour are considered 'normal' or 'average', and discriminate against those who do not appear or act 'normal' or 'average'. Such ableist attitudes can be discerned in the way audiences who watched *Freaks* perceived disabled people as inferior and objected to the idea of an able-bodied person having a relationship with a little person.

Scholars critical of the film argued that the film continued the tradition of the freak show. Jay McRoy and Guy Crucianelli (2009) acknowledged that, on the one hand, the film is engaged in eliciting sympathy for the 'freaks' since the able-bodied Cleopatra and

Hercules figure as villains in the overarching narrative. The same can be said of the scenes that take place outside the circus tent, which portray the disabled performers in a backstage context. They are busy doing some chores, eating, relaxing, chatting, and flirting. Yet, whereas those who 'defend' the film argued that these scenes underscore the performers' humanness and treat them on a par with able-bodied people (see below), McRoy and Crucianelli argued that the film's mise-en-scène and narrative remain invested in 'othering' the disabled performers: "Instead of the performers being freed from their stage personas, they are grounded further within them. Browning allows us a glimpse into the 'ordinary' lives of 'extraordinary' performers only to, essentially, poke fun at them" (p. 261).

Figure 41. Photograph of *Freaks* (1932). Hercules (Henry Victor) and Cleopatra (Olga Baclanova) manipulate Hans (Harry Earles). Photo credit: Metro Goldwyn Mayer/Album. © Imageselect/Alamy.

Fiona Whittington-Walsh (2002) disagreed with this way of reasoning as she underscored that the film should be assessed within the historical context in which it was produced and seen. Whereas disabled people were (and are) played by able-bodied actors, *Freaks* was one of the first film productions that hired actors with physical and mental disabilities to perform disabled characters. Further, she did not agree that the film exploits its disabled actors or puts them on display, since the different actors are allowed to showcase "their diversity without shame" (p. 706). Compared to common stereotypes, *Freaks* does not depict a disabled person as isolated. On the contrary, the many disabled characters are part of a strong circus community, in which able-bodied and disabled 'freak' performers treat each other equally and respect each other's diverse embodied and lived experiences.

At the same time, the violent and horror-like ending – where the 'freaks' avenge the assault on Hans (as well as on able-bodied Venus) by presumably killing Hercules and by turning Cleopatra into a 'freak' herself (a Hen-lady, a woman who is half woman, half chicken) – complicates the emancipatory reading of the film. If this film wants to emancipate 'freakishness', why does the ending represent 'freakishness' as a punishment? The film remains an ambiguous text. It nudges audiences to feel sympathy for the 'freaks' but also to experience fear. Yet, the key question remains whether, for instance, the decision to show 'Armless girl' (Frances O'Connor) eat and drink with her foot is turning her into a spectacle, or whether it is an ableist gaze – which stipulates how one 'normally' eats – that makes people argue that this scene, along with the overall film, is a spectacle?

Figure 42. *Meet the Superhumans* was a promotional campaign by Channel 4 to promote its coverage of the 2012 Paralympics. Photo credit: Howard Davies, © Imageselect/Alamy.

Last, there is the stereotype known as 'the Super Cripple' (Barnes, 1992) or 'Supercrip' (Nelson, 2000). It can be described as a benevolent stereotype as it intends to represent disabled people as "remarkable achievers, 'supercrips' who, against all odds, triumph over the tragedy of their condition" (Harnett, 2000, p. 22). In news content, factual formats, fiction, and advertisements, the stereotype has been used to demonstrate how disabled people have been able to not only adjust to society but even thrive in it. The stereotype of the supercrip is a dominant trope in news reports on sports events for disabled athletes. For instance, David McGillivray et al. (2021) demonstrated how the supercrip discourse was prevalent in British print and online news reports about the Paralympics in 2012 and 2016, which represented the British Paralympians as 'Superhumans' with lots of guts and determination (see figure 42).

The most extreme examples can be found in fiction, especially superhero fiction. Take, for instance, Marvel superhero Daredevil, the moniker of Matthew Murdock. Matthew became blind when he was still a young boy. Through training, however, he developed his other senses to levels exceeding human standards, allowing him to become a vigilante fighting crime in Manhattan. Netflix decided to turn the comic book into a series, which ran for three seasons (*Daredevil*, 2015–2018). By introducing mainstream television audiences to a series whose main character is blind, Netflix defied a common trope of treating disabled characters as supporting characters. Matthew (Charlie Cox) is presented as a layered, complex character who is not defined by his blindness. At the same time, the series does not ignore his blindness, as the way he navigates rooms and engages with media and technology are accurate representations. However, the series also frames his blindness as an impairment that had to be compensated by his other senses, which resulted in his superhuman qualities. Even though the superhero genre expects its main heroes to be 'supernatural', it perpetuates the idea that all disabled people are capable of anything, even though "they are limited by their bodies and the world in which they live, just like everyone else" (Grue, 2016, p. 846). On top of that, it also implies that most disabled people are not worthy of mainstream media attention unless they can go above and beyond (Barnes, 1992).

3.2. Ableist representations of disability

Yet, whereas we may be able to pick up quickly on disablist stereotypes, ableist imagery is more difficult to discern. A first and common trope is the practice of representing disabled people as desiring to be able-bodied and/or as able-bodied as possible. Such practices of representation reinforce ableism: by representing disabled characters as having internalised an ableist standard of how one should live their life and/or striving to be as able-bodied as possible, these representations do not question the rigid interpretation of the human standard in Western society and do not explore different ways of living, being, and thinking about bodies and selves. For instance, there are quite a few examples in which people who need a wheelchair to be mobile are represented as desiring to walk (again). Especially when working with able-bodied actors, we have seen fiction films and series that feature dream sequences in which the characters are walking or dancing (Ellis & Goggin, 2015). In the Belgian film *Hasta La Vista* [Come As You Are] (Geoffrey Enthoven, 2011), three male friends in their twenties go on a road trip to Spain to lose their virginity. They each have a physical disability: Philip (Robrecht Vanden Thoren) is paraplegic and uses an electric wheelchair to get around; Lars (Gilles De Schryver) is terminally ill due to a brain tumour and dependent on a wheelchair; and the vision of Jozef (Tom Audenaert) is severely reduced. Knowing their parents would not allow them to go to a brothel that 'caters' to disabled people, they tell their parents they want to do a wine tour in France.

The film's set-up defies an outdated disablist stereotype; instead of representing disabled people as desexualised or unable to have sex (Barnes, 1992), the film underscores the disabled men's sexual desires. Second, as Eduard Cuelenaere et al. (2019) pointed out, the film aligns with the social model of disability; the three protagonists provoke the 'medical' model of disability by reclaiming their right to sexuality and resisting the (often) limited expectations able-bodied people have of disabled people. The three men succeed in their mission to lose their virginity. However, what caused criticism is the use of an ableist lens that depicts how the men *feel* after having had sex for the first time. In a dream-like scene that uses overexposure and slow motion, the three men walk toward each other, confident and smiling. Importantly, there are no signs of their assistive devices (i.e. the wheelchair, cane, and glasses). According to Cuelenaere et al. (2019), the scene suggests that disabled people "often dream of being, or even aim to be able-bodied, which fits in the dominant cultural ableism" (p. 12).

Second, plenty of popular media texts feature ableist language. In different languages, we can find expressions that rely on metaphors of impairment to articulate frustrations, fear, disgust, and annoyance. Think, for instance, of 'being deaf to a person's pleas', 'being left without a leg to stand on', 'the blind leading the blind', or the terms 'crazy', 'spastic', or 'lame'. The expressions dehumanise people with disabilities and turn their disabilities into pejorative metaphors. Moreover, we should become aware that these expressions are basically stating that people with disabilities are inferior, not 'normal', and less capable (Andrews, 2019; Mogk, 2013). Even though these expressions and metaphors have often been used spontaneously and with no intention of harm or discrimination, their effective use has been increasingly questioned. This context helps us grasp why Beyoncé was called out for using an ableist slur on her 2022 album *Renaissance*. The criticism came as a surprise since the record celebrates black and queer (music) cultures and is dedicated to her older gay cousin Johnny ('Uncle Johnny'), who introduced her to house music. In a letter published ahead of the record's release, she shared that it was her intention "to create a safe place, a place without judgment. A place to be free of perfectionism and overthinking" (Kelly, 2022). Yet, the song 'Heated' (2022) featured the following line: "Spazzin' on that ass, spazz on that ass," in which 'spazz' represents the feeling of freeing oneself from personal constraints and letting go completely. Such an interpretation ignores that the word is derived from the medical term 'spasticity' – a condition in which people experience less control over their muscle movement, resulting in feelings of stiffness and/or involuntary movements of limbs – and its current use as a derogatory slur. Activists, however, lauded the fact that Beyoncé listened to these criticisms voiced by disabled fans and that she changed the lyrics of the song by replacing the word with 'blasting' (Edwards, 2022).

3.3. Accurate and critical representations

However, only focusing on stereotypical and ableist representations would do injustice to the increased and diversified practices of representing disability in popular media culture. In contrast to the stereotypes, well-developed representations cannot be organised according to 'types' or 'stereotypes'. Rather, they are the result of a combination of diverse practices that aim to create a fair and balanced representation of disability.

First, a seemingly obvious practice is representing disabled people as 'normal' and 'accurate'. Writing at the beginning of the 1990s, Barnes (1992) applauded a change in representation in media. Particularly television started representing disabled characters as 'ordinary' or 'normal'. Disabled persons were not represented as heroes, victims, or as the butt of the joke. They were part of the script because of their profession (e.g. a scientist, council official) and not their disability. Yet, Barnes stressed that this alone would not be enough to qualify as an accurate representation. The disabled character should also be given some form of character development, an active role (e.g. having dialogues with other characters, being able to advance the plot), and considerable screen time. Moreover, the script should also feature some reflections on the experience of being disabled. Even though it would be stereotypical to represent a disabled character as solely defined by their disability, not representing the experience of having a disability would ignore what it means to be disabled.

An often-lauded representation concerns teenager Walt White Jr., the son of Walter White in the American crime series *Breaking Bad* (AMC, 2008–2013). Like the character, actor RJ Mitte has cerebral palsy (see figure 43). In the series, Walt Jr.'s cerebral palsy is visibly present (e.g. he walks with crutches, he has a speech impediment) but it does not define him. The storylines that revolve around him focus on being a teenager, figuring out his identity (e.g. changing his name to Flynn), and hanging around with friends, while also persuading his father to pursue cancer treatment and caring for his mother and baby sister. Another praised example can be found in Marvel Cinematic Universe's *Eternals* (Chloé Zhao, 2021). One of the American film's main superheroes is Makkari, a Deaf superhero of colour performed by Deaf actress Lauren Ridloff (see figure 44). In the comics, the character is a hearing white man, but Marvel Studios wanted to reimagine and diversify the cast of superheroes. In the film, Makkari uses American Sign Language to communicate. This demonstrates how the production team acknowledged her disability and took it seriously. At the same time, her role in the narrative is not written around her being Deaf. The example illustrates that representing 'normal' and 'accurate' representations does not preclude fantasy, science-fiction content, or *even* superhero characters.

Figure 43. On-set photograph with RJ Mitte as Walt Jr. in *Breaking Bad* (2008–2013). Photo credit: Landmark media, © Imageselect/Alamy.

Importantly, representations that allow for recognition do not always demand an explicit naming of a disability, even in the case of invisible disabilities. Take, for instance, the Australian series *Please Like Me* (ABC/ABC2, 2013–2016). Comedian Josh Thomas, who created the series, shared in interviews that he felt there was a need for television series that brought a nuanced portrait of mental illness and suicide (see figure 45). At the same time, as a comedian, he wanted to explore how a series tackling these themes can still be funny (Barash, 2021). Throughout the four seasons of the series, we are introduced to several characters who have a mental illness or cognitive disability. Rose (Debra Lawrance), the mother of Josh, the main character (performed by Josh Thomas), has bipolar disorder; Arnold

Figure 44. On-set photograph with Lauren Ridloff as Makkari in *Eternals* (2021).
Photo credit: Marvel Studios/TSG Entertainment/Album, © Imageselect/Alamy.

(Keegan Joyce) has an anxiety disorder; and Hannah (Hannah Gadsby) copes with depression. Yet, although not explicitly stated, the series also recounts a narrative of autism. Like Hannah Gadsby, Josh Thomas has autism spectrum disorder. Although the series creator/actor was not diagnosed at the time of making *Please Like Me*, he was surprised to find out how his autism was already expressed in the way he represented Josh (Barash, 2021). In a study that explored what autistic people found of the way autism was represented in television fiction, several participants named *Please Like Me* as an example of a show that represented autism as accurate, not sensationalised, and not stereotypical (Jones, 2022).

Yet, as scholars in media and cultural studies stressed, it is debatable and relative what qualifies as 'accurate' since the experience of being disabled is diverse and context-dependent. They would likely agree that *Breaking Bad* and *Eternals* provide well-developed disabled characters but argue that a person with cerebral palsy may have different experiences than Walt White Jr. in the series. It illustrates the difficulty of assessing the accuracy of a representation. Furthermore, the narrative and aesthetic qualities of popular media culture allow for critical representations of disability that do not seem 'normal' or 'accurate' – they may even come across as stereotypical. Yet, before jumping to conclusions, such representations may challenge practices of stereotyping through the practice of cripping (see above). That is why such representations should be read and interpreted in the broader context of the product or programme. In doing so, we may be able to discern critical representations of disabled characters that are created to provoke and/or question ableism and disablism. Susan Vertoont et al. (2022) argued that popular culture features narratives or portrayals intended to deconstruct hegemonic discourses on disability and able-bodiedness. It concerns representations of "discriminating practices in relation to feelings of friction, frustration and uneasiness" (p. 8). These narratives and images are concerned with showing "disabled characters and/or their surroundings rebelling, contradicting or parodying the related feelings of friction and injustice" (p. 8).

Vertoont et al. (2022) illustrated their argument by discussing *Tytgat Chocolat* (VRT, 2017), a Flemish television drama series. It tells the story of Jasper Vloemans (Jelle Palmaerts), a young man with Down Syndrome, who works in a sheltered workshop of a chocolate factory. Jasper falls in love with Tina (Mira Bryssinck), a woman with autism and a refugee from Kosovo. She is not granted asylum and is deported to Kosovo, something that could have been prevented were Jasper able to marry her. However, the series makes explicit their frustration as Jasper is legally not allowed to marry because of his prolonged minority status. Vertoont et al. (2022) explained that "[a]lthough he is of adult age, he is considered a minor who lives under the custody of his parents and, therefore, cannot marry. Throughout the series, we see Jasper resisting and rebelling against this unequal treatment and his inability to make this life decision independently of his parents" (p. 8).

Figure 45. On-set photograph from *Please Like Me* (2013–2016), with Josh Thomas as Josh. Photo credit: Australian Broadcasting Corporation (ABC)/Album, © Imageselect/Alamy.

4. ACCESSIBILITY AND ACCESS TO PRODUCTION

A pivotal aspect when studying the interconnections between disability and popular media culture is accessibility. Elizabeth Ellcessor (2017) argued that even though well-developed representations of disabled people are essential, they are not enough when the goal is to establish an inclusive popular media culture environment. What is the point of creating media content about disabled people if it cannot be consumed by disabled people due to a lack of access? Ellcessor (2017) described accessibility as "the means by which people with disabilities can use media, often entailing specialized features or assistive devices" (p. 34). Enabling access can refer to film theatres and music festivals accommodating wheelchair users, or streaming services and public service broadcasters providing audio descriptions and closed captions for their content. Similarly, several devices (e.g. computers, smartphones, game consoles) have built-in screen readers that can read written text out loud. As Katie Ellis (2019) stressed, it is no surprise that disabled people are early adopters of new media technologies since these technologies have often helped remove barriers and facilitate access.

For instance, the invention of Braille – a language system of raised dots that can be read through touch, devised by Louis Braille in 1824 – made it possible for blind people to use a standardised language to write and read. Yet, the popularisation of radio in the 1920s also gave blind people an easier, instant, and less intensive medium to use (e.g. listening to a person reading a newspaper). Likewise, blind people have successfully adopted the internet and digital technologies (e.g. creating their own media content). As a consequence, (the teaching of) Braille has been in decline (Ellis & Goggin, 2015), although disability activists and academics lament the phasing out of Braille instruction. For instance, Lindsay Harris et al. (2023) demonstrated that it is incorrect to assume that teaching Braille is less efficient than auditory word learning. Further, they stressed that Braille literacy is a human right as much as literacy is a human right for sighted people. Either way, Braille and other new media technologies succeeded in helping remove barriers for blind people to participate.

At the same time, the introduction of new media has not always simplified the lives of all disabled people. First, not all new media have been accessible and beneficial to disabled people. For instance, whereas the popularisation of radio improved the quality of life of blind people, the medium excluded Deaf people and it raised obstacles for people who have a speech impediment (e.g. what does this medium mean for politicians with a stutter who are being interviewed live on radio?) (Ellis & Goggin, 2015). Second, the incorporation of new media technologies as assistive devices in media content is not widespread and not always well executed. For instance, Ellis (2019) found that many disabled Australian television viewers continued to experience a recurring lack of audio descriptions or captions. A related issue concerns the use of audio descriptions or captions of questionable quality. Ellis (2017) illustrated this by pointing out how YouTube uses automatic captions, which tend to feature spelling mistakes, incorrect decoding of words, and incorrect use of punctuation, resulting in a difficult viewing experience for people who are Deaf or hard of hearing.

Nonetheless, despite all of this, the necessity to acknowledge and enable access to media and communication technology has been recognised by the United Nations. In 2006, the United Nations Convention on Rights of Persons with Disabilities (CRPD) was adopted by the General Assembly. It is:

> [...] intended as a human rights instrument with an explicit, social development dimension. It adopts a broad categorization of persons with disabilities and reaffirms that all persons with all types of disabilities must enjoy all human rights and fundamental freedoms. It clarifies and qualifies how all categories of rights apply to persons with disabilities and identifies areas where adaptations have to be made for persons with disabilities to effectively exercise their rights and areas where their rights have been violated, and where protection of rights must be reinforced. (United Nations, 2006)

From a media and democracy perspective, article 21 is important. It underscores that the countries that ratified the UNCRPD "shall take all appropriate measures to ensure that persons with disabilities can exercise the right to freedom of expression and opinion, including the freedom to seek, receive and impart information and ideas on an equal basis with others and through all forms of communication of their choice" (United Nations, 2006). Concretely, the article formulates five objectives:

a) Providing information intended for the general public to persons with disabilities in accessible formats and technologies appropriate to different kinds of disabilities in a timely manner and without additional cost;
b) Accepting and facilitating the use of sign languages, Braille, augmentative and alternative communication, and all other accessible means, modes and formats of communication of their choice by persons with disabilities in official interactions;
c) Urging private entities that provide services to the general public, including through the Internet, to provide information and services in accessible and usable formats for persons with disabilities;

d) Encouraging the mass media, including providers of information through the Internet, to make their services accessible to persons with disabilities;
e) Recognizing and promoting the use of sign languages.
(United Nations, 2006)

The objectives illustrate how nation-states should invest in making sure disabled people can take part in society and democracy, and acknowledge that media and communication technology play an important role in those processes.

Besides accessibility, Ellcessor (2017) also drew attention to access to media production. Ellcessor (2017) argued that "a lack of accessible tools, discrimination, and passive neglect are possible causes for a pervasive underrepresentation in all capacities related to media production" (p. 35). However, Ellis and Merchant (2020) underscored that, as opposed to studies on the representation of people with disability, little (systematic) research has been conducted about disabled media workers. Nonetheless, some assumptions can be made based on the few studies conducted. First, studies indicated an 'employer fear' among able-bodied employers, which refers to a fear that disabled professionals will be less productive and may demand costly structural changes in the workplace to accommodate access (Ellis & Goggin, 2015; Ellis & Merchant, 2020). On the side of prospective employees, there is a reluctance to share information about their disability with the employer out of fear that they may be perceived as less productive and more demanding (Ellis & Merchant, 2020).

Yet, thanks to Web 2.0. and accessible, affordable production software, disabled media creators have found a way to work around the traditional mainstream media industries and turn to online media (blogs, social media platforms, video sharing platforms) to upload and distribute content (Ellcessor, 2017). Web series, for instance, turned out to be an alternative format for disabled writers and/or actors to showcase their talents and tell the stories they want to tell, often after experiencing difficulties in being hired as a media professional. An example of a successful web series that deconstructs Hollywood's ableist perspective is *My Gimpy Life* (2012-2014), created by Teal Sherer. The American series, loosely based on her own experiences as a paraplegic actor, attracted a loyal audience (Ellis & Merchant, 2020). Thanks to a successful crowdfunding campaign that emphasised the importance of its politics of representation, a second season was made. The series demonstrates both the viability of disability-centred media and the potential of independent media making, on the condition that a crowdfunding action is successful (Ellcessor, 2017).

CHAPTER 6

SOCIAL CLASS

Setting the scene: Filthy Rich and Homeless

From 2017 to 2020, Australian audiences could watch three seasons of *Filthy Rich and Homeless*, a reality television series broadcast by SBS Australia, one of Australia's three national broadcasting companies. On its official homepage, SBS Australia presents itself as 'the most diverse broadcaster' in the country, concerned with fostering an inclusive society. In this context, it is worth examining to what extent this reality/documentary programme contributes to the company's goal to promote inclusivity. The programme explored homelessness in Australia through a 'social experiment'. Each season revolved around five wealthy Australians who became voluntarily homeless for ten days. Through their experiences, the programme tried to offer reflections on what it meant or felt like to be homeless. The producers underlined that not all candidates were born wealthy. For instance, in season 1, one of the candidates, Jellaine Dee, had lived in family refuges as a child. Nonetheless, at the time of filming, all five participants belonged to the upper class and were symbolically and materially removed from people living on the streets.

To kick off this chapter, I ask you to watch the television trailer created to announce the first season of *Filthy Rich and Homeless*. The trailer opens with shots of people moving about on Melbourne's busy streets, juxtaposed with shots of anonymised homeless people on those same streets. A dramatic piano-led soundtrack underscores the seriousness of the programme's topic. The trailer continues with brief interview statements from the five wealthy candidates who articulate prejudices (e.g. "they get money, they go straight to the pub") or express deliberate ignorance (e.g. "If I'm honest, I'd probably rather not even think about it"). Halfway through the trailer, the programme hosts are introduced. They meet the five candidates, who are carrying huge travelling bags, in an empty hall. One of the hosts announces the set-up of the show: "You're about to spend ten days, living among the homeless." The announcement is followed by a shot of one of the candidates, whose jaw drops upon (allegedly) hearing the set-up for the first time. From this moment on, the tone of the trailer shifts: dramatic up-tempo music colours the shots that show the hardships of the 'homeless' celebrities, while a male voice-over, in a serious tone, explains that "[i]n a three-night special event, SBS shines a light on the crisis of homelessness as five wealthy Australians trade privilege for the pavement." We catch a glimpse of what is to come: shots of the protagonists sleeping underneath blankets on the street, experiencing cold, seeking shelter, and carrying their belongings in a big plastic bag. Furthermore, scenes of emotional breakdowns are interspersed with brief scenes that create suspense. For instance, to the soundtrack of a rapidly beating heart, we see doors being kicked in, hear screams of a person not shown on screen, and watch a police car arrive with sirens blaring, without any clarification on what these short scenes are about and whether or not they are connected.

Even though the programme has been discussed at length in Australian media, the television trailer is also worthy of discussion. It announces *Filthy Rich and Homeless* as a serious programme rooted in everyday life as well as a 'special event' with twists, cliffhangers, and emotionally upsetting scenes. In other words, the programme still aims to entertain. We should ask the question of *who* it wants to entertain. Although social stratification is a complex process and the distinction between social classes is not clear-cut (see below), it can be argued that television companies tend to imagine their target audiences as belonging to the middle class (Bullock et al., 2001; Mantsios, 1995). In this programme in particular, middle-class audiences are the prime audiences. Yet, they are inconspicuously absent in the content of this programme, which allows middle-class audiences to distance themselves from the rich *and* the poor. This is facilitated by representing the wealthy individuals as 'filthy rich' and unworldly, and the homeless people as pitiable and lacking agency. Upon watching the first season, television critics acknowledged that the intent may have been emancipatory but found the program refraining from tackling the political, economic, and sociocultural reasons underpinning an increase in homelessness in Australia (e.g. income inequality, housing affordability, and domestic violence). In the end, middle-class individuals may have experienced empathy and/or considered charity, but they were not prodded to question structural forms of inequality (Delaney, 2018).

Australia is not the only Western country where reality programmes are made around the disparity between rich and poor people. The British programme *Rich House, Poor House* (Channel 5, 2017–present), and its adaptations, such as *Steenrijk, straatarm* (SBS6, 2017–present) in the Netherlands and *Plötzlich arm, plötzlich reich* (SAT.1, 2018–2021) in Germany, illustrate how television companies are well aware of the commercial potential of formats that merge entertainment, reality, and poverty. These programmes, at times, have been dubbed 'poverty porn' (see below) because they objectify and demean poor people for entertainment purposes instead of critically examining structural reasons that create poverty and social inequalities. At the same time, it is worth pointing out that reality formats about poverty are increasingly scrutinised and criticised on social media and in news media. For instance, in Belgium, *Astrid and Natalia: Back to Reality* (VTM, 2024) was pulled off the air after the first episode provoked a media backlash. In the programme, broadcast on Flemish commercial television channel VTM, two famous, wealthy Flemish celebrities had to live in a modest house as single mothers with a minimum wage for a month. Several journalists, media scholars, and other well-known Flemish celebrities spoke out against the way the programme handled poverty. Importantly, single mothers living in poverty also shed their light on the programme. The main critiques concerned the fact that it is simply not possible to experience and fathom, as a wealthy person, what it feels like to be a poor single mother in just one month, especially when factoring in that the two celebrities did not have to go through the trouble of finding a house and were given enough budget to afford a car (Bosmans, 2024). The question that prompts itself is whether commercial as well as public service broadcasters will steer clear of tackling timely issues that relate to social class and inequality, or whether they will look for formats, be it fictional or factual, that do succeed in taking poor, working-poor, and working-class people seriously.

1. REFLECTIONS ON SOCIAL CLASS

Compared to some of the axes of identity discussed in the previous chapters, 'social class' holds a slightly different position. Whereas gender, sexual, and racial identities are constructed around bodily traits, social class is mainly formed around a person's socioeconomic status. Second, scholars in social sciences and humanities have decried a decreased interest in research and politics for understanding class stratification and challenging class discrimination, even though contemporary Western society remains highly unequal (Crompton, 2008; Deery & Press, 2017; O'Neill & Wayne, 2017a). This has also been visible in a disinterest in studying social class in media, communication, and popular culture (O'Neill &

Wayne, 2017a; Skeggs & Wood, 2011). For instance, whereas social-class-based issues were at the heart of the early British cultural studies tradition, exemplified by the work of Richard Hoggart, Raymond Williams, and E. P. Thompson (see below), concerns over class in media and cultural studies declined from the 1990s on (James, 1999; Sparks, 1996). Nonetheless, to assess the material and symbolic impact of social stratification on the lives of all people in contemporary Western society, there is an ongoing need for research that centres social class in social sciences and humanities.

Rosemary Crompton (2008) stressed that "[a]ll complex societies are characterized, to varying extents, by the unequal distribution of material and symbolic rewards" (p. 9). An important shift in thinking about social and economic inequalities was the consensus that these inequalities are "not 'natural' or divinely ordained, but rather emerge as a consequence of human behaviours" (p. 9). However, the concepts and approaches developed to assess, measure, or reflect on these forms of inequalities have been a constant topic of discussion and debate (Crompton, 2008; Levine, 2006). As such, there is no consensus on what social class encompasses, how class-based societies are made, and how class-based societies can be undone. In itself, this is not an issue as the development of knowledge demands ongoing discussions to advance knowledge. Hence, this chapter provides an insight into modern and contemporary theories of social class, with the disclaimer that other scholars may have defined the same concepts differently.

1.1. *Modern class theory: Marx, Althusser, and Bourdieu*

The development of modern class theory in Western society started in the nineteenth century, with the writings of Karl Marx, Max Weber, and Friedrich Engels as fundamental sources. With the scope of this chapter in mind, we begin by revisiting the work of philosopher Karl Marx. He was concerned with understanding class formation and class struggle in a capitalist society. To grasp his theory on social class, we start with his argument that each society throughout history has been organised around a specific mode of production that provided the essential means to live (Marx, 1904; Storey, 2021). Each mode of production consists of the 'forces of production' – which refers to the means of production (i.e. non-human, physical, and non-financial material such as raw materials, tools, and factories) and the labour power in a given society – and the 'relations of production' that are formed around the means of production (Barker, 2012; Marx, 1904; Storey, 2021). For Marx, social class refers to the collectivity of individuals who share the same relationship to the means of production. In a capitalist mode of production, this comes down to classes who own capital (i.e. the bourgeoisie) and classes who only possess their labour (i.e. the proletariat). Since the bourgeoisie's main interest is profit, they exploit the workers by paying the labourers less than the full value of the commodity (e.g. grain, coffee, clothes, furniture) the labourers created. This leads to an antagonistic relationship between both types of classes due to the opposing interests of the bourgeoisie and the proletariat (Crompton, 2008; Levine, 2006; Marx & Engels, 1970/2006).

However, to defy this situation of exploitation, the proletariat has to become *aware* of their shared class interests and, more generally, of the fact that they form a class. Marx used the metaphors of 'base' and 'superstructure' to explain this. Whereas base refers to the dominant mode of production in a given society, superstructure refers to political, legal, educational, and cultural institutions used to legitimate (but also question) the conditions of this dominant mode of production and the ideological discourses shaped by these institutions. According to Marx, those who own the 'means of production' also control the institutions of the superstructure and are, thereby, able to present the ideology of the ruling class as universal and natural, arguing that the current mode of production benefits all, and to nudge the subordinated classes to accept their position (Marx, 1904; Storey, 2021). Following this argument, Marx would agree that elites and upper-class individuals would be able, via the media they own or control, to influence the public by only allowing the creation of content that does not question the social status quo or the capitalist mode of production. For Marx, to become aware of one's subordinated position, a social consciousness (or 'class consciousness') needs to be developed at the level of the superstructure. For working-class people, this implies an awareness of the fact that they are exploited and the ability to develop practices to engender social equality; if a working-class consciousness is lacking, people within the working class will not engage in collective action (Crompton, 2008; Marx, 1904; Levine, 2006). In other words, people can objectively be part of a social class, based on whether they have access to the means of production, but lack a class consciousness if they are not aware they are part of a specific class or exploited as members of that class.

Whereas Marx's approach to understanding social inequality has been criticised for accrediting much power to economic modes of production and creating a binary outlook on class stratification (i.e. the proletariat versus the bourgeoisie) (Crompton, 2008; Storey, 2021), other scholars provided more multidimensional approaches. Philosopher Louis Althusser (1971) focused on understanding the role of ideology in the *reproduction* of modes of production that serve the ruling classes. His work drew from Marxism but was also informed by other essential theories, like Gramsci's conceptualisation of hegemony and ideology (see Chapter 1). He argued that such a reproduction depends on systems and practices that ensure the availability of means of production and labour power. Importantly, "the reproduction of labour power requires not only a reproduction of its skills, but also, at the same time, a reproduction of its submission to the rules of the established order, i.e. a reproduction of submission to the ruling ideology for the workers, and a reproduction of the ability to manipulate the ruling ideology correctly for the agents of exploitation and repression, so that they, too, will provide for the domination of the ruling class 'in words'" (pp. 132–133). Althusser agreed with Marx that the superstructure is tasked with preserving the dominant mode of production but added depth and nuance by distinguishing repressive state apparatuses (RSAs) from ideological state apparatuses (ISAs). RSAs and ISAs ensure that the dominant mode of production is not questioned or challenged, but their means to do so differ. RSAs, which encompass governmental, administrative, military, and judicial institutions, reproduce the mode of production by violent and nonviolent means of repression. ISAs, on the other hand, refer to a wide variety of public and private institutions (e.g. religious organisations, media and communication organisations, cultural institutions, families) that use ideology to achieve the same goals. Since these ideological discourses are hegemonic, many people involved in ISAs participate in reiterating discourses that may not benefit their own living conditions. They simply reproduce what is presented to them as normal and universal. Althusser spoke of interpellation when describing how ideology hails people into subjects (e.g. hailing people as 'workers') that fit the dominant mode of production (e.g. capitalist mode). People are often not aware of this practice, as these interpellations happen daily and are expressed by the many ISAs people come into contact with. Not only family members but also media and popular culture nudge people into specific roles. Yet, like Marx, Althusser believed that the ruled classes could resist the ruling classes. He argued that ISAs have the potential to serve as a site where the ruled classes can challenge the ruling classes. In contrast to the RSAs, ISAs are much more complex to govern and control from the top down, making it possible for the exploited classes to express their resistance to the dominant mode of production and expose how that mode only benefits the ruling classes.

Like Althusser, sociologist Pierre Bourdieu aimed to think beyond the role of economic capital in the process of shaping social classes. Without dismissing the importance of economic capital, he argued that social and cultural factors also contribute to the formation, experience, and expression of social class (Storey, 2021). For him, social stratification in society should be seen as the outcome of relationships "between the universe of economic and social conditions and the universe of lifestyles" (Bourdieu, 1984, pp. xi–xii). Social divisions result from the volume and composition of forms of capital (i.e. economic, social, and cultural capital) within a given society. Economic capital refers to money and other material resources (e.g. property) that can be converted into money; social capital refers to connections and group memberships that can advance one's position in society (i.e. social mobility); cultural capital refers to cultural competencies, practices, or skills that can accredit a person with standing and authority (Bourdieu, 1984, 1987; Weininger, 2005). As such, some classes have a great volume of capital, which Bourdieu referred to as the 'dominant classes', and there are those that do not. At the same time, he also underscored that the composition of capital within classes differs (e.g. there are those with more economic capital than cultural capital and vice versa), resulting in class fractions.

For the scope of this chapter, I zoom in on his ideas about culture and social class. Bourdieu argued that social classes and class fractions represent themselves as a class through cultural practices of consumption, lifestyle, and taste (Bourdieu, 1984; Weininger, 2005). He based his claims on empirical research, which forms the basis for his seminal work *Distinction* (1984), originally published in 1979. To inquire into the taste cultures in France and whether they varied according to a person's educational capital and/or social origin, he conducted two surveys by questionnaire in the 1960s. His aim was not to demonstrate how consumption, taste, and lifestyles vary across classes, but to reveal how they were used to reproduce and secure hierarchical class relations based on economic inequalities (Storey, 2021). For instance, expressions of taste in music may seem or feel like a personal statement, but they function as means of social distinction and markers of class, especially when factoring in that certain forms of music are discursively constructed as more legitimate than others (see below). Crucially, such processes not only include expressions of taste but also distaste (Stillerman, 2015). For instance, Elliot Weininger (2005) rephrased Bourdieu's argument as follows:

> To appreciate a certain type of music is, implicitly or explicitly, to spurn other available forms of music; to find some types of cuisine particularly appetizing is to find others unappealing; and to find certain schools of painting inspiring is to find others dull. In each of these cases, the rejected practices or objects carry an association with the social actors who engage in or possess them. For Bourdieu, in other words, the aesthetic sensibility that orients actors' everyday choices in matters of food, clothing, sports, art, and music—and which extends to things as seemingly trivial as their bodily posture—serves as a vehicle through which they *symbolize* their *social similarity* with and their *social difference* from one another. (p. 141, emphasis in original)

Bourdieu also demonstrated the presence of 'homology' across different cultural fields (e.g. literature, music, visual arts, fashion, food). This means that although each field has its own ways of differentiating between legitimate and popular tastes and practices, homologous patterns across fields were noted that aligned one's lifestyle and consumption patterns across different fields with the same social class fraction (Bennett et al., 2009; Bourdieu, 1984; Weininger, 2005).

Last, Bourdieu stressed that there are struggles *within* social classes over what kind of lifestyle and taste is considered legitimate and/or how to express one's social status. Those with the greatest economic and/or cultural capital have been able to establish which lifestyles and forms of culture are legitimate and superior. Yet, whereas fractions with great economic capital (e.g. industry employers) distinguish themselves via luxury goods, expensive design, and modes of travelling, fractions with great cultural capital (e.g. intellectuals) distinguish themselves via an investment in 'complex' or 'intellectual' forms of culture (e.g. opera, canonical works of literature). At the same time, there are class fractions lacking these forms of capital. Not only are they excluded from the struggle over what qualifies as legitimate culture, but their lifestyles are also represented by the other classes as undesirable (Bourdieu, 1984; Weininger, 2005).

Focus on social class, taste cultures, and taste in music

Bourdieu's work has particularly been informative for studies within the traditions of the sociology of culture and cultural sociology (see below). To illustrate, I focus on studies that inquired into the relationship between music taste and social class. At the basis of these studies is Bourdieu's concept of homology. As argued before, homology implies that each class fraction is likely to express similar taste patterns across a variety of fields (Bourdieu, 1984; Perchard et al., 2022). As a result, a hierarchy emerged of three distinct taste cultures, namely highbrow, middlebrow, and lowbrow culture. Highbrow culture encompasses the cultural preferences and practices of the dominant classes, which are claimed to be legitimate and sophisticated. The taste cultures have been set out by a class fraction of the dominant classes that is less wealthy but holds much cultural capital (e.g. intellectuals and university professors). The works considered highbrow are presumed to be difficult, abstract, and removed from everyday life. Think of arthouse cinema, abstract art, but also baroque music or instrumental jazz. To appreciate these art forms, time, education, etiquette, and aesthetic literacy are allegedly required. Middlebrow culture refers to the taste cultures of the middle class (described by Bourdieu as 'the petit bourgeoisie'), which comprises "the minor works of the major arts [...] and the major works of the minor arts" (Bourdieu, 1984, p. 16). Think of mainstream films or series made by decorated arthouse directors, popular classical compositions (e.g. songs from Broadway musicals), or songs made by popular singers that are lauded for their level of alleged artistic sophistication. Middle-class individuals aim to emulate the highbrow taste cultures but due to a lack of capital, time, and/or education, they turn to works that are comprehensible yet sufficiently 'sophisticated' to allow middle-class consumers to dissociate from the working class. The taste cultures of working-class people have been derogatorily referred to as 'lowbrow' culture and comprise 'popular' taste cultures. They encompass works and other forms of entertainment that are appreciated because of their function/use rather than form and their connection with everyday life. Think of soap operas, amateur theatre, or Schlager music – a genre popular in Western European countries with sentimental songs that are easy to sing along to (see figure 46). These forms of culture provide instant pleasure, and they do not require education or etiquette, allowing everyone to participate. Furthermore, unlike middle-class consumers, working-class people feel much less pressure to take part in a status game with the hope that this will lead to social mobility (Bourdieu, 1984; Perchard et al., 2022; Stillerman, 2015; Veenstra, 2015).

Figure 46. Belgian schlager singer and accordionist Thomas Julian at the summer edition of the Belgian Schlagerfestival, 2023. Photo credit: Belga photo, Kurt Desplenter.

Yet, while this distinction could very well represent taste cultures in the 1960s, taste cultures became more complex from the 1990s on (Peterson & Kern, 1996). An alternative perspective was launched by Richard A. Peterson. He argued that upper-class individuals distinguished themselves from middle- and working-class people by their ability to become cultural omnivores (Peterson & Kern, 1996). This refers to the elite's "desire and ability to consume a multitude of diverse cultural forms, including diverse musical styles" (Veenstra, 2015, p. 138), unlike working-class people, who are described as 'univores' due to their alleged lack of knowledge of and participation in multiple cultural forms. Peterson and Roger M. Kern (1996) found evidence among American high-status persons that supported the idea that the highbrow snob was gradually being replaced by the cultural omnivore. Their study focused on taste in music and to what extent high-status persons liked middlebrow genres (e.g. Broadway musicals, big band) and lowbrow genres (e.g. bluegrass, blues). The results indicated an increased interest in both middlebrow and lowbrow genres. Yet, another study on music tastes, conducted by Gerry Veenstra (2015) in Canada, found that the music taste of Canadian adults was still very homologous with social class; adults with higher class education tended to prefer classical and choral music, opera, and jazz, whereas adults with less than a high school diploma tended to dislike these genres except for jazz music. Vice versa, genres such as country, easy listening, and golden oldies were appreciated by working-class adults while disliked by higher-class individuals.

Although these studies underscored the ongoing role social class plays in shaping taste in music, it could also be argued that these quantitative studies, based on surveys, did not inquire whether people liked certain genres better than others or whether they distinguished between artists within these genres. Similarly, while many artists increasingly defy the reliance on music genres to create music, audiences too can question the use of genres to articulate and curtail their taste in music. Further, terms such as 'highbrow' and 'lowbrow' tend to reiterate normative assumptions about music, as they imply that genres allocated to highbrow culture, say classical music, are considered culturally more distinguished than, for instance, Schlager music. Moreover, scholars (e.g. Bennett et al., 2009) demonstrated how music taste could also be explained by other dimensions of identity such as age, gender, or ethnicity. Last, as Andy Bennett (2008) highlighted, it is vital to explore *how* people experience/make sense of the music they listen to, which often happens in quite reflexive and nuanced ways and is shaped by the local and everyday context in which the music is experienced. For instance, hip-hop music can no longer be considered a genre that marks a black working-class status as the genre has been appropriated and consumed by people from diverse classes and racial backgrounds around the world (Bennett, 1999; Riley, 2005). In such instances, social class can only be one of many factors that need to be taken into account when studying which values and meanings consumers attach to hip-hop music.

1.2. *Contemporary reflections*

Even today, scholars have demonstrated that it is difficult to establish a working-class consciousness and successfully expose and challenge persistent social inequalities and class-based hierarchies (Langston, 2000; O'Neill & Wayne, 2017a). Among other institutional spheres, education and media have been blamed for consolidating class stratification through the repetition of certain myths and practices. To explore this further, I turn to ethnic studies professor Donna Langston (2000). A myth that has been successful in stalling the creation of a working-class consciousness is the myth of a classless society. Langston pointed out how this myth articulates that personal traits like responsibility and ambition, on the one side, and equality of opportunity, on the other, are sufficient for a person to be successful and move ahead in Western society. Such a belief has been central to the idea of meritocracy, which refers to a societal system in which people improve their living conditions because of their skills, achievements, and meritocratic traits (e.g. assertiveness, competitiveness, self-reliance), instead of their wealth or class privileges (Mijs, 2016). In a classless and meritocratic society, failure to succeed is then attributed to lacking traits or skills rather than the economic and political power relations that benefit from a class-based society. This way of thinking places all responsibility on the individual. Further, it disregards that what qualifies as 'meritocratic' is far from neutral and has changed throughout time and obfuscates that 'personal failures' are often the result of structural inequalities (e.g. people not being able to afford home tutoring, lacking the financial means to elite education) (Langston, 2000; Mijs, 2016). Besides reiterating the myth of a classless society, tokenism has been used to prevent working-class people from questioning class-based systems. Tokenism refers to the creation of a few visible tokens of people who were able to achieve social mobility. By highlighting those few who succeed, false hope is created. At the same time, these practices confirm middle- and upper-class groups in their superiority since their socioeconomic status and lifestyles are represented as desirable and the norm all people should aim for (Langston, 2000).

For Langston (2000), the myth of the classless society and tokenism illustrate how society has been ignorant about social class being all-encompassing. Echoing Bourdieu, she argued that social class comprises both one's socioeconomic status as well as one's cultural background:

> As a result of the class you are born into and raised in, class is your understanding of the world and where you fit in, it's composed of ideas, behavior, attitudes, values, and language; class is how you think, feel, act, look, dress, talk, move, walk; class is what store you shop at, restaurants you eat in; class is the schools you attend, the education you attain; class is the very jobs you will work at throughout your adult life. (p. 398)

Consequentially, working-class, working-poor, and poor people will experience classism based on their lack of money and/or based on their cultural practices (e.g. language, housing, taste cultures). Akin to racism and sexism, classism refers to "a set of individual and institutional beliefs, systems, and practices that assigns value to people according to their class ranking and creates an economic inequality affording economic privilege to some while targeting others for oppression" (Holtzman & Sharpe, 2014, p. 148).

To research social class then is first to acknowledge that social class comprises a (relatively) objective and subjective dimension. The objective dimension has often been studied by measuring a person's socioeconomic status (SES), which "indexes one's position within a power hierarchy via relatively objective indicators of power, prestige, and control over resources, such as income, wealth, education level, and occupational prestige" (Diemer et al., 2013, p. 79). The subjective dimension has been studied by exploring a person's subjective social status (SSS), measured by one's perception of their social class, using qualitative methods and subjective methods (Diemer et al., 2013). This implies that researchers need to understand a given society's economic mode of production, patterns of social stratification, and dominant sociocultural discourses on social class. Research that factors in the objective and subjective dimension will likely encounter people who may situate themselves in a social class different from the one they are 'objectively' part of.

Second, it also pertains to approaching social class from an intersectional lens, as being white and/or male within a working-class community has come with privileges that people of colour and/or women lack (Langston, 2000; Levine, 2006). Rhonda Levine (2006), for instance, reflected on the relationship between class inequality and gender inequality by demonstrating how the disproportionate role women assume in the domestic sphere (e.g. homemaking, childcare) has an impact on the kinds of jobs they consider, their wages, or means of making promotion. Similarly, racial inequality intersects with class inequality as the structural hindrances people of colour experience in getting access to education, being invited for a job interview, and being able to rent houses in certain neighbourhoods impact the class position of racial and ethnic minorities (Levine, 2006).

Last, it is crucial to be aware of the arbitrariness of the classifications of social class (see also Bourdieu, 1987). These classifications of social class are context-dependent (e.g. some countries have a large middle class, whereas others do not) and have been defined differently (e.g. which qualifications are used to decide who 'belongs' to which social class). Nonetheless, the following categories are often used in Western society: 'poor and homeless', 'working class', 'middle class', and 'upper class' (e.g. Kendall, 2016). In some more recent models, the number of categories has increased and diversified. For instance, the European socioeconomic classification (ESeC), which uses occupation as the main indicator, consists of ten classes (i.e. 'higher salariat', 'lower salariat', 'higher white collar', 'petit bourgeois', 'small farmers', 'higher grade blue collar', 'skilled manual', 'semi/-unskilled', and 'unemployed') (Rose & Harrison, 2007). Nonetheless, for the sake of clarity, this chapter uses the broader and more common class categories (e.g. 'middle class', 'working class').

2. RESEARCHING SOCIAL CLASS AND POPULAR MEDIA CULTURE

In surveying the academic literature published on social class and popular media culture, it may appear that not that much was published about social class and popular media culture at the turn of the twenty-first century compared to research about gender, sexual diversity, and ethnic and racial diversity in popular media culture. Nonetheless, going back in time to especially the third quarter of the twentieth century, we notice that concerns over social stratification and class informed quite a lot of work that (in)directly dealt with culture and communication. In this section, I discuss three major traditions that have provided theoretical and empirical approaches to researching social class and popular media culture. At the same time, I explain why there was a decline in interest in studying these topics.

2.1. Cultural studies and social class

Social class and (popular) culture used to be one of the main topics in the tradition of cultural studies. Richard Hoggart, Raymond Williams, and E. P. Thompson are seen as founders of the British cultural studies tradition. In the work they published in the 1950s and early 1960s, Hoggart, Williams, and Thompson contemplated the state of the British working class in late modern societies. They not only demonstrated the presence of a distinct working-class culture but also stressed its social and cultural value. In their writings, they were critical of capitalism and believed mass media and capitalist popular culture posed a threat to working-class culture. At the same time, they also believed that working-class culture and minority media had the political power to resist the imposing threat of capitalist culture (Sparks, 1996; Storey, 2021). Their work and arguments are generally described as culturalist, as they focused on the lived experiences of working-class individuals and underscored the agency of people to create their own meanings and to have an impact as individuals (Sparks, 1996; Storey, 2021; Turner, 2003). It is important to highlight that not all were inspired by Marx – Hoggart is considered a scholar who dismissed Marx's ideas – while Williams and Thompson each critically engaged with Marx's writings (Sparks, 1996).

The works of these scholars served as foundational texts for the Birmingham Centre for Contemporary Cultural Studies, in particular in the works of Stuart Hall. In the papers of the CCCS, social class was seen as the prime category of analysis. This remained the case throughout the 1970s and 1980s, although the culturalist approach made way for a more structuralist approach. In this period, the theories of Marx and Althusser took on a more central position, which resulted in increased attention to ideology and its role in shaping society and, consequently, social class. In contrast to the culturalist approach, the structuralist approach in cultural studies led to the assumption that audiences had less agency in decoding culture and were, therefore, less equipped to critically decode dominant ideologies embedded in (popular) culture (Turner, 2003). By the 1990s, when cultural studies had developed into a mainstream and international research tradition, other dimensions of identity were taken up by cultural studies (e.g. gender, race, ethnicity, sexuality, and age), often at the cost of social class (James, 1999). Moreover, whereas the bulk of studies focused on ideological meanings in cultural texts and how they engendered social inequalities, little attention was given to exploring the *material* conditions underpinning social inequalities (Sparks, 1996).

2.2. Political economy and social class

Contrary to cultural studies, the tradition of political economy prioritised the study of the material conditions of mainstream media and popular culture. For a tradition at times referred to as Marxist political economy, it is self-evident that Marx's writings were essential to the tradition's theoretical foundations. Yet, whereas cultural studies, at times, used Marxist insights to explore how ideology was negotiated in cultural texts and consumption, political economists used Marxist theory to study the economic structure that underpins media culture. As Graeme Turner (2003) argued, political economists assume "that those who own the media control the way it produces culture; and those who control cultural production are themselves enclosed within a dominant capitalist class in whose interests the media represent reality" (p. 161). Prominent political economist Nicholas Garnham (1995) stated that an exclusive focus on consumption – which he reproached cultural studies of doing – ignored that a dominant class "determines which meanings circulate and which do not, which stories are told and about what, which arguments are given prominence and what cultural resources are made available and to whom" (p. 65). As such, among other issues, political economists were concerned with the increasing role of private business in the sphere of cultural production and the impact of the concentration of media power. For them, increased control over the production of culture implied increased control over content.

A seminal work illustrating this argument is Edward S. Herman and Noam Chomsky's *Manufacturing Consent: The Political Economy of the Mass Media*, originally published in 1988. In this book, Herman and Chomsky argued that news media in the United States "serve, and propagandize on behalf of, the powerful societal interests that control and finance them" (2002, p. xi). They demonstrated how the increased commercialisation of mass media led to a small group of media conglomerates controlling a big portion of the market, including diverse news media that are deployed to increase profit rather than encourage discussion and contribute to a well-functioning public sphere. As such, a media ecology was fostered in which news media increasingly depended on advertisers who were averse to societal debate and critical voices that questioned the established order in society. To attract and please advertisers and elite investors, news media framed stories in such a way that the social status quo was maintained and, as such, 'manufactured consent'. Even though Herman and Chomsky demonstrated that journalists and other media professionals working with these media experienced some autonomy and were able to 'dissent' by covering inconvenient truths, they also pointed out how these acts of dissent were limited in scope and impact and did not prevent the creation of an increasingly depoliticised consumer culture (Herman & Chomsky, 2002), making it difficult for working-class newspapers to survive and working-class concerns to be heard and addressed.

Although cultural studies and political economy drew from Marxism and were concerned with advancing the condition of the working class, they nonetheless got caught up in a debate in the 1990s that has been described as lively and unproductively antagonistic, while partly based on misunderstandings of arguments on both sides (see Grossberg, 1995). Nonetheless, it is worth pointing out that some of the criticisms were gradually addressed. For instance, the critique that cultural studies were mainly concerned with textual analyses of cultural texts led to studies that not only took audiences seriously but also aspects related to production and the cultural industries. David Morley (1980), for instance, demonstrated the necessity for ethnographic approaches in cultural studies to explore how audiences make sense of television content, while Angela McRobbie (1997) focused explicitly on production when discussing the fashion industry, highlighting how the creation of a fair industry demands an analysis that joins aspects of production (e.g. manufacturing, designing, retailing) to aspects of consumption (e.g. audience awareness of sustainability or labour conditions of female workers in the industry). On top of that, political economy and cultural studies have grown closer together, as each tradition adopted methods, theories, and approaches from the other tradition. To this end, we can see them as distinct but related approaches in the field of media and cultural studies. Furthermore, political economic insights not only enriched media and cultural studies but also communication sciences (e.g. Evens & Donders, 2018).

2.3. *The sociology of culture, cultural sociology, and social class*

Last, the discussion of Pierre Bourdieu and music taste in the previous section also demonstrated the attention given to popular culture in sociology. This part highlights two sociological traditions that have explored social class and popular culture. First, the sociology of culture has been concerned with the sociological study of arts and popular culture, with attention to studying decision-making processes in cultural organisations and institutions and exploring cultural participation. Typically, such studies start from (post-)positivist premises (see Chapter 1) and, for instance, examine whether correlations can be found between social categories (such as social class) and film taste, attending museums, or learning musical instruments (Hanquinet, 2022; Wolff, 1999). Although the quantitative data revealed trends and changes, the tradition tended to look at arts and popular culture through lenses that stress economic, material, and structural factors (Back et al., 2012; Wolff, 1999). Think, for instance, of the postulation that one's class status is an important determinant of one's taste in arts.

The younger tradition of cultural sociology, however, recentred culture and interpreted it in the broadest sense of the word, including values, norms, and beliefs.

The tradition questioned the idea that participation in cultural activities and experience of cultural texts has been shaped by non-cultural factors (e.g. class relations, elite influence in the production of media) and accredited relative autonomy to culture in affecting how people engage with popular culture and the arts (Wolff, 1999). In other words, they postulated that sociologists should inquire *how* people make sense of popular culture and arts rather than assume that cultural dispositions or socially shared meanings are predetermined. Similar to contemporary media and cultural studies, the tradition ascribed agency to individuals in how they make sense of popular culture and argued that the best way to study this is by adopting an interpretative approach and relying on qualitative research methods (see Chapter 1). At the same time, cultural sociologists disagreed with some scholars in media and cultural studies that interpreted practices of cultural resistance (e.g. liking or making cultural texts that resist or provoke hegemonic ideologies in society) as forms of class resistance (Back et al., 2012). Nonetheless, akin to the rapprochement of cultural studies with political economy, cultural studies scholars and cultural sociologists have worked together and have often been part of the same department at universities. If anything, it illustrates how the disciplinary boundaries between the different traditions in practice are rather porous, with research combining theories, concepts, and methods from cultural sociology, political economy, and/or cultural studies.

2.4. *Decline and revival*

Yet, despite this history of studying social class in relation to media and (popular) culture, several scholars pointed out that a decline of interest in studying these issues had set from the 1990s on (Deery & Press, 2017; James, 1999; O'Neill & Wayne, 2017a). Beverley Skeggs and Helen Wood (2011) indicated that there was a hesitancy to make grand statements about social class and popular culture to avoid being reductionist or essentialist (e.g. arguing that all cultural texts produced within a capitalist logic reflect the dominant classes' ideologies). At the same time, this hesitancy coincided with the continuation of the dismantling of the public sphere. Deirdre O'Neill and Michael Wayne (2017a, 2017b), echoing arguments made by political economy, located this dismantling at the level of media, education, and politics:

> The public sphere where decisions are made and discussed, in the media, education and politics, have been occupied completely by a middle class dedicated to managerialist approaches to public life and market focused insistence on competitive individualism that removes the potential for collective action. (2017a, p. 6)

Traditional news media no longer succeed in playing their role as a critical watchdog as they cater increasingly to the middle and upper classes. Rather than creating a forum where policy-making and political power can be discussed from both hegemonic and counterhegemonic perspectives, O'Neill and Wayne argued that traditional news media tend to give a platform to middle-class intellectuals who show little awareness about how class divisions impact their rhetoric or standpoints. However, since the 2010s, a new wave of research among scholars in media and cultural studies as well as communication sciences has begun to emerge that takes social class and popular media culture seriously (Deery & Press, 2017; Polson et al., 2020).

Whereas aspects of production and consumption have already been discussed in the first two sections of this chapter, the next two sections are reserved for an exploration of how social class has been represented in audiovisual culture. The first section provides an in-depth discussion of three films from the first decades of cinema that qualify as milestones in the history of imagining social class in film. The second section focuses on television and explores how each class has commonly been represented in television content made from the 1990s onward.

3. MILESTONES IN THE REPRESENTATION OF SOCIAL CLASS IN FILM

Compared to some of the minoritised identities tackled in previous chapters, working-class and poor people figured prominently on the big screen from the very beginnings of cinema. One of the first films ever made, Louis Lumière's *La Sortie de l'usine Lumière à Lyon* [*Workers Leaving the Lumière Factory in Lyon*] (1895) documents the end of the working day, showing numerous female and male employees leaving a factory (see figure 47). During the formative years of cinema, up to roughly the mid 1920s, quite a lot of films featured the working class as their main subject. Steven J. Ross (1998), talking about the emergence of film culture in the United States, argued that this was not that surprising if we look at this period's production and consumption of silent film.

On the one hand, the majority of film audiences were working-class people. Film was an inexpensive leisure activity and did not require specific forms of literacy, dubbed 'the poor man's amusement'. Its popularity led to the construction of many movie theatres in working-class and immigrant neighbourhoods. On the other hand, working-class individuals were also active in the production of film, ranging from being wage labourers on film sets to creators of films. The latter was possible because the production costs of film were relatively low and the demand for films was very high. Similarly, reform organisations and labour unions understood that films could reach more audiences than newspapers could. It was no surprise that such a favourable environment led to the production of many so-called 'working-class films'. Ross (1998) distinguished three categories of working-class films:

> [O]ne, a vast number of innocuous romances, melodramas, comedies, and adventures that used workers and immigrants as their protagonists, but could just as easily have used middle-class or elite characters; two, a more modest number of social-problem films that depicted the general hardships of working-class life; and three, a smaller group of highly politicized labor-capital films [...] that focused on the often violent confrontations between employers and employees. (p. 45)

Figure 47. Still from *La Sortie de l'usine Lumière à Lyon* (1895). Photo credit: World History Archive, © Imageselect/Alamy.

For instance, in Edwin S. Porter's *The Kleptomaniac* (1905), an upper-class woman and a poor woman are caught stealing. The first woman stole several items in a department store while the woman with hungry children at home felt forced to steal a loaf of bread. Both women are tried in court. However, while the poor woman is sentenced by the judge, the rich woman is released. The film reads as an unequivocal critique of class justice as it demonstrates how the judicial systems are not impartial and benefit those with more means and, consequentially, access to better forms of legal advice and legal representation. The film's last two shots reveal the critical standpoint of the film. One shot features the word 'justice' – which, at this point, can only be read as an ironic comment on the functioning of justice. The other shot emphasises this critique, as it features an image of a half-blindfolded Lady Justice whose pair of scales is no longer in balance since a loaf of bread cannot compete with the literal and symbolic weight of a bag of gold.

Yet, toward the end of the 1920s, it became much harder to produce critical working-class films. Several factors could be mentioned, including the increased cost of making films, the increased power of Hollywood studios, industry leaders refusing to distribute and exhibit these films, and state censorship boards that demanded cuts in films that dealt with labour-management discords or civil strife (Black, 1989; Ross, 1998). What did increase were films that used stereotypical representations of poor, working-poor, and working-class individuals, films that celebrated the lives of the middle and upper classes, and films that promised social mobility (Benshoff & Griffin, 2021). Nonetheless, despite the increased difficulties of making audiovisual content about class hierarchies and class struggle, several films have been made in the United States and other Western countries that took social class issues seriously and questioned social class hierarchies. In the next section, we explore three such canonical films.

3.1. *Metropolis*

The first film worth discussing in depth is *Metropolis*, a German film made in 1927 and directed by Fritz Lang (see figure 48). The film is often considered one of the last films made within the wave of German Expressionism, a silent film movement that found its origins in arts and theatre around 1908.

Expressionist art turned away from realism and looked for radical manners to represent and visualise subjective and internalised feelings. German Expressionist films, which were produced between 1910 and 1927, were characterised by abstract and symbolic depictions of reality. Concretely, the films made use of exaggerated and highly stylised settings, decors, costumes, and acting codes (e.g. unnatural facial expressions and gestures) (Bordwell & Thompson, 2003). In *Metropolis*, Lang channelled the wave's interest in fantasy and science fiction by representing a dystopian twenty-first-century society. The city, named Metropolis, is denoted as totalitarian and is organised around a rigid class hierarchy, envisioned in the decors that represent the city. The fact that Fritz Lang was also trained as an architect came in handy when designing the film's cityscape (Cook, 1996).

Metropolis shows affinities with Marxist theory, such as Marx's binary approach to social class, as it imagines a society that comprises two distinct classes: the upper class, who owns the gigantic machines on which the city runs, and the working class, whose physical labour is needed to run the machines. Expressionist visual techniques underscore how the city is organised. The top level of the cityscape (i.e. 'the upper city') is reserved for the upper classes. Here, we witness the upper class indulge in leisure activities, such as dancing, sports, and courting. The middle level is reserved for the industrial machines, which are manned by the working class. The city's underground (i.e. 'the worker's city') is where the workers live, represented as an uninviting and inhospitable space (Byrne, 2003). Even though the labourers are essential for the functioning of the city, they are represented as passive dupes unaware of their agency to overthrow the unjust system. In other words, they are shown to lack a working-class consciousness.

Figure 48. Film poster of *Metropolis* (1927). Photo credit: Historic Illustrations, © Imageselect/Alamy.

The film's main protagonist is Freder Fredersen (Alfred Abel), the son of the master of Metropolis, who becomes gradually aware of how his class exploits the working class. Together with Maria (Brigitte Helm), a working-class woman, they try to figure out a way to bring the classes together. The ending, however, is bleak and ambiguous. A mad professor creates a false Maria who incites the workers to destroy the machines. As a consequence, the workers flood their own quarters and nearly kill their own children (Byrne, 2003). In the end, the upper class remains unthreatened while the working class is represented as a group of men lacking responsibility and rationality. Despite not offering solutions to engender social change, the film did raise pertinent questions about social inequality, capitalism, and exploitation. It is also a good illustration of how a film style has been used to expose unjust class hierarchies and class relationships through cinematographic and narrative tactics.

3.2. *Ladri di biciclette*

The second film, *Ladri di biciclette* [Bicycle Thieves], is an Italian film from 1948 directed by Vittorio De Sica. De Sica is considered one of the leading filmmakers of Italian Neorealism, a film movement that emerged in a post-war climate and spanned a period from the 1940s to the early 1950s. Italian cinema, which was known for its magnificent settings and decors, had to reinvent itself as the major film studios were destroyed during the Second World War. Several filmmakers, such as Roberto Rossellini and Luchino Visconti, embraced a realistic outlook by filming on location and immersing themselves in real-life environments rather than using artificial studio settings. In terms of narrative themes and topics, they explored the ramifications of the war on Italian society, such as inflation and unemployment. The films' main narratives revolved around the everyday lives of working-class individuals and communities, with particular attention to their struggles to survive (Cook, 1996; Piepergerdes, 2015; Bordwell & Thompson, 2003).

In *Ladri di biciclette*, the audience is introduced to Antonio Ricci (Lamberto Maggiorani). He has been unemployed for quite a while but is eventually offered a job as a bill poster. Even though a bicycle is required to perform the work, Antonio is expected to provide his own bike (see figure 49). Yet, on his very first day on the job, his bike gets stolen. Together with his son Bruno (Enzo Staiola), he seeks the thief as well as help from established institutions (i.e. the police, the Church, and the labour union). Yet, no one seems willing or able to help. In the end, a desperate Antonio tries to steal a bicycle himself but gets caught in the act. The bicycle owner, however, shows compassion because of Antonio's son and drops the charges (Cook, 1996). *Ladri di biciclette* gives due weight to the condition of the working class and unemployed. De Sica explained that he felt the need to represent the lives of those who were being ignored in mainstream newspapers and to ensure that bourgeois film audiences were unable to ignore the ramifications of living in a class-based society. To this end, he crafted a film that encourages audiences to identify with Antonio and to feel his frustration with the way established institutions are treating him unjustly. Similarly, audiences are made aware of how the theft of a bike may be a trivial thing for the bourgeoisie, but catastrophic for a worker (Ben-Ghiat, 2001). Last, by casting an ordinary worker as the lead and filming the characters in the streets of Rome, the film represents the scale, impact, and lived experience of being part of the working class and/or unemployed. Ruth Ben-Ghiat (2001) described it as follows:

> As Antonio and his son Bruno undertake a desperate search through Rome, De Sica charts a geography of the dispossessed. We see squalid alleyways, over-flowing soup kitchens, and neighborhood brothels and everywhere hordes of unemployed men whose frustration gives the film an urgent energy. (p. 42)

Figure 49. Still from *Ladri di biciclette* (1948), with Lamberto Maggiorani as Antonio and Enzo Staiola as Antonio's son Bruno. Photo credit: Photo 12, Produzioni De Sica, © Imageselect/Alamy.

De Sica's film demonstrates, first, that Antonio and the thief are not that different: both 'bicycle thieves' are no aggressors. Rather, their actions should be seen in the light of a state that fails to address the worries, concerns, and precarious living conditions of the poor and working class (Ben-Ghiat, 2001). Second, rather than giving us a romanticised and naïve representation of being poor, the film shows, as realistically as possible, what it means when a person or family lacks the means to provide food, clothing, and a home.

3.3. *All That Heaven Allows*

The third film, *All That Heaven Allows*, is a Hollywood film from 1955 made by German director Douglas Sirk. Melodrama films were a popular genre from the 1940s up to the 1960s. Many melodrama films revolve around the conflicts and tensions of a middle-class family. The main character is often the mother, brother, or daughter, and their personal and emotional traumas or conflicts – in many cases, an intergenerational conflict – are at the centre of the narrative (Mercer & Shingler, 2004). The conflicts and tensions are often represented implicitly, as Hollywood conventions (e.g. the necessity of a happy ending), commercial considerations, and the dominance of the Production Code Administration (e.g. certain themes considered difficult or forbidden to represent, see Chapter 3) forced filmmakers to look for other ways to tackle societal issues (Elsaesser, 2013; Mercer & Shingler, 2004). To understand the critical subtext, one had to read the film's main narratives together with the way the mise-en-scène, décor, props, or double entendres in the dialogues were deployed.

To illustrate, we turn to Sirk. Many of his films revolve around a middle-aged woman who feels trapped in her own life. In *All That Heaven Allows*, the lead character is Cary Scott (Jane Wyman), a widow. She lives in an upscale American suburban neighbourhood, where she spends her days with social activities organised by a female friend and accommodating her two young adult children who are off to college. She seems lonely and bored, but that changes when she falls for a young gardener named Ron Kirby (Rock Hudson) (see figure 50). Gradually, audiences experience how she feels trapped in the mores and values of middle-class society and finds herself being drawn to Ron's way of living. At the same time, she is very much aware that a relationship with somebody from the working class would be frowned upon and/or lead to social rejection by her friends and family. When she tells her children of her love for Ron, they take action to prevent the relationship from happening. They argue that it is only proper for her to remarry with an equally established man. She first gives in at the request of her children, only to figure out that it brings her no happiness.

In a pivotal scene around Christmas, she confesses to her daughter that she regrets her decision to try and find happiness in her domestic environment. However, the heartfelt conversation is interrupted by her son entering the living room. Unwilling or unable to read the room, he starts telling his mother that she should consider selling the house out of economic considerations, without allowing his mother to express her own thoughts on the matter. Next, a salesman enters the living room with a gift from her son. The son tells his mother that the gift is a way to compensate for the fact that her children are no longer living at home. It turns out to be a television set, the middle-class commodity at the time. The salesman tries to pitch the advantages of television to her: "All you have to do is turn that dial, and you have all the company you want, right there on the screen. Drama, comedy… life's parade at your fingertips." Yet, the only thing she sees is her own reflection, which reminds her of the fact that she is – like her reflection on the screen – still trapped. Whereas the middle-class lifestyle is generally represented as 'normal' and thereby invisible (also referred to as 'ex-nomination', see below), the modes of representation used in this film turn the 'normal' into something 'strange'. Like the house, the television entraps Cary into a normative middle-class culture, something she escapes from by the end of the film when she chooses to live with Ron.

Figure 50. Still from *All That Heaven Allows* (1955). Cary (Jany Wyman) and Ron (Rock Hudson) at a Christmas tree sale. Photo credit: RGR Collection, © Imageselect/Alamy.

4. MAKING SENSE OF CLASS REPRESENTATIONS ON TELEVISION

This chapter began with a discussion of the television industry and highlighted how television content, in particular, has been produced by and for middle-class people. Although many commercial television companies are owned by upper-class individuals, the media and creative professionals making the programmes are part of the middle class. Furthermore, most of the content we see on television either features middle-class individuals (both in fiction and factual formats) and/or is created with a middle-class audience in mind (Bullock et al., 2001; Fiske, 1987; Mantsios, 1995). As a consequence, middle-class cultures, including their sets of norms, values, and practices, tend to form the dominant ideological framework underpinning plenty of television content, ranging from serious and news-oriented formats to fiction and entertainment (Bullock et al., 2001; Butsch, 1995). At the same time, many audiences are not *aware* of the ideological discourses embedded in the content they consume.

Roland Barthes's (1957) ex-nomination allows us to make sense of this. Barthes used the concept to discuss how the bourgeoisie took on the role of 'the social class which does not want to be named', thereby becoming invisible and allegedly apolitical and non-ideological. In contemporary society, the (upper-)middle class has become the *invisible* class. Although presumed to be non-ideological, middle-class media and cultural professionals have played an important part in setting out which practices, norms, and values are legitimate and which ones are not through the content they create. Since this content is also consumed by subordinated classes, it is fair to say that they may feel pressured to reflect upon their own class identities and taste cultures through the middle-class lenses that shape plenty of popular culture content. This argument resembles Marx's and Althusser's argument about the role of the superstructure in upholding the social status quo. In this instance, Althusser (1971) would argue that television should be understood as an ISA that hails its audiences as subjects that support the capitalist mode of production. Television, like other media, presents us with a sense of realism that originates from a middle-class perspective, but which is framed as the 'normal' way of living one's life and thereby implied to be non-ideological (Althusser, 1971; Bullock et al., 2001; Fiske, 1987; Kendall, 2016). Consequentially, media and popular culture prompt working-poor and working-class audiences to question their lifestyles and cultural practices – which are represented as not legitimate – and aspire to embody or emulate middle-class lifestyles.

A first practice of ex-nomination concerns the way middle-class people are represented in television content. In effect, most of the people we see on television are part of the middle class. The sheer volume of middle-class characters implies a wide range of diversity as they are shown in a plethora of professions and represented in a more nuanced way when compared to the other classes and, as such, are able to amply demonstrate their lifestyles as normal and/or the norm people from subordinated classes should aspire to. In other words, drawing on Bourdieu, television has been able to articulate middle-class culture as a legitimate culture (Skeggs, 2009). In contrast, there is a sheer volume of programmes that tend to stereotype the other classes (see below).

A second practice of ex-nomination involves the act of literally removing middle-class individuals from the screen but retaining their gaze. At the start of this chapter, *Filthy Rich and Homeless* and *Astrid and Natalia: Back to Reality* (see above) served as illustrations of programmes in which topics such as homelessness, poverty, and upper-class lifestyles are represented as issues that are out of the ordinary. These and other programmes tend to depict rich people as unworldly and naïve, poor people as pitiful, and working-class people as uncultured. Although middle-class individuals may not be at the centre of these programmes, their taste cultures, norms, and values surely act as reference points.

Bearing this in mind, it is interesting to explore the practices used to represent different social classes. So far, it should be clear that both communication scientists and cultural and media scholars have an interest in studying whether or not people are being stereotyped. Even though the two approaches hold different assumptions about how stereotypes function and how they impact audiences (see Chapters 1 and 2), their descriptions and discussions of class stereotypes can be valuable to both. That is why this chapter's last part simultaneously draws on authors and concepts from both traditions.

The main source of inspiration is Diana Kendall's (2016) analysis of social class in American media culture. Kendall is a sociologist who relied on framing theory (see Chapter 4) to discuss how the different social classes were represented. However, rather than only discussing the frames she found, I extended her work by incorporating other practices of representing the social classes on television.

4.1. The upper classes

Broadly speaking, the televised representations of the upper classes – especially of those with great economic capital – fall into two broad categories. On the one hand, there is television content that glorifies the lifestyles of the upper classes.

Kendall (2016) elaborated on the positive framing she found in American television content. She discussed three types of framing: consensus framing, admiration framing, and emulation framing. First, consensus framing refers to images that present the wealthy as ordinary people. This corresponds to, for instance, reality series about the everyday lives of famous and/or rich individuals (e.g. *Keeping Up with the Kardashians* (E!, 2007–2021), *Astrid in Wonderland* (VIJFtv, 2011–2013)), zooming in on mundane moments that allow for recognition. In other words, these programmes aim to represent upper-class individuals as resembling the audience, which is imagined as middle-class. Second, admiration framing refers to images of the wealthy as caring and generous individuals who reach out to the world. They are still represented as rich and privileged, but the privilege is framed as a means to engage in charity and do good deeds. Kendall is particularly concerned about the third type, emulation framing, which "suggests that people in all classes should reward themselves with a few of the perks of the wealthy, such as a larger house, a more luxurious vehicle, or better jewelry" (p. 24). This type of framing implies that consumerism can be used to symbolically move up the class ladder: social mobility is there if you want it, just dress differently, live differently, tidy up your house, and clean up your act. In reality, though, such programmes may push middle- and working-class individuals into large debts.

On the other hand, there is television content that criticises the lifestyles of the upper classes. Many will think of the rather unsubtle accounts of rich, one-dimensional villains in plenty of children's animation. Yet, there is also the genre of fictional satire about upper-class people. In these accounts, upper-class characters are not represented as easy-to-beat villains or helping hands in the process of climbing the social ladder, but as people who are unaware of their class status, privileges, and social impact on the other classes. Some recent examples include *Succession* (HBO, 2018–present), *Knokke Off* [High Tides] (VRT, 2023–present), and *The White Lotus* (HBO, 2021–present). *The White Lotus*'s first season, for instance, takes place at a Hawaiian holiday resort and documents the experiences of both the staff and the wealthy guests. Despite portraying a few of the upper-class characters as sympathetic, it becomes clear that none of them has any profound interest in questioning their class position. Instead, they assume that their class status entitles them to expect that the staff should respond to every whim or act as an emotional sounding board. Since the upper management of these upscale resorts demands their personnel to subordinate themselves to the guests, the working-class staff have no other choice but to weigh their options: accommodate the rich's often ridiculous requests or run the risk of becoming unemployed. For instance, only minutes after arriving at the hotel, Tanya (Jennifer Coolidge), a wealthy white woman, tells the staff that she is in dire need of a massage. She prods Belinda (Natasha Rothwell), a black woman who manages the hotel's spa, to help her out even though there is no one available. Throughout her stay, Tanya increasingly relies on Belinda and even promises to help her by investing in her own spa business, a promise that is not kept by the end of the season (see figure 51). This storyline is but one of many in the series. Taken together, these narratives expose the unequal impact a class-based society has upon individuals.

Figure 51. Still from *The White Lotus* (2021–present). Belinda (Natasha Rothwell) gives a massage to Tanya (Jennifer Coolidge). Courtesy Everett Collection.

4.2. Poor and homeless persons

Poor and homeless people are, in general, kept out of sight (Bullock et al., 2001; Kendall, 2016). If represented, classist stereotypes are often used. For instance, Heather Bullock et al. (2001) found that representations about poor people suggested that poor people's class status was the result of individual, characterological deficiencies and moral failings, such as crime or substance abuse. Similarly, welfare recipients have been represented as immoral, lacking initiative, and neglectful, especially when it concerns single mothers who are also held responsible for breaking up the nuclear family. Tracey Jensen (2014, 2018) explored this as well by reflecting on a series of British reality-television programmes, such as

Benefits Street (Channel 4, 2014–2015), that dealt with poverty in an apolitical manner. These programmes are sometimes referred to as 'poverty porn' as they objectify poor people to entertain the other classes. Jensen argued that these programmes participate in distributing unfounded and popularised ideas about welfare. The poor people are "presented as undisciplined, lazy and shameless, neither legitimate citizen nor consumer, exiled from the routine of the working day and forever trying to grasp yet more from the very benefits system that has created their condition of dependence" (Jensen, 2018, p. 152). In framing poverty as an individual problem – by, for instance, arguing that one is poor due to a lack of self-discipline, resilience, and a history of bad choices – rather than a structural problem – by contextualising poverty vis-à-vis austerity politics – television has been able to distance its audiences from taking structural inequality seriously. Kendall too wrote about these practices in exploring the framing of poor people. She referred to this practice as episodic framing, which is used when media highlight some problems of poverty but refrain from linking the personal situations of poor and homeless people "to such larger societal problems as limited educational opportunities, high unemployment rates, and jobs that pay depressingly low wages" (2016, p. 27).

Last, concerning news media, Kendall mentioned the practice of thematic framing. This practice is used when the poor and homeless only figure as 'faceless' statistics in reports on poverty. These reports frame the poor and homeless as figures of otherness, to be pitied at most. Yet, they do not create opportunities for empathy or identification, in contrast to the practice of admiration framing used to depict upper-class individuals.

4.3. *The working classes*

Working-class people and working-class issues are of little concern to television or even mainstream media in general. Kendall (2016) highlighted how there is little room in mainstream media to focus on issues that are pertinent to working-class communities: low wages, lack of benefits, and hazardous working conditions. Akin to the portrayal of poor people, classist stereotypes have been used to represent the working class. Kendall applied the concept of caricature framing to describe how mainstream media mock and demean the lifestyles of working-class people. Following Bourdieu, it becomes apparent that a lack of cultural capital is often used to belittle working-class individuals. This type of framing is particularly deployed in reality-television programmes or comedy content (e.g. Lockyer, 2010).

Especially makeover television has been prone to using classist stereotypes. In many makeover television programmes, a working-class individual has to be transformed into a new and improved subject. Programmes such as *What Not to Wear* (BBC, 2001–2007), *The Biggest Loser* (NBC, 2004–2016), *Extreme Makeover: Home Edition* (ABC, 2004–2012), and *Supernanny* (Channel 4, 2004–2008) centre on working-class people who, at the start of the programme, are depicted as persons who are unable to keep their houses clean, raise their children, dress well, or stay healthy. With the 'help' of (upper-)middle-class experts and hosts, participants are taught that self-work, self-development, and taking responsibility are essential meritocratic traits, while being nudged to exercise, dress properly (making sure the colours match), act and talk correctly, and develop appropriate tastes (e.g. house decoration). As should be clear by now, these traits, practices, and taste cultures are all rooted in middle-class lifestyles (Allen & Mendick, 2013; Kendall, 2016; McRobbie, 2004a; Skeggs & Wood, 2011). Angela McRobbie (2004a), speaking of women-centric programmes such as *What Not to Wear*, was appalled by how these programmes denigrated women through acts of symbolic violence. Using Bourdieu's concept of symbolic violence, which refers to the subtle ways class distinctions and hierarchies are reinforced, she argued that these programmes enabled young middle-class women to use humiliation, hurtful comments, and insult – under the pretext of irony – to 'improve' working-class women. Recent makeover television programmes, such as *Queer Eye* (Netflix, 2018–present) and its adaptation *Queer Eye Germany* (Netflix, 2022), have tried to be more mindful of sociocultural diversity in Western society (e.g. choosing candidates with diverse minoritised identities). Yet, since these formats too are commercial by nature, emphasised by, for instance, the product placement and the programme's hosts being part of the (upper-)middle-class in society, they fail to take working-class individuals seriously. This can be discerned in the hosts' discourses of self-improvement, which remain rooted in neoliberal, meritocratic, and middle-class principles, norms, and values, even though these shows are intended to help the (oftentimes) working-class subjects find their 'true' selves.

However, there has been an increase in fictional and factual programmes that offer balanced portrayals of working-class communities while looking for ways to let middle-class audiences become aware of their privileges, such as HBO's *Treme*.

Focus on *Treme*

An example of a television series that succeeds in bringing a nuanced, well-informed, and critical representation of class inequality is *Treme* (HBO, 2010-2013). The drama series is created by Eric Overmeyer and David Simon. *Treme* is set in New Orleans, three months after Hurricane Katrina hit the city in 2005. The series explores how several characters, diverse in age, gender, ethnic/racial background, and social class, deal with the aftermath of the storm. The name of the series refers to its main setting, the Faubourg Tremé neighbourhood, "known for its early engagement with the civil rights movement and known also as the birthplace of Jazz" (Gendrin et al., 2012, pp. 290-291).

In *Treme*, social class and race intersect. Many episodes illustrate how, first, the floods disproportionally impacted impoverished black neighbourhoods. Second, it also depicts how (predominantly) white politicians, real estate agents, and insurance companies have not been of any help and, even worse, have hampered or counteracted the material and symbolic recovery of working-class neighbourhoods. This is made tangible in the story of Albert Lambreaux (Clarke Peters), an older man whose house got damaged during the floods but who refuses to leave the neighbourhood (see figure 52). He is also known as Big Chief of the Guardians of the Flame, one of the Black Mardi Gras Indian tribes. Black Mardi Gras Indian culture is a unique culture that goes back to Louisiana in the eighteenth century when enslaved African and indigenous people were able to escape and establish communities together. Informed by their shared ancestry and experiencing exclusion, slavery, and racism, Mardi Gras tribes developed, which were originally intended as mutual aid societies. Nowadays, the tribes use their participation in the annual carnival as a means to articulate "a renewed expression of core values and beliefs that operate in the everyday life of Black workers in New Orleans" (Gendrin et al., 2012, p. 293), including resistance to practices and discourses that express white supremacy. An important ritual is the creation of suits that are informed by the Indian dress of the Plains Indians and the beadwork of the Yoruba people of Nigeria (Gendrin et al., 2012).

Especially remarkable is a scene that is shown at the end of 'Right Place, Wrong Time' (season 1, episode 3). Albert Lambreaux and a few people are mourning the death of a friend. They engage in an

Indian ritual that is used during funeral processions. The ritual is interrupted by a white bus that stops outside the house where the ritual is held. It is a tourist bus that offers 'Katrina Tours'. Not only does the bus disturb the ritual, but its invisible passengers also intrude on the mourners by flashing their cameras. The bus and its passengers represent the (upper-)middle class. They are able to afford to travel and are often unaware, by being symbolically and literally remote from working-class communities, about the everyday lives and challenges of working-class people. In this scene, the series criticises the bus and its passengers: the bus represents yet another commercial company making a profit from other people's misery – presenting disaster tourism as a form of poverty porn – while the passengers are represented as unaware of their privileges. The scene seems created to nudge its audiences, which are mainly (upper-)middle-class individuals since not everyone can afford to pay for HBO or other subscription-based television content, to look inward.

Figure 52. On-set photograph from *Treme* (2010–2013), with Clarke Peters as Albert. Photo credit: Blown Deadline Productions/Bolen, Skip/Album, © Imageselect/Alamy.

4.4. The middle classes

Last, the classes that are represented the most are also the ones that are – in terms of their class identity – the least stereotyped. For Kendall, it is clear that media frame the middle classes as the value centre and backbone of a given nation. Hence, she argued that mainstream media generally engage in middle-class-values framing, which is used to imply that "the mores of this class hold the nation together" (2016, p. 29). Despite economic and social insecurities experienced by many middle-class families in the twenty-first century (Kendall, 2016; Polson et al., 2020), many television programmes tend to avoid broaching these insecurities and continue to represent middle-class identities as aspirational. In other words, rather than accumulating a certain proportion of economic capital, one can belong to the middle class by appropriating middle-class lifestyles. Following Bourdieu, different middle-class fractions resulted in different middle-class lifestyles, creating the impression of a diversity in cultural tastes and styles. In general, the diverse middle-class lifestyles represented on screen are deemed to be legitimate and not in opposition to the interests of the television industry. Especially commercial television companies have invested in content that represents and/or attracts the middle classes as they are the favoured target consumers of advertisers (Kendall, 2016).

In her conclusion, Kendall (2016) stressed the difficulty of truly challenging the dominance of middle-classness. She pointed out the reality of increased concentrated media ownership and strong ties between the corporate-media elites and the upper class. She found it quite unlikely that mainstream media would ever contribute to raising awareness and creating class consciousness, as a crisis between the classes would not be in the interest of media owners. Like many other scholars (e.g. O'Neill & Wayne, 2017a), she has set her hope on journalism, particularly civic journalism and alternative digital news media. As Kendall (2016) stressed:

> Just as more journalists have become aware of the importance of fair and accurate representations of people based on race, gender, age, disability, and sexual orientation, we may be able to improve media representations of class. Rather than pitting the middle class against the working class and the poor, for example, the media might frame stories in such a way as to increase people's awareness of their shared concerns in a nation where members of the upper class typically get portrayed as more important and more deserving than the average citizen. (p. 39)

If news media would succeed at that, the question remains whether audiovisual *fiction* – which is expensive, time-consuming, and difficult to produce outside of a capitalist production industry – could also reach that point. Especially if the goal is to have critical television content broadcast to large audiences on public or commercial broadcasting channels, hoping for impact, rather than to niche audiences via online channels.

Epilogue

"Michelle Yeoh Is Oscars' First Asian Best Actress Winner: 'This is a Beacon of Hope and Possibilities'" (Sun, 2023)

"Troy Kotsur becomes first Deaf man to win acting Oscar" (Linton, 2022)

"Kim Petras and Sam Smith become the first transgender and nonbinary winners of the Grammy for Best Pop Duo Performance" (Mandler, 2023)

Arriving at the end of this book, some readers may wonder whether things are looking up for the representation of sociocultural diversity in popular media culture. My selection of headlines highlighting first-time wins at major award ceremonies indicates some patterns are being challenged. Simply scroll back to the pages highlighting the gendered and racialised double standards at work in the music industry to understand the value of these wins. After years of calling out the underrepresentation of diversity in nominated artists in music, television, and film awards, minoritised media professionals are finally recognised for their artistic contributions. In turn, they are able to serve as role models for aspiring artists, directors, or content creators.

The headlines also illustrate something else, namely the news media's awareness of the historical significance of these first-time triumphs. Although some journalists could have done their homework better – the first trans woman to win at the Grammy's was composer Wendy Carlos, taking home three awards for her classical-meets-electric debut *Switched-On Bach* (1968) – they understood that to write about these victories was to situate them in a long history of omission, underrepresentation, and trivialisation. One could argue that by focusing on the minoritised identity of the winners, the headlines downplayed their artistic qualities. Although such scepticism is not unwarranted, the critical acknowledgement or popularity of minoritised music artists or content creators is rarely based on their (minoritised) identity alone. Take, for instance, the commercial and critical successes of female music artists in the summer of 2024: Sabrina Carpenter scored a global hit with 'Espresso' (2024); Billie Eilish established herself with her third album *Hit Me Hard and Soft*, which overtly references her same-sex desires; and Chappell Roan convinced global audiences with her impassioned pop music and queer aesthetics. Not to mention Taylor Swift's ambitious career-spanning Eras Tour, which (so far) has collected 1 billion dollars in revenue, something only Coldplay had succeeded in doing.

Figure 53. Left: Charli xcx on stage at Roskilde Festival 2024, Denmark. Right: Album cover of *BRAT*. Photo credit image: Gonzales Photo, Bo Kallberg, © Imageselect/Alamy. Photo credit album cover: Asylum, Atlantic and Warner UK, Wikimedia public domain.

Yet, writing this epilogue at the end of a summer dubbed by digital enthusiasts a 'brat summer' after Charli xcx's album *BRAT* (2024), the British artist too deserves a spot here (see figure 53). While many people wanted to capitalise on Charli xcx's success – the distinct lime-green cover art became a popular filter on social media, for better or worse – Charli xcx used her popularity and music to present an alternative femininity. Columnist Zoe Williams (2024), trying to grasp what brat as a phenomenon meant, did not consider being 'brat' a feminine ideal, "because it rejects the social surveillance that requires all young women to be the same way" (Williams, 2024). Rather, she felt that it pertained to hedonistic pleasures, sexual agency, or trashy aesthetics, illustrated in the way Charli xcx described the essentials for a brat summer to be a "pack of cigs, a Bic lighter and a strappy white top with no bra" (Williams, 2024). Most of all, the audacity of *BRAT* – accentuated in the lyrics, music videos, hyper-pop sounds, clubbing and party aesthetics, and the string of remixes with artists such as Billie Eilish and Troye

Sivan – has come across as freeing oneself from socially imposed norms, of which many are gendered. It is not simply a pose as the stakes are real. Noteworthy is the remix of 'Girl, so confusing', which features vocals by Lorde. In the original version, Charli xcx sings honestly and directly about feeling uncertain about a friendship with another female musician, implied to be Lorde: "Yeah, I don't know if you like me / Sometimes I think you might hate me / Sometimes I think I might hate you / Maybe you just wanna be me." Prior to the release of the album, she reached out to Lorde with a voice note about the song. The original version, featuring a line that predicts a collaboration between the two would make the internet go crazy, may have compelled Lorde to suggest that they should make a new version of the song together (Robinson, 2024). Lorde's verse on the remix reveals how she was grappling with her own issues and insecurities, including body dissatisfaction, which had an impact on how she approached her friendship with Charli xcx: "I was so lost in my head / And scared to be in your pictures / Cause for the last couple years / I've been at war with my body." In acknowledging each other's insecurities vis-à-vis a society that projects its gendered norms, values, and expectations on celebrities and tabloid media vying for feuds between female stars, Charli xcx and Lorde represent female friendship in all its complexities. As Lorde said to *Billboard*, "I love that we truly did work it out on the remix. There's something very *brat* about that, something very meta and modern" (Robinson, 2024).

But let us not get complacent and fall into the trap postfeminist thinking did when proclaiming that equality was achieved when several women attained notable positions in political, economic, and cultural institutions. One swallow does not make a (brat) summer. If anything, this book aimed to demonstrate how an academic perspective on sociocultural diversity and popular media culture can provide depth, nuance, and insights. Rather than making big unfounded statements, scholars of communication sciences and media and cultural studies will ask diverse and complex questions to grasp, for instance, gender inequalities in the music industry in-depth. How much money do female artists make annually compared to male artists? How much airplay do female artists receive compared to male artists? How do women experience working in the music industry? Why have music journalists framed this summer as a successful summer for female artists? Which discourses and images of femininity are represented by the artists seen as successful and to what extent do they challenge the music industry's pattern of hegemonic masculinity? Scholars will also have to factor in aspects that relate to intersectionality and explore whether there are differences when we look at one's age or racial and ethnic background. The diverse questions illustrate how one type of study alone will not provide conclusive answers and demonstrate the necessity of having researchers from different research fields study the same topic.

With this book, I wanted to display the work already done. Scholars in communication sciences and media and cultural studies have provided rich histories that allow us to comprehend how minoritised identities have been represented in the past and to what extent the politics of representation became more inclusive. They developed concepts and theories that enable us to understand how mundane media production processes have been racialised, how much television entertainment starts from middle-class norms and values, and why certain expressions in everyday speech are ableist. Furthermore, they showed that the meaning of certain practices of representation, such as stereotyping or self-deprecating humour, is far from unequivocal. At the same time, this book has restricted itself to a selection of identity axes, which is why it does not explore the identity axis of age and only touches upon religion briefly. Further, the book only covers a limited number of authors, topics, and cases. Hence, subjects like the manosphere, body positivity, or the gendered dimensions of horror did not make the cut, although they are certainly worthy of exploring.

Moreover, new media developments are demanding novel approaches and concepts. Especially artificial intelligence (AI) is booming and impacting many aspects of contemporary society, including the production and consumption of media and popular culture. Think of AI-generated porn platforms that create unrealistic gendered body ideals and reiterate heteronormative and patriarchal tropes (Wiggers, 2022) or the widespread distribution of nonconsensual deepnudes (AI-generated nudes) of predominantly female celebrities (Robertson, 2024). These are but a few new challenges for students and scholars in communication sciences and media and cultural studies. With this book, I hope to have given those interested in these timely topics a solid introduction and to have whet your appetite to explore matters of representation yourself.

Acknowledgements

I want to start by thanking the two anonymous peer reviewers for making time to read the entire manuscript and providing me with helpful notes, fresh ideas, and essential comments. Further, I am grateful to Sander De Ridder, Hanne Van Haelter, Wiebe Copman, Jorn Verschuere, Alexander De Man, Ben De Smet, Florian Vanlee, Laurens Dhaenens, Eduard Cuelenaere, and Salma Mediavilla Aboulaoula for providing me with critical and encouraging feedback on parts and aspects of this book. I also want to thank Sofie Van Bauwel, Lies Van de Vijver, Daniel Biltereyst, Stijn Joye, Tom Evens, and Koen Ponnet for their tips and tricks. Another thank you goes to Beatrice De Keyzer and her colleagues at Academia Press for their care in producing this book and going the extra mile to arrange images. I also want to thank the many students I had the pleasure of teaching and whose feedback strengthened the ideas expressed in this book. Last, a heartfelt thank you goes out to my friends, family, and Maarten for their encouragement, feedback, and support.

References

Aaron, M. (Ed.). (2004). *New queer cinema: A critical reader.* Rutgers University Press.

Adriaens, F. (2014). 'Diaspora girls doing identities': Creating ideal television programmes and narratives of the self. *European Journal of Cultural Studies, 17*(2), 101-117.

Adriaens, F., & Van Bauwel, S. (2014). *Sex and the City*: A postfeminist point of view? Or how popular culture functions as a channel for feminist discourse. *Journal of Popular Culture, 47*(1), 174-195.

Allen, K., & Mendick, H. (2013). Keeping it real? Social class, young people and 'authenticity' in reality TV. *Sociology, 47*(3), 460-476.

Allington, D. (2007). "How come most people don't see it?": Slashing *The Lord of the Rings*. *Social Semiotics, 17*(1), 43-62.

Althusser, L. (1971). *Lenin and philosophy, and other essays.* New Left Books.

Andrews, E. E. (2019). *Disability as diversity: Developing cultural competence.* Oxford University Press.

Ang, I. (1996). *Living room wars: Rethinking media audiences for a postmodern world.* Routledge.

Armstrong, E. A., & Crage, S. M. (2006). Movements and memory: The making of the Stonewall myth. *American Sociological Review, 71*(5), 724-751.

Arnesen, A. L., & Allan, J. (2009). *Policies and practices for teaching sociocultural diversity: Concepts, principles and challenges in teacher education.* Council of Europe.

Avila-Saavedra, G. (2009). Nothing queer about queer television: Televized construction of gay masculinities. *Media, Culture & Society, 31*(1), 5-21.

Back, L., Bennett, A., Edles, L. D., Gibson, M., Inglis, D., Jacobs, R., & Woodward, I. (2012). *Cultural sociology: An introduction.* John Wiley & Sons.

Banet-Weiser, S. (2018). Postfeminism and popular feminism. *Feminist Media Histories, 4*(2), 152-156.

Baptista, I., & Marlier, E. (2022). *Social protection for people with disabilities in Europe: An analysis of policies in 35 countries.* Publications Office of the European Union.

Barash, A. (2021, April 5). *Josh Thomas's comedy of self-diagnosis.* The New Yorker. https://www.newyorker.com/magazine/2021/04/12/josh-thomas-comedy-of-self-diagnosis

Barkan, E. (1992). *The retreat of scientific racism: Changing concepts of race in Britain and the United States between the World Wars.* Cambridge University Press.

Barker, C. (2012). *Cultural studies: Theory and practice* (4th ed.). SAGE.

Barnes, C. (1992). *Disabling imagery and the media: An exploration of the principles for media representations of disabled people.* Ryburn Publishing.

Baroutsis, A., Eckert, C., Newman, S., & Adams, D. (2023). How is autism portrayed in news media? A content analysis of Australian newspapers articles from 2016-2018. *Disability & Society, 38*(6), 963-986.

Barrios, R. (2003). *Screened out.* Routledge.

Barthes, R. (1957). *Mythologies.* Éditions du Seuil.

Battles, K., & Hilton-Morrow, W. (2002). Gay characters in conventional spaces: *Will & Grace* and the situation comedy genre. *Critical Studies in Media Communication, 19*(1), 87-105.

Bayton, M. (1997). Women and the electric guitar. In S. Whiteley (Ed.), *Sexing the groove: Popular music and gender* (pp. 37-49). Routledge.

Beasley, C. (2008). Rethinking hegemonic masculinity in a globalizing world. *Men and masculinities, 11*(1), 86-103.

Behdad, A. (2010). Orientalism Matters. *MFS Modern Fiction Studies, 56*(4), 709-728.

Bell-Metereau, R. (2019). *Transgender cinema*. Rutgers University Press.

Ben-Ghiat, R. (2001). The Italian cinema and the Italian working class. *International Labor and Working-Class History, 59*, 36-51.

Bennett, A. (1999). Rappin' on the Tyne: White hip hop culture in Northeast England-an ethnographic study. *The Sociological Review, 47*(1), 1-24.

Bennett, A. (2008). Towards a cultural sociology of popular music. *Journal of Sociology, 44*(4), 419-432.

Bennett, T., Savage, M., Silva, E. B., Warde, A., Gayo-Cal, M., & Wright, D. (2009). *Culture, class, distinction*. Routledge.

Benshoff, H. M., & Griffin, S. (2021). *America on film: Representing race, class, gender, and sexuality at the movies*. John Wiley & Sons.

Berkers, P., & Eeckelaer, M. (2014). Rock and roll or rock and fall? Gendered framing of the rock and roll lifestyles of Amy Winehouse and Pete Doherty in British broadsheets. *Journal of Gender Studies, 23*(1), 3-17.

Bernstein, M. (2002). Identities and politics: Toward a historical understanding of the lesbian and gay movement. *Social Science History, 26*(3), 531-581.

Bernstein, M. (2005). Identity politics. *Annual Review of Sociology, 31*, 47-74.

Bhabba, H. K. (1994). *The location of culture*. Routledge.

Billard, T. J. (2016). Writing in the margins: Mainstream news media representations of transgenderism. *International Journal of Communication, 10*, 4193-4218.

Billard, T. J., & Zhang, E. (2022). Toward a transgender critique of media representation. *JCMS: Journal of Cinema and Media Studies, 61*(2), 194-199.

Black, G. D. (1989). Hollywood censored: The Production Code Administration and the Hollywood film industry, 1930-1940. *Film History, 3*(3), 167-189.

Bogaert, A. F. (2015). Asexuality: What it is and why it matters. *Journal of Sex Research, 52*(4), 362-379.

Bogdan, R. (1996). The social construction of freaks. In R. Garland-Thomson (Ed.), *Freakery: Cultural spectacles of the extraordinary body* (pp. 23-38). New York University Press.

Bond, B. J. (2013). Physical disability on children's television programming: A content analysis. *Early Education & Development, 24*(3), 408-418.

Bonneure, K. (2020, July 22). *VRT schrapt aflevering "FC De Kampioenen" wegens racisme: "Past niet meer bij de tijdsgeest van vandaag"* [VRT cancels episode of "FC De Kampioenen": "Does not fit today's zeitgeist"]. VRT NWS. https://www.vrt.be/vrtnws/nl/2020/07/17/vrt-schrapt-aflevering-fc-de-kampioenen-wegens-racisme-past-ni/

Bordages, A. (2023, January 31). *L'épisode 3 de "The Last of Us" est tout simplement miraculeux* [The third episode of "The Last of Us" is simply miraculous]. Slate. https://www.slate.fr/story/239851/pourquoi-episode-3-the-last-of-us-deja-un-des-plus-beaux-annee-serie-tele-long-time

Bordwell, D., & Thompson, K. (2003). *Film history: An introduction*. McGraw-Hill.

Bosmans, G. (2024, February 21). *Alleenstaande moeder reageert op "Astrid en Natalia: back to reality"* [Single mother reacts to "Astrid and Natalia: back to reality"] VRT NWS. https://www.vrt.be/vrtnws/nl/2024/02/21/veel-kritiek-op-astrid-en-natalia-back-to-reality/

Bourabain, D., Verhaeghe, P., & Stevens, P. (2023). School of choice or schools' choice? Intersectional correspondence testing on ethnic and class discrimination in the enrolment procedure to Flemish kindergarten. *Race Ethnicity and Education, 26*(2), 184-204.

Bourdieu, P. (1984). *Distinction*. Harvard University Press.

Bourdieu, P. (1987). What makes a social class? On the theoretical and practical existence of groups. *Berkeley Journal of Sociology, 32*, 1-17.

Bracewell, L. N. (2016). Beyond Barnard: Liberalism, antipornography feminism, and the sex wars. *Signs: Journal of Women in Culture and Society, 42*(1), 23-48.

Brackett, D. (1994). The politics and practice of "crossover" in American popular music, 1963 to 1965. *The Musical Quarterly, 78*(4), 774-797.

Brackett, D. (2003). What a difference a name makes: Two instances of African-American popular music. In M. Clayton, T. Herbert, & R. Middleton (Eds*.), The cultural study of music: A critical introduction* (pp. 238-250). Routledge.

Brah, A., & Phoenix, A. (2004). Ain't I a woman? Revisiting intersectionality. *Journal of International Women's Studies, 5*(3), 75-86.

Brickell, C. (2006). The sociological construction of gender and sexuality. *The Sociological Review, 54*(1), 87-113.

Brisenden, S. (1986). Independent living and the medical model of disability. *Disability, Handicap & Society, 1*(2), 173-178.

Brockes, E. (2018, January 15). #MeToo founder Tarana Burke: 'You have to use your privilege to serve other people.' The Guardian. https://www.theguardian.com/world/2018/jan/15/me-too-founder-tarana-burke-women-sexual-assault

Broos, D., & Van den Bulck, H. (2012). One religion, many identities? The reception of Islam related news items by Muslim women with Turkish, Moroccan and Flemish roots in Flanders. *Middle East Journal of Culture and Communication, 5*(2), 116-134.

Brubaker, R. (2005). The 'diaspora' diaspora. *Ethnic and Racial Studies, 28*(1), 1-19.

Buckingham, D. (1993). Introduction: Young people and the media. In D. Buckingham (Ed.), *Reading audiences: Young people and the media* (pp. 1-23). Manchester University Press.

Bullock, H. E., Wyche, K. F., & Williams, W. R. (2001). Media images of the poor. *Journal of Social Issues, 57*(2), 229-246.

Bullock, K., & Zhou, Z. (2017). Entertainment or blackface? Decoding Orientalism in a post-9/11 era: Audience views on Aladdin. *Review of Education, Pedagogy, and Cultural Studies, 39*(5), 446-469.

Bulut, S. (2022, March 2). *Charlotte Adigéry and Bolis Pupul on Their Political, "Club-Ready" Album*. AnOther Magazine. https://www.anothermag.com/design-living/13922/charlotte-adigery-bolis-pupul-on-their-political-club-ready-album-topical-dancer

Burch, L. (2020). 'The stuff of nightmares": Representations of disability on the online bulletin board Reddit. In J. Johanssen & D. Garrisi (Eds.), *Disability, media, and representations: Other bodies* (pp. 19-24). Routledge.

Butler, J. (1993). Imitation and gender insubordination. In H. Abelove, M. A. Barale, & D. M. Halperin (Eds.), *The Lesbian and Gay Studies Reader* (pp. 307-320). Routledge.

Butler, J. (1999). *Gender trouble: Feminism and the subversion of identity* (2nd ed.). Routledge.

Butler, J. (2024). *Who's afraid of gender?* Allen Lane.

Butsch, R. (1995). Ralph, Fred, Archie and Homer: Why television keeps recreating the white male working-class buffoon. In G. Dines & J. Humez (Eds.), *Gender, race, and class in the media: A text-reader* (pp. 403-412). SAGE.

Buxton, R. A. (1997). Sexual orientation and television. In H. Newcomb (Ed.), *Encyclopedia of television* (pp. 1477-1482). Fitzroy Dearborn.

Byrne, D. C. (2003). The top, the bottom and the middle: Space, class and gender in *Metropolis. Literator, 24*(3), 1-14.

Cammaerts, B. (2022). The abnormalisation of social justice: The 'anti-woke culture war' discourse in the UK. *Discourse & Society, 33*(6), 730-743.

Campbell, E. (1991). Obscenity, music and the First Amendment: Was the crew 2 lively? *Nova Law Review, 15*(1), 159-240.

Campbell, F. K. (2012). Stalking ableism: Using disability to expose 'abled' narcissism. In D. Goodley, B. Hughes, & L. Davis (Eds.), *Disability and social theory* (pp. 212-230). Palgrave Macmillan.

Capuzza, J. C., & Spencer, L. G. (2017). Regressing, progressing, or transgressing on the small screen? Transgender characters on US scripted television series. *Communication Quarterly, 65*(2), 214-230.

Center for Intersectionality and Social Policy Studies (n.d.). *Center for Intersectionality and Social Policy Studies.* https://intersectionality.law.columbia.edu/

Cervulle, M. (2021). *Dans le blanc des yeux. Diversité, racisme et médias [In the whites of your eyes. Diversity, racism and the media]*. Éditions Amsterdam.

Chambers, S. A. (2009). *The queer politics of television*. I. B. Tauris.

Changing Faces (n.d.). *I am not your villain: Equal representation of visible difference in film*. https://www.changingfaces.org.uk/get-involved/campaign-with-us/i-am-not-your-villian/

Charlotte Adigéry & Bolis Pupul (2019). *Charlotte Adigéry - High Lights*. YouTube. https://youtu.be/hCkTyEsCNL4

Chilton, L. (2023a, January 31). *The Last of Us director says he wanted to 'trick' viewers into watching episode three's gay romance*. The Independent. https://www.independent.co.uk/arts-entertainment/tv/news/last-of-us-episode-3-nick-offerman-b2272921.html

Chilton, L. (2023b, March 15). *The Last of Us episodes 'review-bombed' by homophobic trolls*. The Independent. https://www.independent.co.uk/arts-entertainment/tv/news/last-of-us-rotten-tomatoes-lgbt-b2301761.html

Cho, A. (2018). Default publicness: Queer youth of color, social media, and being outed by the machine. *New Media & Society, 20*(9), 3183-3200.

Church, D. (2011). Freakery, cult films, and the problem of ambivalence. *Journal of Film and Video, 63*(1), 3-17.

Clark, C., & Kaiser, W. (2003). Introduction: The European culture wars. In C. Clark & W. Kaiser (Eds.), *Culture wars: Secular-catholic conflict in nineteenth-century Europe* (pp. 1-10). Cambridge University Press.

Clawson, M. A. (1999). Masculinity and skill acquisition in the adolescent rock band. *Popular Music, 18*(1), 99-114.

Clayton, D. M. (2018). Black Lives Matter and the Civil Rights Movement: A comparative analysis of two social movements in the United States. *Journal of Black Studies, 49*(5), 448-480.

Coates, N. (1997). (R)Evolution now? Rock and the political potential of gender. In S. Whiteley (Ed.), *Sexing the groove: Popular music and gender* (pp. 50-64). Routledge.

Coleman, M. N., Reynolds, A. A., & Torbati, A. (2020). The relation of Black-oriented reality television consumption and perceived realism to the endorsement of stereotypes of Black women. *Psychology of Popular Media, 9*(2), 184-193.

Connell, R. (1997). Hegemonic masculinity and emphasized femininity. In L. Richardson, V. Taylor, & N. Whittier (Eds.), *Feminist frontiers IV* (pp. 22-25). McGraw-Hill.

Connell, R. (2005). *Masculinities*. Polity.

Connell, R. (2014). The study of masculinities. *Qualitative Research Journal, 14*(1), 1-14.

Connell, R. W., & Messerschmidt, J. W. (2005). Hegemonic masculinity: Rethinking the concept. *Gender & Society, 19*(6), 829-859.

Cook, (1996). *A history of narrative film* (3rd ed.). W. W. Norton & Company.

Cooper, R., Coles, A., & Hanna-Osborne, S. (2017). *Skipping a beat: Assessing the state of gender equality in the Australian music industry*. The University of Sydney.

Cottle, S. (2000). A rock and a hard place: Making ethnic minority television. In S. Cottle (Ed.), *Ethnic minorities and the media* (pp. 100-117). McGraw-Hill Education.

Cover, R., & Prosser, R. (2013). Memorial accounts: Queer young men, identity and contemporary coming out narratives online. *Australian Feminist Studies, 28*(75), 81-94.

Crenshaw, K. (1991). Mapping the margins: Intersectionality, identity politics, and violence against women of color. *Stanford Law Review, 43*(6), 1241-1299.

Crompton, R. (2008). *Class and stratification* (3rd ed.). Polity Press.

Cuelenaere, E., Willems, G., & Joye, S. (2019). Remaking identities and stereotypes: How film remakes transform and reinforce nationality, disability, and gender. *European Journal of Cultural Studies, 22*(5-6), 613-629.

Cumberbatch, G., & Negrine, R. (1992). *Images of disability on television*. Routledge.

Cunningham, S., & Sinclair, J. (Eds.). (2001). *Floating lives: The media and Asian diasporas*. Rowman & Littlefield.

Davis, N. A. (2005). Invisible disability. *Ethics, 116*(1), 153-213.

D'Emilio, J. (2007). Progress and representation. In K. Barnhurst (Ed.), *Media queered: visibility and its discontents* (pp. 23-26). Peter Lang Publishing.

D'Heer, J., De Vuyst, S., & Van Leuven, S. (2022). Gendering in the electoral run: A media monitoring study of women politicians' representation in Belgian news. *Journalism, 23*(11), 2289-2310.

D'Souza, R. A., & Rauchberg, J. S. (2020). Neoliberal values & queer/disability in *Margarita with a Straw*. *Journal of International and Intercultural Communication, 13*(2), 183-196.

Dastgeer, S., & Gade, P. J. (2016). Visual framing of Muslim women in the Arab Spring: Prominent, active, and visible. *International Communication Gazette, 78*(5), 432-450.

Davies, H. (2001). All rock and roll is homosocial: The representation of women in the British rock music press. *Popular Music, 20*(3), 301-319.

Davis, G., & Needham, G. (2009). Introduction: The pleasures of the tube. In G. Davis & G. Needham (Eds.), *Queer TV: Theories, histories, politics* (pp. 1-11). Routledge.

De Bens, E., & De Smaele, H. (2001). The inflow of American television fiction on European broadcasting channels revisited. *European Journal of Communication, 16*(1), 51-76.

De Boise, S. (2014). Cheer up emo kid: Rethinking the 'crisis of masculinity' in emo. *Popular Music, 33*(2), 225-242.

de Lauretis, T. (1991). Queer theory: Lesbian and gay sexualities. *differences: A Journal of Feminist Cultural Studies, 3*(2), iii-xviii.

De Man, A., Willems, G., & Biltereyst, D. (2024). Discourses of cultural diversity and inclusion in film policy: The case of Flanders (2002-2022). *European Journal of Cultural Studies*. Advance online publication: https://doi.org/10.1177/13675494241228937

De Smet, B., & Dhaenens, F. (2024). Heteromasculinity and queer reappropriation in music streaming practices exploring homonegative curation by ordinary Spotify users. *Feminist Media Studies, 24*(4), 695-712.

De Swert, K., Kuypers, I., & Walgrave, S. (2021). *Monitor Diversiteit 2021: Een kwantitatieve studie naar de zichtbaarheid van diversiteit op het scherm in Vlaanderen* (Presentation). https://www.vrt.be/content/dam/vrtbe/over-de-vrt/prestaties/Monitor%20Diversiteit%202021_Extern_JV.pdf

Deery, J., & Press, A. L. (2017). *Media and class: TV, film, and digital culture*. Routledge.

DEEWEE (n.d.). *Charlotte Adigéry & Bolis Pupul*. DEEWEE. https://deew.ee/catalogue/055

Deiter, N. E. (1976). The last minority: Television and gay people. *Television Quarterly, 13*(3), 69-72.

Delaney, B. (2018, August 15). *Filthy rich and homeless: Can empathy alone really change how we view disadvantage?* The Guardian. https://www.theguardian.com/tv-and-radio/2018/aug/15/filthy-rich-and-homeless-can-empathy-alone-really-change-how-we-view-disadvantage

Dennis, R. M. (1995). Social Darwinism, scientific racism, and the metaphysics of race. *Journal of Negro Education, 64*(3), 243-252.

Dhaenens, F. (2012a). *Gays on the small screen: A queer theoretical study into articulations of queer resistance in contemporary television fiction* (Doctoral dissertation, Ghent University).

Dhaenens, F. (2012b). Queer cuttings on YouTube: Re-editing soap operas as a form of fan-produced queer resistance. *European Journal of Cultural Studies, 15*(4), 442-456.

Dhaenens, F. (2012c). Reading gays on the small screen: A reception study among Flemish viewers of queer resistance in contemporary television fiction. *Javnost-The Public, 19*(4), 57-72.

Dhaenens, F. (2023). "Timeless" rock masculinities: Understanding the gendered dimension of an annual Belgian radio music poll. *Feminist Media Studies, 23*(1), 154-169.

Dhaenens, F., & De Ridder, S. (2015). Resistant masculinities in alternative R&B? Understanding Frank Ocean and The Weeknd's representations of gender. *European Journal of Cultural Studies, 18*(3), 283-299.

Dhaenens, F., Mediavilla Aboulaoula, S., & Lion, A. (2023). 'I'm just not gay-gay': Exploring same-sex desire and sexual minority identity formation in *SKAM* and its Western European remakes. *European Journal of Cultural Studies, 26*(6), 863-879.

Dhaenens, F., & Van Bauwel, S. (2017). Sex in sitcoms: Unravelling the discourses on sex in *Friends*. In C. Smith, F. Attwood, & B. McNair (Eds.), *The Routledge companion to media, sex and sexuality* (pp. 300-308). Routledge.

Dhaenens, F., & Van Bauwel, S. (2022). Textual Analysis: A practical introduction to studying texts in media and cultural studies. In P. A. J. Stevens (Ed.), *Qualitative data analysis: Key approaches* (pp. 271-289). SAGE.

Dhaenens, F., Van Bauwel, S., & Biltereyst, D. (2008). Slashing the fiction of queer theory: Slash fiction, queer reading, and transgressing the boundaries of screen studies, representations, and audiences. *Journal of Communication Inquiry, 32*(4), 335-347.

Diemer, M. A., Mistry, R. S., Wadsworth, M. E., López, I., & Reimers, F. (2013). Best practices in conceptualizing and measuring social class in psychological research. *Analyses of Social Issues and Public Policy, 13*(1), 77-113.

Donaldson, J. (1981). The visibility and image of handicapped people on television. *Exceptional Children, 47*(6), 413-416.

Doty, A. (1993). *Making things perfectly queer: Interpreting mass culture*. University of Minnesota Press.

Doty, A. (2000). *Flaming classics*. Routledge.

Downing, J. D. H., & Husband, C. (2005). *Representing 'race': Racisms, ethnicity and the media*. SAGE.

Driessens, O. (2013). Celebrity capital: Redefining celebrity using field theory. *Theory and Society, 42*, 543-560.

Dubois, W. E. B. (2008). *The souls of black folk.* Oxford University Press. (Original work published 1903)

Duggan, L. (2003). *The twilight of equality? Neoliberalism, cultural politics, and the attack on democracy*. Beacon.

Duncombe, S. (2002). Introduction. In S. Duncombe (Ed.), *Cultural resistance reader* (pp. 1-15). Verso.

Durham, M. G. & Kellner, D. M. (Eds.) (2006). *Media and cultural studies: Keyworks* (Rev. ed.). Blackwell.

During, S. (2005). *Cultural studies: A critical introduction*. Routledge.

Dworkin, A. (1985). Against the male flood: Censorship, pornography, and equality. *Harvard Women's Law Journal, 8*, 1-30.

Dwyer, D. (2022, June 24). *Supreme Court overturns Roe v. Wade in landmark case on abortion rights*. ABC News. https://abcnews.go.com/Politics/supreme-court-overturns-roe-wade-landmark-case-abortion/story?id=85160781

Dyer, R. (1979). In Defense of Disco. *Gay Left, 8*, 20-23.

Dyer, R. (1993). *The matter of images: Essays on representations*. Routledge.

Dyer, R. (1997). *White*. Routledge.

Dyer, R. (2002). *The culture of queers.* Routledge.

Dyer, R. (2003). *Now you see it: Historical studies in lesbian and gay film* (2nd ed.). Routledge.

Dyer, R. (2006). Stereotyping. In M. G. Durham & D. M. Kellner (Eds.), *Media and cultural studies: Keyworks* (Rev. ed., pp. 353-365). Blackwell. (Reprinted from *Gays and film*, pp. 27-39, by R. Dyer (ed.), 1984, Zoetrope)

Dyer, R. (Ed.). (1977). *Gays and film*. British Film Institute.

Edwards, J. (2022, August 2). *Beyoncé used 'ableist' slur in a new song. After uproar, she's deleting it*. The Washington Post. https://www.washingtonpost.com/nation/2022/08/02/beyonce-spaz-slur/

Ellcessor, E. (2017). Kickstarting community: Disability, access, and participation in *My Gimpy Life*. In E. Ellcessor & B. Kirkpatrick (Eds.), *Disability media studies* (pp. 31-51). New York University Press.

Ellcessor, E., & Kirkpatrick, B. (2019). Studying disability for a better cinema and media studies. *JCMS: Journal of Cinema and Media Studies, 58*(4), 139-144.

Ellcessor, E., Hagood, M., & Kirkpatrick, B. (2017). Introduction: Toward a disability media studies. In E. Ellcessor & B. Kirkpatrick (Eds.), *Disability media studies* (pp. 1-28). New York University Press.

Ellis, K. (2014). Cripples, bastards and broken things: Disability in *Game of Thrones*. *M/C Journal, 17*(5). https://doi.org/10.5204/mcj.895

Ellis, K. (2015). *Disability and popular culture: Focusing passion, creating community and expressing defiance*. Ashgate.

Ellis, K. (2019). *Disability and digital television cultures: Representation, access, and reception.* Routledge.

Ellis, K., & Goggin, G. (2015). *Disability & the media.* Palgrave.

Ellis, K., & Merchant, M. (2020). Disability media work. In K. Ellis, G. Goggin, B. Haller, & R. Curtis (Eds.), *The Routledge companion to disability and media* (pp. 387–399). Routledge.

Ellis, K., Goggin, G., Haller, B. & Curtis, R. (2020). Introduction. Disability and media – an emergent field. In K. Ellis, G. Goggin, B. Haller, & R. Curtis (Eds.), *The Routledge companion to disability and media* (pp. 1–9). Routledge.

Ellis-Petersen, H. (2017, May 26). *Miranda Hart: 'I used to think fame would justify my whole existence'.* The Guardian. https://www.theguardian.com/tv-and-radio/2017/may/26/miranda-hart-fame-would-justify-existence-comedian-interview

Elsaesser, T. (2013). Tales of sound and fury: Observations on the family melodrama. In B. K. Grant (Ed.), *Film genre reader IV* (pp. 433–462). University of Texas Press.

Ene, L., Fioroni, M., Fontaine, G., Grece, C., Kanzler, M., Lacourt, A., Munch, E., Radel, J., Schneeberger, A., Simone, P., & Valais, S. (2024). *Yearbook 2023/2024: Key trends.* European Audiovisual Observatory.

Entman, R. M. (1993). Framing: Toward clarification of a fractured paradigm. *Journal of Communication, 43*(4), 51–58.

Erni, J. N. (2001). Media studies and cultural studies: A symbiotic convergence. In T. Miller (Ed.), *A companion to cultural studies* (pp. 187–213). Blackwell.

Evens, T., & Donders, K. (2018). *Platform power and policy in transforming television markets.* Palgrave Macmillan.

Fanon, F. (2008). *Black skin, white masks* (C. L. Markmann Trans.). Pluto Press. (Original work published 1952)

Fausto☐Sterling, A. (1993). The five sexes. *The Sciences, 33*(2), 20–24.

Fawlty Towers: The Germans episode to be reinstated by UKTV (2020, June 13). BBC News. https://www.bbc.com/news/entertainment-arts-53032895

Fejes, F., & Petrich, K. (1993). Invisibility, homophobia and heterosexism: Lesbians, gays and the media. *Critical Studies in Mass Communication, 10*(4), 396–422.

Feldstein, R. (2005). "I don't trust you anymore": Nina Simone, culture, and black activism in the 1960s. *The Journal of American History, 91*(4), 1349–1379.

Fenimore, C. (2022, August 19). *Five fits with: Genre-defying singer-songwriter Tamino.* Esquire. https://www.esquire.com/style/mens-fashion/a40941860/five-fits-with-tamino/

Ferber, A. (2020, September 22). *Judith Butler on the culture wars, JK Rowling and living in "anti-intellectual times".* The New Statesman. https://www.newstatesman.com/long-reads/2020/09/judith-butler-culture-wars-jk-rowling-living-anti-intellectual-times

Ferguson, A. (1984). Sex war: The debate between radical and libertarian feminists. *Signs: Journal of Women in Culture and Society, 10*(1), 106–112.

Fischer, M. (2018). Queer and feminist approaches to transgender media studies. In D. Harp, J. Loke, & I. Bachmann (Eds.), *Feminist approaches to media theory and research* (pp. 93–107). Palgrave Macmillan.

Fisher, D., Hill, D., Grube, J., & Gruber, E. (2007). Gay, lesbian, and bisexual content on television: A quantitative analysis across two seasons. *Journal of Homosexuality, 52*(3–4), 167–188.

Fiske, J. (1987). *Television culture.* Routledge.

Florestal, (2021, 28 October). *The N word, a slur reclaimed.* Speakeasy Stage. https://www.speakeasystage.com/2021/10/28/the-n-word-a-slur-reclaimed/

Foster, J., & Pettinicchio, D. (2023). # DisabilityTikTok. In M. S. Jeffress et al. (Eds.), *The Palgrave handbook of disability and communication* (pp. 273–291). Springer International Publishing.

Foucault, M. (1998). *The will to knowledge: The history of sexuality volume 1* (R. Hurley, Trans.). Penguin. (Original work published 1976)

Friedan, B. (1963). *The feminine mystique.* W. W. Norton.

Frith, S. (1978). *The sociology of rock.* Constable.

Galupo, M. P. (2018). Plurisexual identity labels and the marking of bisexual desire. In D. Swan & S. Habibi (Eds.), *Bisexuality* (pp. 61–75). Springer.

Garnham, N. (1995). Political economy and cultural studies: Reconciliation or divorce? *Critical Studies In Mass Communication, 12*(1), 62–71.

Garofalo, R. (1994). Culture versus commerce: the marketing of black popular music. *Public Culture, 7*(1), 275–287.

Garton, S. (2004). *Histories of sexuality: Antiquity to sexual revolution.* Routledge.

Gauntlett, D. (2008). *Media, gender, and identity: An introduction* (2nd ed.). Routledge.

Gendrin, D. M., Dessinges, C., & Hajjar, W. (2012). Historicizing the Mardi Gras Indians in HBO's *Treme*: An emancipatory narrative. *Intercultural Communication Studies, 21*(1), 290–307.

Georgiou, M. (2005). Diasporic media across Europe: Multicultural societies and the universalism–particularism continuum. *Journal of Ethnic and Migration Studies, 31*(3), 481–498.

Gerbner, G. (1998). Cultivation analysis: An overview. *Mass Communication and Society, 1*(3-4), 175–194.

Gerbner, G., & Gross, L. (1976). Living with television: The violence profile. *Journal of Communication, 26*(2), 172–199.

Gill, R. (2007). *Gender and the media.* Polity.

Gilroy, P. (1987). *There ain't no black in the Union Jack: The cultural politics of race and nation.* Hutchinson.

Gilroy, P. (1993). *The black Atlantic: Modernity and double consciousness.* Harvard University Press.

GLAAD (2021). *Where We Are on TV Report – 2020-2021.* https://www.glaad.org/whereweareontv20

GLAAD (2024). *Where We Are on TV 2023-2024.* https://glaad.org/whereweareontv23/

Glynn, P. (2018, August 31). *The importance of being Idles: 'You are safe to be vulnerable'.* BBC News. https://www.bbc.com/news/entertainment-arts-45037339

Goethals, T., Mortelmans, D., & Van Hove, G. (2018). Toward a more balanced representation of disability? A content analysis of disability coverage in the Flemish print media. *Développement Humain, Handicap et Changement Social, 24*(1), 109–120.

Goodley, D. (2014). *Dis/ability studies: Theorising disablism and ableism.* Routledge.

Goodley, D. (2018). The dis/ability complex. *DiGeSt. Journal of Diversity and Gender Studies, 5*(1), 5–22.

Gramsci, A. (1971). *Selections from the prison notebooks.* Lawrence and Wishart.

Gray, J. (2006). *Watching with The Simpsons: Television, parody, and intertextuality.* Routledge.

Gross, L. (1991). Out of the mainstream: Sexual minorities and the mass media. *Journal of Homosexuality, 21*(1-2), 19–46.

Grossberg, L. (1995). Cultural studies vs. political economy: Is anybody else bored with this debate? *Critical Studies in Mass Communication, 12*(1), 72–81.

Grossberg, L., Nelson, C., & Treichler, P. A. (Eds.) (1992). *Cultural studies.* Routledge.

Grosz, E. (1984/85). Criticism, feminism and the institution: An interview with Gayatri Chakravorty Spivak. *Thesis Eleven,* (10-11), 175–187.

Grue, J. (2016). The problem with inspiration porn: A tentative definition and a provisional critique. *Disability & Society, 31*(6), 838–849.

Guba, E. G., & Lincoln, Y. S. (1994). Competing paradigms in qualitative research. In N. K. Denzin & Y. S. Lincoln (Eds.), *Handbook of qualitative research* (pp. 105–117). SAGE.

Hahn, H. (1988). The politics of physical differences: Disability and discrimination. *Journal of Social Issues, 44*(1), 39–47.

Halberstam, J. (2005). *In a queer time and place: Transgender bodies, subcultural lives.* New York University Press.

Halberstam, J. (2011). *The queer art of failure.* Duke University Press.

Halberstam, J. (2018). *Trans*: A quick and quirky account of gender variability.* University of California Press.

Hall, S. (1980). Encoding/decoding. In S. Hall et al. (Eds.), *Culture, media, language: Working papers in cultural studies, 1972-79* (pp. 128–138). Hutchinson.

Hall, S. (1996). New ethnicities. In D. Morley & K.-H. Chen (Eds.), *Stuart Hall: Cultural dialogues in cultural studies* (pp. 442–451). Routledge.

Hall, S. (1997). *Representation: Cultural representations and signifying practices.* SAGE.

Hall, S. (2005). Notes on deconstructing 'the popular'. In R. Guins & O. Zaragoza (Eds.), *Popular culture: A reader* (pp. 64-71). SAGE.

Hall, S. (2017). *The fateful triangle: Race, ethnicity, nation*. Harvard University Press.

Hall, S. (2019). Thinking the diaspora: Home-thoughts from abroad [1999]. In D. Morley (Ed.), *Essential essays vol. 2: Identity and diaspora* (pp. 206-226). Duke University Press.

Hall, S. (2021). Race, the floating signifier: What more is there to say about "race"? [1997]. In C. Hall & B. Schwarz (Eds.), *Stuart Hall: Selected writings* (pp. 359-373). Duke University Press.

Hamilton, R. (2020). The very quintessence of persecution: Queer anti-fascism in 1970s Western Europe. *Radical History Review*, (138), 60-81.

Hammer, R. & Kellner, D. (Eds.) (2009). *Media/cultural studies: Critical approaches*. Peter Lang.

Hanquinet, L. (2022). Who?, Why? and How? The contribution of sociology to the study of arts audiences. In M. Reason, L. Conner, K. Johanson, & B. Walmsley (Eds.), *Routledge companion to audiences and the performing arts* (pp. 68-82). Routledge.

Harding, X. (2017, September 6). *Keeping 'Insecure' lit: HBO cinematographer Ava Berkofsky on properly lighting black faces*. Mic. https://www.mic.com/articles/184244/keeping-insecure-lit-hbo-cinematographer-ava-berkofsky-on-properly-lighting-black-faces

Hardy, M. (2019). The East is least: The stereotypical imagining of Essos in *Game of Thrones*. *Canadian Review of American Studies*, 49(1), 26-45.

Harnett, A. (2000). Escaping the 'evil avenger' and the 'supercrip': Images of disability in popular television. *The Irish Communications Review*, 8(1), 21-29.

Harris, L. N., Gladfelter, A., Santuzzi, A. M., Lech, I. B., Rodriguez, R., Lopez, L. E., ... & Li, A. (2023). Braille literacy as a human right: A challenge to the "inefficiency" argument against braille instruction. *International Journal of Psychology*, 58(1), 52-58.

Harrison, M. (2018). Power and punishment in *Game of Thrones*. In A. E. George & J. L. Schatz (Eds.), *The image of disability: Essays on media representations* (pp. 28-43). McFarland.

Haynes, J. (2016). Race on *The Wire*: a metacritical account. *Journal for Cultural Research*, 20(2), 157-170.

Heathcott, J. (2003). Urban spaces and working-class expressions across the Black Atlantic: Tracing the routes of ska. *Radical History Review*, 87(1), 183-206.

Hebdige, D. (1979). *Subculture: The meaning of style*. Routledge.

Hegewisch, A., & Hartmann, H. (2014). *Occupational segregation and the gender wage gap: A job half done*. Institute for Women's Policy Research.

Hellekson, K., & Busse, K. (2014). Introduction: Why a fan fiction studies reader now? In K. Hellekson & K. Busse (Eds.), *The fan fiction studies reader* (pp. 1-18). University of Iowa Press.

Hekma, G. (1999). Same-sex relations among men in Europe, 1700-1990. In F. X. Eder, L. A. Hall & G. Hekma (Eds.), *Sexual cultures in Europe: Themes in sexuality* (pp. 79-103). Manchester University Press.

Herman, D. (2003). "*Bad Girls* changed my life": Homonormativity in a women's prison drama. *Critical Studies in Media Communication*, 20(2), 141-159.

Herman, E. S., & Chomsky, N. (2002). *Manufacturing consent: The political economy of the mass media*. Pantheon Books.

Hermes, J. (2024). *Cultural citizenship and popular culture: The art of listening*. Routledge.

Holmes, J. A. (2020). "The dress-clad, out loud singer of queer punks": Bradford Cox and the performance of disability. *Journal of the Society for American Music*, 14(3), 250-279.

Holtzman, L., & Sharpe, L. (2014). *Media messages: What film, television, and popular music teach us about race, class, gender, and sexual orientation* (2nd ed.). M. E. Sharpe.

hooks, b. (2004). *We real cool: Black men and masculinity*. Routledge.

Houston, T. M. (2012). The homosocial construction of alternative masculinities: Men in indie rock bands. *The Journal of Men's Studies*, 20(2), 158-175.

Hunt, D., & Ramón, A. C. (2021a). *Hollywood diversity report 2021 part 1: Film*. UCLA College: Social Sciences.

Hunt, D., & Ramón, A. C. (2021b). *Hollywood diversity report 2021 part 2: Television*. UCLA College: Social Sciences.

i-D Staff & Maicki, S. (2016, October 1). *The punk inspirations behind Solange's new album*. Vice. https://i-d.vice.com/en_uk/article/d3va4q/the-punk-inspirations-behind-solanges-new-album

IFPI (2024). *Global music report 2024*. IFPI.

Ivory, A. H., Gibson, R., & Ivory, J. D. (2009). Gendered relationships on television: Portrayals of same-sex and heterosexual couples. *Mass Communication and Society, 12*(2), 170-192.

Iwamoto, D. (2003). Tupac Shakur: Understanding the identity formation of hyper-masculinity of a popular hip hop artist. *The Black Scholar, 33*(2), 44-49.

Jagose, A. (1996). *Queer theory: An introduction*. New York University Press.

James, D. (1999). Is there class in this text? The repression of class in film and cultural studies. In T. Miller & R. Stam (Eds.), *A companion to film theory* (pp. 182-201). Blackwell Publishing.

Jeffries, M. P. (2010). Can a thug (get some) love? Sex, romance, and the definition of a hip hop 'thug'. *Women and Language, 32*(2), 35-41.

Jenkins, H. (1992). *Textual poachers*. Routledge.

Jenkins, R. (2014). *Social identity* (4th ed.). Routledge.

Jenkins, S. (2021). Constructing ableism. *Genealogy 5*(3), 66. https://doi.org/10.3390/genealogy5030066

Jensen, J. (1992). Fandom as pathology: The consequences of characterization. In A. Lewis (Ed.), *The adoring audience: Fan culture and popular media* (pp. 9-29). Routledge.

Jensen, T. (2014). Welfare commonsense, poverty porn and doxosophy. *Sociological Research Online, 19*(3), 277-283.

Jensen, T. (2018). *Parenting the crisis: The cultural politics of parent-blame*. Policy Press.

Johnson, E. P. (2003). *Appropriating blackness: Performance and the politics of authenticity*. Duke University Press.

Jones, O. (2011). *Chavs: The demonization of the working class*. Verso.

Jones, S. (2006). *Antonio Gramsci*. Routledge.

Jones, S. C. (2022). Hey look, I'm (not) on TV: Autistic people reflect on autism portrayals in entertainment media. *Disability & Society*, 39(6), 1484-1501.

Joseph, T., & Golash-Boza, T. (2021). Double consciousness in the 21st century: Du Boisian theory and the problem of racialized legal status. *Social Sciences, 10*(9), 345.

Joye, S., & Loisen, J. (2017). *On media and communication: An introduction to communication sciences*. Acco.

Kanai, A., & Gill, R. (2020). Woke? Affect, neoliberalism, marginalised identities and consumer culture. *New Formations, 102*, 10-27.

Kanobana, S. R. (2021). A black perspective on the language of race in Dutch. *Journal of Linguistic Anthropology, 31*(2), 271-274.

Kanzler, M., & Simone, P. (2023). *Focus 2023: World film market trends - Tendances du marché mondial du film*. Marché du Film.

Karaian, L., & Mitchell, A. (2009). Third wave feminisms. In N. Mandell (Ed.), *Feminist issues: Race, class and sexuality* (5th ed., pp. 63-86). Pearson Prentice Hall.

Karim, K. H. (2018). Migration, diaspora and communication. In K. H. Karim & A. Al-Rawi (Eds.), *Diaspora and media in Europe: Migration, identity, and integration* (pp. 1-24). Palgrave Macmillan.

Karim, K. H., & Al-Rawi, A. (Eds.). (2018). *Diaspora and media in Europe: Migration, identity, and integration*. Palgrave Macmillan.

Katz, J. N. (1995). *The invention of heterosexuality*. The University of Chicago Press.

Kearney, M. C. (2017). *Gender and rock*. Oxford University Press.

Kellner, D. (1995). *Media culture: Cultural studies, identity and politics between the modern and the postmodern*. Routledge.

Kellner, D. (2023). Cultural Marxism, British cultural studies, and the reconstruction of education. *Educational Philosophy and Theory, 55*(13), 1423-1435.

Kelly, D. (2022, July 28). *Beyoncé shares letter to fans ahead of 'Renaissance' album release,* Hypebeast. https://hypebeast.com/2022/7/beyonce-letter-fans-renaissance-album-release

Kelly, E. A. (2005). Review essay: A new generation of feminism? Reflections on the third wave. *New Political Science, 27*(2), 233-243.

Kendall, D. (2016). Framing class, vicarious living, and conspicuous consumption. In S. Lemke & W. Schniedermann (Eds.), *Class divisions in serial television* (pp. 21-46). Palgrave Macmillan.

Kennedy, H. (1999). *The ideal gay man: The story of Der Kreis.* Routledge.

Kern, R. (2014). Imagining community: Visibility, bonding, and *L Word* audiences. *Sexualities, 17*(4), 434-450.

Khan, Z., & Bruschke, J. (2016). Media coverage of Muslims, perceived threats, ethnocentrism, and intercultural contact: Applying cultivation theory, integrated threat theory, and the contact hypothesis. *Northwest Journal of Communication, 44*(1), 7-34.

Kooijman, J. (2019). After *Will & Ellen*: Uneventful queer television. *Critical Studies in Television, 14*(4), 451-455.

Kovács, Z. (2021, June 24). *Portrayal and promotion – Hungary's LGBTQI+ law explained.* Euractiv. https://www.euractiv.com/section/non-discrimination/news/portrayal-and-promotion-hungarys-latest-anti-lgbt-law-explained/

Krijnen, T., & Van Bauwel, S. (2022). *Gender and media: Representing, producing, consuming.* Routledge.

Kroon, A. C., Kluknavská, A., Vliegenthart, R., & Boomgaarden, H. G. (2016). Victims or perpetrators? Explaining media framing of Roma across Europe. *European Journal of Communication, 31*(4), 375-392.

Krüger, S. (2021). Gendering music in popular culture. In K. Ross (Ed.), *The international encyclopedia of gender, media, and communication* (pp. 658-666). Wiley Blackwell.

Kuipers, G. (2011). Cultural globalization as the emergence of a transnational cultural field: Transnational television and national media landscapes in four European countries. *American Behavioral Scientist, 55*(5), 541-557.

Lancee, B. (2021). Ethnic discrimination in hiring: Comparing groups across contexts. Results from a cross-national field experiment. *Journal of Ethnic and Migration Studies, 47*(6), 1181-1200.

Langston, D. (2000). Tired of playing monopoly. In M. Adams et al. (Eds.), *Readings for diversity and social justice* (pp. 397-402). Routledge.

Larsen, R., & Haller, B. A. (2002). Public reception of real disability: The case of "Freaks". *Journal of Popular Film & Television, 29*(4), 164-172.

Lay, F. (2000). "Sometimes we wonder who the real men are" - Masculinity and contemporary popular music. In R. West & R. Lay (Eds.), *Subverting masculinity* (pp. 227-246). Brill.

Leibetseder, D. (2016). *Queer tracks: Subversive strategies in rock and pop music.* Routledge.

Leonard, M. (2007). *Gender in the music industry: Rock, discourse and girl power.* Ashgate.

Leonard, M. (2016). Girls at work: Gendered identities, sex segregation, and employment experiences in the music industries. In A. Adrian & J. Warwick (Eds.), *Voicing girlhood in popular music* (pp. 47-65). Routledge.

Levine, R. F. (2006). Introduction. In R. F. Levine (Ed.), *Social class and stratification* (2nd ed., pp. 1-16). Rowman & Littlefield Publishers.

Lind, R. A. (Ed.) (2023). *Race/gender/class/media: Considering diversity across audiences, content, and producers.* Routledge.

Linton, C. (2022, March 28). *Troy Kotsur becomes first Deaf man to win acting Oscar.* CBS News. https://www.cbsnews.com/news/troy-kotsur-oscar-deaf-man-coda/

Lion, A., & Dhaenens, F. (2023). 'Just kidding?'–an exploratory audience study into the ways Flemish youth with a minoritized ethnic identity make sense of ethnic humor and the politics of offense. *HUMOR, 36*(3), 375-395.

Lippmann, W. (1922). *Public opinion.* The Free Press.

Lockyer, S. (2010). Dynamics of social class contempt in contemporary British television comedy. *Social Semiotics, 20*(2), 121-138.

Loist, S. (2012). A complicated queerness: LGBT film festivals and queer programming strategies. In J. Ruoff (Ed.), *Coming soon to a festival near you: Programming film festivals* (pp. 157-172). St Andrews Film Books.

Lugowski, D. (1999). Queering the (New) Deal: Lesbian and gay representation and the Depression-era cultural politics of Hollywood's Production Code. *Cinema Journal, 38*(2), 3-35.

Maenhaut, M. (2019, February 6). *"Ik wil verwonderd blijven": Charlotte Adigéry over nieuwste EP Zandoli. ["I want to continue to be amazed": Charlotte Adigéry about her new EP Zandoli]*. Indiestyle. https://www.indiestyle.be/interviews/ik-wil-verwonderd-blijven-charlotte-adigery-over-nieuwste-ep-zandoli

Malik, S. (2013). "Creative diversity": UK public service broadcasting after multiculturalism. *Popular Communication, 11*(3), 227-241.

Mallett, R., & Mills, B. (2015). Special issue: Disability and television. *Journal of Popular Television 3*(2), 155-161.

Mandler, C. (2023, February 6). *Kim Petras and Sam Smith become the first transgender and nonbinary winners of the Grammy for Best Pop Duo Performance*. CBS News. https://www.cbsnews.com/news/kim-petras-sam-smith-first-transgender-nonbinary-winners-grammy-awards-best-pop-duo/

Mantsios, G. (1995). Making magic: Making class invisible. In P. S. Rothenberg (Ed.), *Race, class, and gender in the United States: An integrated study* (3rd ed., pp. 409-416). St. Martin's Press.

Manzoor, N. (2021, May 10). *Nida Manzoor on writing We Are Lady Parts: 'Why is being honest so scary?'* Inews. https://inews.co.uk/culture/television/we-are-lady-parts-nida-manzoor-channel-4-991333

Markowitsch, C. (2024). "I tried to have a father but instead I had a dad": Defining dad rock. *Rock Music Studies*, Advance online publication: DOI: 10.1080/19401159.2024.2346999

Marks, D. (1997). Models of disability. *Disability and Rehabilitation, 19*(3), 85-91.

Martin, J. J. (2013). Benefits and barriers to physical activity for individuals with disabilities: a social-relational model of disability perspective. *Disability and Rehabilitation, 35*(24), 2030-2037.

Martin, A. L. (2018). Introduction: What is queer production studies/Why is queer production studies? *Journal of Film and Video, 70*(3-4), 3-7.

Marx, K. (1904). *A contribution to the critique of political economy.* Charles H. Kerr & Company.

Marx, K., & Engels, F. (2006). Manifesto of the Communist Party. In R. F. Levine (Ed.), *Social class and stratification* (2nd ed., pp. 19-46). Rowman & Littlefield Publishers. (Reprinted from Selected works in one volume, pp. 35-63, by K. Marx & F. Engels, 1970, International Publishers)

Maultsby, P. K. (1983). Soul music: Its sociological and political significance in American popular culture. *Journal of Popular Culture, 17*(2), 51-60.

McCormack, M., & Anderson, E. (2010). "It's just not acceptable anymore": The erosion of homophobia and the softening of masculinity at an English sixth form. *Sociology, 44*(5), 843-859.

McDermott, M. (2020). *The affective politics of queerbaiting: Fandom, identity and representation* (Doctoral dissertation, La Trobe).

McGillivray, D., O'Donnell, H., McPherson, G., & Misener, L. (2021). Repurposing the (super)crip: Media representations of disability at the Rio 2016 Paralympic Games. *Communication & Sport, 9*(1), 3-32.

McIntosh, P. (1988). *White privilege and male privilege: A personal account of coming to see correspondences through work in women's studies*. Wellesley College Center for Research on Women.

McKay, G. (2013). *Shakin' all over: Popular music and disability*. The University of Michigan Press.

McRobbie, A. (1997). Bridging the gap: Feminism, fashion and consumption. *Feminist Review, 55*(1), 73-89.

McRobbie, A. (2011). Introduction: Queer adventures in cultural studies. *Cultural studies, 25*(2), 139-146.

McRobbie, A. (2004a). Notes on 'What Not To Wear' and post-feminist symbolic violence. *The Sociological Review, 52*(2), 99-109.

McRobbie, A. (2004b). Post-feminism and popular culture. *Feminist Media Studies, 4*(3), 256-264.

McRoy, J., & Crucianelli, G. (2009). "I panic the world": Benevolent exploitation in Tod

Browning's *Freaks* and Harmony Korine's *Gummo*. *The Journal of Popular Culture, 42*(2), 257-272.

McRuer, R. (2019). In Focus: Cripping cinema and media studies: Introduction. *JCMS: Journal of Cinema and Media Studies, 58*(4), 134-139.

Meehan, K., & Friedman, J. (2023, April 20). *Banned in the USA: State laws supercharge book suppression in schools.* Pen America. https://pen.org/report/banned-in-the-usa-state-laws-supercharge-book-suppression-in-schools/

Mercer, J., & Shingler, M. (2004). *Melodrama: Genre, style and sensibility*. Columbia University Press.

Mercer, K. (1987). Black hair/style politics. *New Formations, 3*, 33-54.

Mercer, K. (1990). Black art and the burden of representation. *Third Text, 4*(10), 61-78.

Messerschmidt, J. W. (2012). Engendering gendered knowledge: Assessing the academic appropriation of hegemonic masculinity. *Men and Masculinities, 15*(1), 56-76.

Messerschmidt, J. W. (2019). The salience of "hegemonic masculinity". *Men and Masculinities, 22*(1), 85-91.

Metoomvmt.org (n.d.). *History & inception*. https://metoomvmt.org/get-to-know-us/history-inception/

Meyenburg, B., & Sigusch, V. (1977). Sexology in West Germany. *Journal of Sex Research, 13*(3), 197-209.

Meyers, J. (1977). *Homosexuality and literature: 1890-1930*. Athlone.

Mijs, J. J. (2016). The unfulfillable promise of meritocracy: Three lessons and their implications for justice in education. *Social Justice Research, 29*, 14-34.

Milestone K., & Meyer, A. (2012). *Gender and popular culture*. Polity.

Miller, K. (2005). *Communication theories: Perspectives, processes, and contexts.* Macgraw-Hill.

Miller, P., Parker, S., & Gillinson, S. (2004). *Disablism: How to tackle the last prejudice*. Demos.

Miranda starts filming with an all-star cast for her new sitcom on BBC Two. (2009, June 18). BBC. https://www.bbc.co.uk/pressoffice/pressreleases/stories/2009/06_june/18/miranda.shtml

Mogk, M. E. (2013). Introduction: An invitation to disability. In M. E. Mogk (Ed.), *Different bodies: Essays on disability in film and television* (pp. 1-16). McFarland & Co.

Monaghan, W. (2021). Post-gay television: LGBTQ representation and the negotiation of 'normal' in MTV's *Faking It*. *Media, Culture & Society, 43*(3), 428-443.

Moore, T. O. (2005). A Fanonian perspective on double consciousness. *Journal of Black Studies, 35*(6), 751-762.

Morley, D. G. (1980). *The Nationwide audience*. British Film Institute.

Morrison, T., Dinno, A., & Salmon, T. (2021). The erasure of intersex, transgender, non-binary, and agender experiences through misuse of sex and gender in health research. *American Journal of Epidemiology, 190*(12), 2712-2717.

Moser, C. (2016). Defining sexual orientation. *Archives of Sexual Behavior, 45*(3), 505-508.

Motmans, J., & van der Ros, J. (2015). Trans activism and LGB movements: Odd bedfellows? In D. Paternotte & M. Tremblay (Eds.), *The Ashgate research companion to lesbian and gay activism* (pp. 163-178). Routledge.

Moya, P. M. L. (2000). Reclaiming identity. In P. M. L. Moya & M. R. Hayes-García (Eds.), *Reclaiming identity: Realist theory and the predicament of postmodernism* (pp. 1-26). University of California Press.

Muli, E. (2015). *Why the term 'world music' is bullshit*. True Africa. https://trueafrica.co/article/endeguenamulu-aka-ethiopian-records-on-world-music/

Mullens, F., & Zanoni, P (2019). "'Mothering the artist': Women artist managers crafting an occupational identity in the Flemish music industry." *Tijdschrift voor Genderstudies, 22*(1), 7-26.

Mulvey, L. (1975). Visual pleasure and narrative cinema. *Screen, 16*, 6-18.

Myers, O. (2020, July 12). *Belgian singer Tamino merges Arabic sounds with Western sensibilities*. GQ. https://www.gq-magazine.co.uk/culture/article/tamino-interview

Navarro, L. (2010). Islamophobia and sexism: Muslim women in the Western mass media. *Human Architecture: Journal of the Sociology of Self-Knowledge, 8*(2), 95-114.

Neal, A. (1997). Sold out on soul: The corporate annexation of black popular music. *Popular Music and Society, 21*(3), 117-135.

Nelson, C., & George, H. (1995). White racism and "The Cosby show": a critique. *The Black Scholar, 25*(2), 59-61.

Nelson, J. A. (2000). The media role in building the disability community. *Journal of Mass Media Ethics, 15*(3), 180-193.

Ng, E. (2013). A "post-gay" era? Media gaystreaming, homonormativity, and the politics of LGBT Integration. *Communication, Culture and Critique, 6*(2), 258-283.

Ng, E. (2020). No grand pronouncements here…: Reflections on cancel culture and digital media participation. *Television & New Media, 21*(6), 621-627.

Nibert D. A. (1995). The political economy of developmental disability. *Critical Sociology, 21*(1), 59-80.

Nicholson, L. (2010). Identity and identity politics. *Washington University Journal of Law & Policy, 33*(1), 43-74.

Norden, M. (1990). Victims, villains, saints, and heroes: Movie portrayals of people with physical disabilities. In P. Loukides & L. K. Fuller (Eds.), *Beyond the stars: Stock characters in American popular films* (pp. 222-233). Bowling Green State University Popular Press.

Nylund, D. (2007). Reading Harry Potter: Popular culture, queer theory and the fashioning of youth identity. *Journal of Systemic Therapies, 26*(2), 13-24.

O'Brien, A., & Kerrigan, P. (2020). Gay the right way? Roles and routines of Irish media production among gay and lesbian workers. *European Journal of Communication, 35*(4), 355-369.

O'Neill, D., & Wayne, M. (2017a). Introduction. In M. Wayne & D. O'Neill (Eds.), *Considering class: Theory, culture and the media in the 21st century* (pp. 1-12). Brill.

O'Neill, D., & Wayne, M. (2017b). On intellectuals. In M. Wayne & D. O'Neill (Eds.), *Considering class: Theory, culture and the media in the 21st century* (pp. 166-184). Brill.

Ocean, F. (2012). Untitled [Blog post]. http://frankocean.tumblr.com/post/33700009336

Oliver, M. (1990). *The politics of disablement*. Macmillan.

Oliver, M. (1998). Theories in health care and research: Theories of disability in health practice and research. *BMJ, 317*(7170), 1446-1449.

Olveira-Araujo, R. (2023a). The (r)evolution of transsexuality in the news media: The case of the Spanish digital press (2000-2020). *Journalism, 24*(10), 2270-2293.

Olveira-Araujo, R. (2023b). Who drives news coverage of trans issues? Intermedia agenda setting dynamics in Spanish digital press. *Journalism*. Advance online publication: https://doi.org/10.1177/14648849231222701

Omi, M., & Winant, H. (2015). *Racial formation in the United States* (3rd ed.). Routledge.

Ono, K. A., & Pham, V. N. (2009). *Asian Americans and the media (Vol. 2)*. Polity.

Paasonen, S. (2014). Diagnoses of transformation: "Pornification," digital media, and the diversification of the pornographic. In L. Coleman & J. Held (Eds.), *The philosophy of pornography: Contemporary perspectives* (pp. 3-16). Rowman & Littlefield.

Paasonen, S., & Saarenmaa, L. (2007). The golden age of porn: Nostalgia and history in cinema. In K. Nikunen, S. Paasonen, L. Saarenmaa (Eds.), *Pornification* (pp. 23-32). Berg.

Pastorello, T. (2010). L'abolition du crime de sodomie en 1791: Un long processus social, répressif et pénal [The abolition of sodomy in 1791: A long social, repressive and criminal process]. *Cahiers d'histoire. Revue d'histoire critique*, (112-113), 197-208.

Peeters, T. (2022, February 23). Charlotte Adigéry & Bolis Pupul: 'It was love at first conversation.' Bruzz. https://www.bruzz.be/culture/music-nightlife/charlotte-adigery-bolis-pupul-it-was-love-first-conversation-2022-02-23

Perchard, T., Graham, S., Rutherford-Johnson, T., & Rogers, H. (2022). *Twentieth-century music in the West: An introduction*. Cambridge University Press.

Pérez, R. (2013). Learning to make racism funny in the 'color-blind' era: Stand-up comedy students, performance strategies, and the (re) production of racist jokes in public. *Discourse & Society, 24*(4), 478-503.

Peterson, R. A., & Kern, R. M. (1996). Changing highbrow taste: From snob to omnivore. *American Sociological Review, 61*(5), 900-907.

Piepergerdes, B. J. (2015). Re-envisioning the nation: Film Neorealism and the postwar Italian condition. *ACME: An International Journal for Critical Geographies, 6*(2), 231-257.

Pitchfork (2023a, December 5). *The 50 Best Albums of 2023*. Pitchfork. https://pitchfork.com/features/lists-and-guides/best-albums-2023/

Pitchfork (2023b, December 4). *The 100 Best Songs of 2023*. Pitchfork. https://pitchfork.com/features/lists-and-guides/best-songs-2023/

Pitchfork (2023c, December 8). *Readers' poll '23*. Pitchfork. https://pitchfork.com/features/lists-and-guides/2023-readers-poll-results/

Poindexter, P. M., Smith, L., & Heider, D. (2003). Race and ethnicity in local television news: Framing, story assignments, and source selections. *Journal of Broadcasting & Electronic Media, 47*(4), 524-536.

Polson, E., Clark, L. S., & Gajjala, R. (2020). Media and class in the twenty-first century. In E. Polson, L. S. Clark, & R. Gajjala (Eds.), *The Routledge companion to media and class* (pp. 1-14). Routledge.

Porfido, G. (2009). Queering the small screen: Homosexuality and televisual citizenship in spectacular societies. *Sexualities, 12*(2), 161-179.

Priestley, M. (2003). *Disability: A life course approach*. Polity.

Quillian, L., Lee, J. J., & Honoré, B. (2020). Racial discrimination in the US housing and mortgage lending markets: a quantitative review of trends, 1976-2016. *Race and Social Problems, 12*, 13-28.

Radway, J. (2016). Girl zine networks, underground itineraries, and Riot grrrl history: Making sense of the struggle for new social forms in the 1990s and beyond. *Journal of American Studies, 50*(1), 1-31.

Rasmussen, A. C. (2014). Causes and solutions: Mainstream and black press framing of racial and ethnic health disparities. *Howard Journal of Communications, 25*(3), 257-280.

Rembis, M., Kudlick, C. J., & Nielsen, K. (2018). Introduction. In M. Rembis, C. J. Kudlick, & K. Nielsen (Eds.), *The Oxford handbook of disability history* (pp. 1-20). Oxford University Press.

Rhodes, C. (2022). *Woke capitalism: How corporate morality is sabotaging democracy*. Bristol University Press.

Rich, B. R. (2013). *New queer cinema*. Duke University Press.

Riley, A. (2005). The rebirth of tragedy out of the spirit of hip hop: A cultural sociology of gangsta rap music. *Journal of Youth Studies, 8*(3), 297-311.

Robertson, A. (2024, January 31). *Lawmakers propose anti-nonconsensual AI porn bill after Taylor Swift controversy*. The Verge. https://www.theverge.com/2024/1/30/24056385/congress-defiance-act-proposed-ban-nonconsensual-ai-porn

Robinson, K. (2024, July 17). *'Brat' unfiltered: Charli xcx on how she stole the summer (and worked it out with Lorde on the remix)*. Billboard. https://www.billboard.com/music/pop/charli-xcx-brat-billboard-cover-story-interview-1235732025/

Romano, A. (2020, October 9). *A history of "wokeness"*. Vox. https://www.vox.com/culture/21437879/stay-woke-wokeness-history-origin-evolution-controversy

Rose, D., & Harrison, E. (2007). The European socio-economic classification: A new social class schema for comparative European research. *European Societies, 9*(3), 459-490.

Ross, S. J. (1998). *Working-class Hollywood: Silent film and the shaping of class in America*. Princeton University Press.

Roth, L. (2009). Looking at Shirley, the ultimate norm: Colour balance, image technologies, and cognitive equity. *Canadian Journal of Communication, 34*(1), 111-136.

Rubin, G. S. (1993). Thinking sex: Notes for a radical theory of the politics of sexuality. In H. Abelove, M. A. Barale, & D. M. Halperin (Eds.), *The lesbian and gay studies reader* (pp. 3-44). Routledge.

Russell, D. (2002). Self-deprecatory humour and the female comic: Self-destruction or comedic construction? *thirdspace: a journal of feminist theory & culture, 2*(1). https://journals.lib.sfu.ca/index.php/thirdspace/article/view/d_russell/3117

Russo, V. (1985). *The celluloid closet*. Harper & Row.

Safran, W. (1991). Diasporas in modern societies: Myths of homeland and return. *Diaspora: A journal of transnational studies, 1*(1), 83-99.

Saha, A. (2018). *Race and the cultural industries*. Polity.

Saha, A. (2021). *Race, culture and media*. SAGE.

Said, E. W. (1979). *Orientalism*. Knopf Doubleday Publishing Group.

Saito, S., & Ishiyama, R. (2005). The invisible minority: Under‐representation of people with disabilities in prime‐time TV dramas in Japan. *Disability & Society, 20*(4), 437-451.

Salfiti, J. (2019, November 27). *Tamino: the Arab-Belgian singer bringing two worlds together*. The Guardian. https://www.theguardian.com/music/2019/nov/27/tamino-the-arab-belgian-singer-bringing-two-worlds-together

Sandahl, C. (2003). Queering the crip or cripping the queer?: Intersections of queer and crip identities in solo autobiographical performance. *GLQ: A Journal of Lesbian and Gay Studies, 9*(1), 25-56.

Sandvoss, C. 2005. *Fans: The mirror of consumption*. Polity Press.

Sax, L. (2002). How common is intersex? A response to Anne Fausto‐Sterling. *Journal of Sex Research, 39*(3), 174-178.

Scanlon, J., & Lewis, R. (2017). Whose sexuality is it anyway? Women's experiences of viewing lesbians on screen. *Feminist Media Studies, 17*(6), 1005-1021.

Scharrer, E., & Warren, S. (2022). Adolescents' modern media use and beliefs about masculine gender roles and norms. *Journalism & Mass Communication Quarterly, 99*(1), 289-315.

Schippers, M. (2007). Recovering the feminine other: Masculinity, femininity, and gender hegemony. *Theory and Society, 36*(1), 85-102.

Schoonover, K., & Galt, R. (2016). *Queer cinema in the world*. Duke University Press.

Sedgwick, E. K. (1993). Queer and now. In E. K. Sedgwick (Ed.), *Tendencies* (pp. 1-20). Duke University Press.

Seida, K., & Shor, E. (2020). *Aggression in pornography: Myths and realities*. Routledge.

Seidman, S. (1988). Transfiguring sexual identity: AIDS & the contemporary construction of homosexuality. *Social Text, 19/20*, 187-205.

Seidman, S. (1996). Introduction. In S. Seidman (Ed.), *Queer theory/sociology* (pp. 1-29). Blackwell.

Semati, M. M., & Sotirin, P. J. (1999). Hollywood's transnational appeal: Hegemony and democratic potential? *Journal of Popular Film and Television, 26*(4), 176-188.

Shakespeare, T. (2013). The social model of disability. In L. J. Davis (Ed.), *The disability studies reader* (4th ed., pp. 214-221). Routledge.

Shakespeare, T. (2018). *Disability: The basics*. Routledge.

Shugart, H. A. (2003). Reinventing privilege: The new (gay) man in contemporary popular media. *Critical Studies in Media Communication, 20*(1), 67-91.

Shuker, R. (2012). *Popular music culture: The key concepts* (3rd ed.). Routledge.

Shuker, R. (2016). *Understanding popular music culture* (5th ed.). Routledge.

Siapera, E. (2010). *Cultural diversity and global media*. Wiley-Blackwell.

Skeggs, B. (2009). The moral economy of person production: The class relations of self-performance on 'reality' television. *The Sociological Review, 57*(4), 626-644.

Skeggs, B., & Wood, H. (2011). Introduction: Real class. In H. Wood & B. Skeggs (Eds.), *Reality television and class* (pp. 1-29). British Film Institute.

Snyder, R. C. (2008). What is third-wave feminism? A new directions essay. *Signs: Journal of Women in Culture and Society, 34*(1), 175-196.

Snyder, S. L., & Mitchell D. T. (2006). *Cultural locations of disability*. The University of Chicago Press.

Sobande, F. (2019). Woke-washing: "intersectional" femvertising and branding "woke" bravery. *European Journal of Marketing, 54*(11), 2723-2745.

Solomos, J. (2022). *Race, ethnicity and social theory*. Routledge.

Somani, I. S., & Guo, J. (2018). Seeing Indian, being Indian: Diaspora, identity, and ethnic media. *Howard Journal of Communications, 29*(1), 63-82.

Sparks, C. (1996). Stuart Hall, cultural studies and Marxism. In D. Morley & K.-H. Chen (Eds.), *Stuart Hall: Critical dialogues in cultural studies* (pp. 71-102). Routledge.

Spongberg, M. (2006). Andrea Dworkin, 1946-2005. *Australian Feminist Studies, 21*(49), 3-5.

Staiger, J. (2005). *Media reception studies*. New York University Press.

Staples, R., & Jones, T. (1985). Culture, ideology and black television images. *The Black Scholar, 16*(3), 10-20.

Stein, A., & Plummer, K. (1996). "I can't even think straight": "Queer" theory and the missing sexual revolution in sociology. In S. Seidman (Ed.), *Queer theory/Sociology* (pp. 129-144). Blackwell.

Stein, J. P., Krause, E., & Ohler, P. (2021). Every (Insta)Gram counts? Applying cultivation theory to explore the effects of Instagram on young users' body image. *Psychology of Popular Media, 10*(1), 87-97.

Stevens, P. A. J. (2022). Introduction: Walking on and off the beaten track. In P. A. J. Stevens (Ed.), *Qualitative data analysis: Key approaches* (pp. 1-16). SAGE.

Stewart, J. B. (2005). Message in the music: Political commentary in black popular music from rhythm and blues to early hip hop. *The Journal of African American History, 90*(3), 196-225.

Stillerman, J. (2015). *The sociology of consumption: A global approach*. Polity.

Stimpson, C. R. (1981). Zero degree deviancy: The lesbian novel in English. *Critical Inquiry, 8*(2), 363-379.

Storey, J. (1996). *Cultural studies & the study of popular culture: Theories and methods*. Edinburgh University Press.

Storey, J. (2021). *Cultural theory and popular culture: A reader* (9th ed.). Routledge.

Streitmatter, R. (2009). *From 'perverts' to 'fab five': The media's changing depiction of gay men and lesbians*. Routledge.

Strong, C. (2010). The Triple J Hottest 100 of All Time and the dominance of the rock canon. *Meanjin, 69*(2), 122-127.

Strong, C., & Raine, S. (Eds.). (2019). *Towards gender equality in the music industry: Education, practice and strategies for change*. Bloomsbury Publishing USA.

Stryker, S. (2008). *Transgender history*. Seal Press.

Stryker, S., & Bettcher, T. M. (2016). Introduction: trans/feminisms. *Transgender Studies Quarterly, 3*(1-2), 5-14.

Sullivan, N. (2003). *A critical introduction to queer theory*. New York University Press.

Sun, R. (2023, March 12). *Michelle Yeoh is Oscars' first Asian Best Actress winner: "This is a beacon of hope and possibilities"*. The Hollywood Reporter. https://www.hollywoodreporter.com/movies/movie-news/michelle-yeoh-first-asian-best-actress-oscars-2023-1235348487/

Surís, A., Holliday, R., & North, C. S. (2016). The evolution of the classification of psychiatric disorders. *Behavioral Sciences, 6*(1), 5. https://doi.org/10.3390/bs6010005

Taylor, J. (2012). *Playing it queer: Popular music, identity and queer world-making*. Peter Lang.

Thompson, C. (2006). Race science. *Theory, Culture & Society, 23*(2-3), 547-549.

Thompson, K. D. (2012). "Deserve got nothing to do with it": Black urban experience and the naturalist tradition in *The Wire*. *Studies in American Naturalism, 7*(1), 80-120.

Tischauser, L. V. (2012). *Jim Crow laws*. ABC-CLIO.

Tomsett, E. (2018). Positives and negatives: Reclaiming the female body and self-deprecation in stand-up comedy. *Comedy Studies, 9*(1), 6-18.

Tøssebro, J. (2004). Introduction to the special issue: Understanding disability. *Scandinavian Journal of Disability Research, 6*(1): 3-7.

Tropiano, S. (2002). *The prime time closet: A history of gays and lesbians on TV*. Applause Theatre & Cinema.

Tuchman, G. (1978). Introduction: The symbolic annihilation of women by the mass media. In G. Tuchman, A. K. Daniels, & J. Benét (Eds.), *Hearth and home: Images of women in the mass media* (pp. 1-38). Oxford University Press.

Turner, G. (2003). *British cultural studies: An introduction* (3rd ed.). Routledge.

Turner, G. (2019). *Essays in media and cultural studies: In transition*. Routledge.

Tyler, P. (1972). *Screening the sexes: Homosexuality in the movies*. Holt, Rinehart and Winston.

United Nations (2006). *Convention on the Rights of Persons with Disabilities (CRPD)*. https://social.desa.un.org/issues/disability/crpd/convention-on-the-rights-of-persons-with-disabilities-crpd

Van Dijk, T. (2006). Ideology and discourse analysis. *Journal of Political Ideologies, 11*(2), 115-140.

Van Goidsenhoven, L. (2017). Crip theory. In J. de Bloois, S. De Cauwer, & A. Masschelein (Eds.), *50 key terms in contemporary cultural theory* (pp. 92-96). Pelckmans Pro.

Van Goidsenhoven, L. (2020). *Autisme in veelvoud. Het potentieel van life writing voor alternatieve vormen van subjectiviteit* [Autism in multiplicity: The potential of life writing for alternative forms of subjectivity]. Garant.

Van Haelter, H., Dhaenens, F., & Van Bauwel, S. (2022). Trans persons on trans representations in popular media culture: A reception study. *DiGeSt-Journal of Diversity and Gender Studies, 9*(1), 75-88.

van Meer, M. M., & Pollmann, M. M. H. (2022). Media representations of lesbians, gay men, and bisexuals on Dutch television and people's stereotypes and attitudes about LGBs. *Sexuality & Culture, 26*, 640-664.

Van Steenkiste, M. (2019, February 13). *Charlotte Adigéry: "Mag dat nog, een beetje zoeken?"* [Charlotte Adigéry: 'Is that still allowed, to search a little?']. Enola. https://www.enola.be/2019/02/13/charlotte-adigery-mag-dat-nog-een-beetje-zoeken/

Van Zoonen, L. (1994). *Feminist media studies*. SAGE.

VanDerWerff, E. (2020, February 19). *Portrait of a Lady on Fire director Céline Sciamma on her ravishing romantic masterpiece.* Vox. https://www.vox.com/culture/2020/2/19/21137213/portrait-of-a-lady-on-fire-celine-sciamma-interview

Vanlee, F. (2019a). Acknowledging/denying LGBT+ difference: Understanding homonormativity and LGBT+ homogeneity in Flemish TV fiction through production research. *European Journal of Communication, 34*(5), 520-534.

Vanlee, F. (2019b). Finding domestic LGBT+ television in Western Europe: Methodological challenges for queer critics. *Continuum, 33*(4), 423-434.

Vanlee, F., Dhaenens, F., & Van Bauwel., S. (2018). *Sexual diversity on the small screen: Mapping LGBT+ characters in Flemish television fiction (2001-2016).* CIMS-Centre for Cinema and Media Studies.

Vanlee, F. H. J., Dhaenens, F., & Van Bauwel, S. (2020). Indifference and queer television studies: Distinguishing norms of existence and coexistence. *Critical Studies in Media Communication, 37*(2), 105-119.

Veenstra, G. (2015). Class position and musical tastes: A sing-off between the cultural omnivorism and Bourdieusian homology frameworks. *Canadian Review of Sociology/Revue Canadienne de sociologie, 52*(2), 134-159.

Verboord, M., & Brandellero, A. (2018). The globalization of popular music, 1960-2010: A multilevel analysis of music flows. *Communication Research, 45*(4), 603-627.

Vertoont, S. (2019). Beperkte beeldvorming: Een exploratieve studie naar televisierepresentaties van handicap in Vlaanderen [Limited representation: An explorative study on television representations of disability in Flanders]. *Tijdschrift voor Communicatiewetenschap, 47*(2), 84-103.

Vertoont, S., Goethals, T., Dhaenens, F., Schelfhout, P., Van Deynse, T., Vermeir, G., & Ysebaert, M. (2022). Un/recognisable and dis/empowering images of disability: A collective textual analysis of media representations of intellectual disabilities. *Critical Studies in Media Communication, 39*(1), 1-14.

Vivarelli, N. (2023, March 14). *'The Last of Us' breaks HBO's SVOD ratings records in Europe.* Variety. https://variety.com/2023/digital/global/the-last-of-smashes-hbo-svod-ratings-europe-1235553491/

Vrangalova, Z., & Savin-Williams, R. C. (2012). Mostly heterosexual and mostly gay/lesbian: Evidence for new sexual orientation identities. *Archives of Sexual Behavior, 41*, 85-101.

VRT (2020). *Beheersovereenkomst 2021-2025.* VRT. https://www.vrt.be/nl/over-de-vrt/beheersovereenkomst

VRT (n.d.). *Charter diversiteit.* VRT. https://www.vrt.be/nl/over-de-vrt/opdracht/omroepthema-s/diversiteit/charter-diversiteit/

Waldschmidt, A. (2017). Disability goes cultural: The cultural model of disability as an analytical tool. In A. Waldschmidt, H. Berressem, & M. Ingwersen (Eds.), *Culture – theory – disability: encounters between disability studies and cultural studies* (pp. 19-28). Transcript Verlag.

Wall, T. (2013). *Studying popular music culture*. SAGE.

Warner, M. (1999). The trouble with normal. Harvard University Press.

Warwick, J. (2015). Midnight ramblers and material girls: Gender and stardom in rock and pop. In A. Bennett & S. Waksman (Eds.), *The Sage handbook of popular music* (pp. 332-345). SAGE.

Watkins, S. C. (2006). *Hip hop matters: Politics, pop culture, and the struggle for the soul of the movement*. Beacon Press.

Weeks, J. (1996). The construction of homosexuality. In S. Seidman (Ed.), *Queer theory/Sociology* (pp. 41-63). Blackwell.

Weininger, E. B. (2005). Pierre Bourdieu on social class and symbolic violence. In E. O. Wright (Ed.), *Approaches to class analysis* (pp. 116-165). Cambridge University Press.

Weitzer, R., & Kubrin C. E. (2009). Misogyny in rap music: A content analysis of prevalence and meanings. *Men and Masculinities, 12*(1), 3-29.

Welch, A. (2023, January 30). *The Last of Us recap episode three – absolutely magical television.* The Guardian. https://www.theguardian.com/tv-and-radio/2023/jan/30/the-last-of-us-recap-episode-three-absolutely-magical-television

West, I. (2018). Queer perspectives in communication studies. In *Oxford research encyclopedia of communication*. https://doi.org/10.1093/acrefore/9780190228613.013.625

Westerfelhaus, R., & Lacroix, C. (2006). Seeing "straight" through Queer Eye: Exposing the strategic rhetoric of heteronormativity in a mediated ritual of gay rebellion. *Critical Studies in Media Communication, 23*(5), 426-444.

Wiggers, K. (2022, September 2). *AI is getting better at generating porn. We might not be prepared for the consequences.* TechCrunch. https://techcrunch.com/2022/09/02/ai-is-getting-better-at-generating-porn-we-might-not-be-prepared-for-the-consequences/

Williams, L. (1989). *Hardcore: Power, pleasure, and the frenzy of the visible.* University of California Press.

Williams, Z. (2024, July 16). *Brat summer: Is the long era of clean living finally over?* The Guardian. https://www.theguardian.com/lifeandstyle/article/2024/jul/16/brat-summer-is-the-long-era-of-clean-living-finally-over

Whiteley, S. (2000). *Women and popular music: Sexuality, identity and subjectivity.* Routledge.

Whiteout, S. (2018). Popularizing wokeness. *Harvard Journal of African American Public Policy 2017-2018*, 63-70.

Whittington-Walsh, F. (2002). From freaks to savants: Disability and hegemony from The Hunchback of Notre Dame (1939) to Sling Blade (1997). *Disability & Society, 17*(6), 695-707.

WHO (n.d.). *Disability.* https://www.who.int/health-topics/disability

Winnow, J. (1992). Lesbians evolving health care: Cancer and AIDS. *Feminist Review, 41*(1), 68-76.

Wise, S. J. (2001). Redefining black masculinity and manhood: Successful black gay men speak out. *Journal of African American Men, 5*(4), 3-22.

Wolbring, G. (2008). The politics of ableism. *Development, 51*(2), 252-258.

Wolff, J. (1999). Cultural studies and the sociology of culture. *Contemporary Sociology, 28*(5), 499-507.

Wood, H. (2024). *Audience.* Routledge.

Yates, C. (2018, May 8). *Childish Gambino's 'This is America' video is a beautiful nightmare.* The Undefeated. https://theundefeated.com/features/childish-gambinos-this-is-america-video-is-a-beautiful-nightmare/

Yousman, B., Yousman, L. B., Dines, G., & Humez, J. M. (Eds.). (2020). *Gender, race, and class in media: A critical reader* (6th ed.). SAGE.

Index

#meToo 24, 30
   MeToo movement 24, 67
2 Live Crew 26, 27, 155
A Christmas Carol 174, 175
able-bodied norms 170, 172
   (compulsory) able-bodiedness 168, 171, 172, 187
ableism 10, 17, 164, 169, 170, 172, 178, 182, 183, 187
   language 183
   representations 182-183, 184
accessibility 17, 172, 188, 190
   media production 188-190
accountability 30
admiration framing 219, 221
aesthetic anxiety 178
All That Heaven Allows 215, 216
Althusser, Louis 195-197, 205, 217
Anders als die Andern 12, 95, 110
assimilation 87, 115, 125
Astrid and Natalia: Back to Reality 194, 218
audio descriptions and captions 188, 189
Barnes, Colin 171, 173, 174, 176, 177, 181, 182, 184
Beauty and the Beast 41, 107
Beyoncé 183
Bhabba, Homi K. 137
Billboard 151, 152, 230
Birmingham Centre for Contemporary Cultural Studies 14, 36-38, 43, 66, 205
Black Lives Matter 29, 49
black popular music 17, 138, 150-158
blues music 151, 152, 201
Bourdieu, Pierre 25, 195, 197-200, 203, 204, 207, 218, 221, 222, 225
   forms of capital 25
Braille 188, 189
BRAT 229
Breaking Bad 184-186

British cultural studies 36, 38, 195, 205
burden of representation 147
Burke, Tarana 24
Butler, Judith 31, 60, 84, 103, 105
cancel culture 9, 16, 28-31
Candida Royalle 82
caricature framing 221
celebrity capital 25
Charli xcx 229, 230
Charlotte Adigéry 124-126
Childish Gambino 48-50
Chomsky, Noam 206
Connell, Raeywyn 56-58, 68, 69, 114
Connell's gender theory 56
   hegemonic masculinity 56, 57, 69
   complicit masculinity 56, 57, 71
   subordinated masculinity 56, 57, 78, 114
   marginalised masculinity 56, 78
   emphasised femininity 53, 58, 69
consensus framing 219
commodification 142
contemporary R&B 154
Crenshaw, Kimberle 25-28, 48, 60, 155
crip theory 171, 172
   cripping 171, 172
cultivation theory 16, 34, 35, 37, 63, 100-103, 137, 138
   gender 100-103
   sexual diversity 16, 37, 41, 93-120
cultural model of disability 168, 169, 172
cultural omnivores 201
cultural resistance 37, 82, 121, 208
cultural sociology 17, 207, 208
culturalism 134
culture wars 10-12
Daredevil 181
De Lauretis, Teresa 103
De Sica, Vittorio 213-215
Deaf people 188

Deep Throat 80, 81
Der Kreis 96, 97
diaspora 13, 17, 38, 127-134, 138, 150, 156
disablism 10, 162, 164, 169, 170, 173, 187
disco music 100, 101
Distinction 198
diversity charter 144
diversity monitor 144
double-consciousness 147
Dubois, W. E. B. 128, 129, 147
Dworkin, Andrea 81, 82
Dyer, Richard 12, 15, 35, 43, 44, 96, 99-101, 104, 110, 112, 113, 148
emulation framing 219
encoding/decoding 37, 67, 140, 189, 205
episodic framing 221
essentialism 21, 23, 56, 59, 96, 104, 128, 157, 208
Eternals 121, 184, 186
ethnic music 130
Euphoria 8, 86, 87
ex-nomination 216-218
fandom 120, 155
    fan fiction 120
    slash fiction 16, 37, 120-122
Fanon, Franz 129, 135
female gaze 91, 92
Filthy Rich and Homeless 192, 193, 218
Foucault, Michel 94
framing theory 17, 137, 138, 218
Frank Ocean 157, 158
Freaks 178-180
Friedan, Betty 62
Game of Thrones 160-162
gay liberation movement 97, 98, 112
Georgiou, Myria 131
Gerbner, George 34., 35, 63, 65, 101
German Expressionism 211
Gilroy, Paul 127, 128, 137
Goodley, Dan 164, 168-170
Grammy Awards 79, 157
Gross, Larry 35, 100-102, 112
Hall, Stuart 12, 21, 35, 37, 39, 40, 44-47, 67, 125, 128-130, 134, 137, 205
Harlem Hit Parade 151
Hart, Miranda 52-54
Hasta La Vista 182
Heated 183
hegemony 15, 36, 37, 56, 58, 76, 166, 196
Herman, Edward S. 115, 206
Heteronormativity 10, 11, 13, 37, 44, 98, 104-107, 115-120, 231
heterosexual recuperation 114
hip-hop 26, 27, 137, 154-156, 202
    gender 154-156
    masculinity 137, 155, 157, 158
Hirschfeld, Magnus 12, 95, 96
homology 198, 199

homonormativity 40, 115, 119
homophile movements 96, 97, 112
hooks, bell 15, 137, 155
hybridity 130, 134, 137
hyperstereotyping 27, 54, 67
identity politics 10, 16, 22-26, 29, 30, 41, 125, 176
identity-based film festivals 40
    LGBTQ-film festivals 40
ideological state apparatuses (ISAs) 197
ideology 36, 37, 62, 66, 72, 127, 168, 196, 197, 205, 206
IDLES 78, 79
If Beale Street Could Talk 47
individual models of disability 166, 167
    medical model of disability 166, 167, 182
    psychological model of disability 162, 166
Insecure 150
interpellation 197
intersectionality 16, 25-28, 47, 60, 146
Italian Neorealism 12, 213
jazz 153, 154, 199, 201, 223
Karim, Karim H. 127, 130, 131, 135, 137
Kendall, Diana 204, 217-222, 225
La Sortie de l'usine Lumière à Lyon 209, 210
Ladri di biciclette 213, 214
Lang, Fritz 211, 212
Langston, Donna 202, 203
legitimacy indicators 85
Lippmann, Walter 42, 43
MacKinnon, Catharine 81, 82
mainstreaming of diversity 9, 146
makeover television 222
male gaze 83, 91, 92
management agreement 143-145
Manufacturing Consent: The Political Economy of the Mass Media 206
Manzoor, Nida 147
Marx, Karl 195-197, 205, 206, 212, 217
Marxism 14, 36, 38, 196, 206, 207, 212
McIntosh, Peggy 148
Me Before You 175, 176
Media Access Awards 161
melodrama films 210, 215
Mercer, Kobena 126, 127, 145, 215
meritocracy 202, 222
Metropolis 211-213
micro-aggression 145, 155
middle-class-values framing 225
Miranda 52-54, 67
Mulvey, Laura 91, 92
My Gimpy Life 130
myth of a classless society 202, 203
narrowcasting 141
new queer cinema 116
Nina Simone 153, 154
non-essentialism 21
Omi, Michael 127, 128

253

Index

Orientalism 17, 135, 136, 161
Paralympics 181
Peterson, Richard A. 200, 201
Please Like Me 8, 185-187
political economy 17, 38, 106, 206-208
    social class 206, 207
politics of production 139
politics of representation 16, 39-42, 48, 67, 84, 88, 137, 139, 190, 231
pop music 27, 70-72, 75, 229
pornography 16, 59, 62, 63, 80-83
    sex wars 80-83
Portrait de la jeune fille en feu 90-92
postcolonial studies 17, 125, 134, 135
postfeminism 60-62, 230
poverty porn 194, 221, 224
Production Code Administration 110, 215
queer reading 16, 37, 121, 172
queer theory 16, 59, 84, 94, 98, 100, 101, 103-107, 115, 171, 172
queerbaiting 42, 106
race music 151
realism 34, 211
relational model of disability 167, 168
Represent 143
repressive state apparatuses (RSAs) 197
review bombing 8, 9
rhythm and blues 15, 152, 154, 157, 158
Riot grrrl 60, 71, 76
rock music 68-76
    canon 71-76
Saha, Anamik 9, 13, 15, 139, 142, 143, 145, 148, 155
Said, Edward 135-137
Sciamma, Céline 90-92
Schippers, Mimi 58, 68, 69
Schippers' gender theory 58
    alternative femininity 58
    alternative masculinity 58, 60
    hegemonic femininity 58, 69
    pariah femininity 58, 69, 72
second wave of feminism 59, 61, 62
self-deprecating humour 54
Siapera, Eugenia 142, 143, 145, 146
Sirk, Douglas 215
SKAM 105, 117-119
social consciousness 196
    class consciousness 17, 196, 202, 225
social constructionism 16, 21-23, 33, 39, 58, 59, 94, 103
social Darwinism 127, 129, 170
social mobility 197, 200, 219
social model of disability 162, 166, 167, 170
socio-economic status (SES) 194, 202, 203
sociology of culture 17, 207
Solange 155, 156
soul 12, 152, 157
Star Trek 122

stereotyping 42-44, 63-65, 112-114, 173-182
    through iconography 43
    through structure 43, 44, 113
Stonewall uprising 97, 98
strategic essentialism 23
structuralism 38, 205
subjective social status (SSS) 203
super cripple/ supercrip 44, 162, 181
Sweet Sweetback's Baadasssss Song 45
symbolic annihilation 35, 63, 65, 101
    sexual minorities 101, 108, 109, 116, 117
    women 63-65
symbolic violence 222
Tamino 133, 134, 137
taste 75, 76, 198-203, 207, 217, 218, 222, 225
The Children's Hour 112, 113
The Cosby Show 46
The Feminine Mystique 62
The Hollywood Diversity Report 2021 140, 142
The Kleptomaniac 210
The Last of Us 7-9
The United Nations Convention on Rights of Persons with Disabilities (CRPD) 189
The White Lotus 219, 220
The Wire 40
thematic framing 221
third wave of feminism 59, 60, 84
This is America 48-50
tokenism 17, 202, 203
trans-coding strategies 16, 44, 45, 48, 137
transnational identifications 131
Treme 222-224
Tuchman, Gaye 35, 63, 65, 66
Tytgat Chocolat 187
VRT 9, 143-145, 173, 187, 219
Warner, Michael 103, 104
We Are Lady Parts 146, 147
white privilege 10, 148
WHO (World Health Organization) 163
Winant, Howard 127, 128
woke 10, 13, 28-31, 67
    corporate wokeness 29
    woke-washing 29

Academia Press
Coupure Rechts 88
9000 Ghent
Belgium

www.academiapress.be

Academia Press is a subsidiary of Lannoo Publishers.

ISBN 978 94 014 44088 | D/2025/45/8 | NUR 670

Frederik Dhaenens
Represent! Studies of Diversity and Popular Media Culture
Ghent, Academia Press, 2025, 256 p.

Cover & Layout: Studio Lannoo (Nele Reyniers)

© Frederik Dhaenens
© Lannoo Publishers

No part of this publication may be reproduced in print, by photocopy, microfilm or any other means, without the prior written permission of the publisher. Every effort has been made to trace copyright holders. If, however, you feel that you have inadvertently been overlooked, please contact the publishers.